EMPOWERED EDUCATORS IN CANADA

How High-Performing Systems Shape Teaching

Carol Campbell
Ken Zeichner
Ann Lieberman
Pamela Osmond-Johnson

with Jesslyn Hollar, Shane Pisani, and Jacqueline Sohn

JOSSEY-BASS™
A Wiley Brand

Published by Jossey-Bass
A Wiley Brand

One Montgomery Street, Suite 1000, San Francisco, CA 94104-4594—www.josseybass.com

Jossey-Bass books and products are available through most bookstores. To contact
Jossey-Bass directly call our Customer Care Department within the U.S. at 800-956-7739,
outside the U.S. at 317-572-3986, or fax 317-572-4002.

Wiley publishes in a variety of print and electronic formats and by print-on-demand.
Some material included with standard print versions of this book may not be included in
e-books or in print-on-demand. If this book refers to media such as a CD or DVD that
is not included in the version you purchased, you may download this material at http://
booksupport.wiley.com. For more information about Wiley products, visit www.wiley.com.

ISBN: 9781119369622
ISBN: 9781119369684
ISBN: 9781119369691

Cover design by Wiley
Cover image: © suriya9/Getty Images, Inc.

FIRST EDITION
PB Printingg   10 9 8 7 6 5 4 3 2 1

CONTENTS

FOREWORD

FEW WOULD DISAGREE THAT, among all the factors that affect how much students learn, the quality of their teachers ranks very high. But what, exactly, do policy makers, universities, and school leaders need to do to make sure that the vast majority of teachers in their jurisdiction are *literally* world class?

Perhaps the best way to answer that question is to look carefully and in great detail at what the countries whose students are performing at the world's top levels are doing to attract the highest quality high school students to teaching careers, prepare them well for that career, organize schools so teachers can do the best work of which they are capable, and provide incentives for them to get better at the work before they finally retire.

It was not hard for us to find the right person to lead a study that would do just that. Stanford professor Linda Darling-Hammond is one of the world's most admired researchers. Teachers and teaching have been lifelong professional preoccupations for her. And, not least, Professor Darling-Hammond is no stranger to international comparative studies. Fortunately for us and for you, she agreed to lead an international comparative study of teacher quality in a selection of top-performing countries. The study, *Empowered Educators: How High-Performing Systems Shape Teaching Quality Around the World*, took two years to complete and is unprecedented in scope and scale.

The volume you are reading is one of six books, including case studies conducted in Australia, Canada, China, Finland, and Singapore. In addition to the case studies and the cross-study analysis, the researchers have collected a range of videos and artifacts (http://ncee.org/empowered-educators)—ranging from a detailed look at how the daily schedules of teachers in Singapore ensure ample time for collaboration and planning to a description of the way Shanghai teachers publish their classroom research in refereed journals—that we hope will be of great value to policy makers and educators interested in using and adapting the tools that the top-performing jurisdictions use to get the highest levels of teacher quality in the world.

Studies of this sort are often done by leading scholars who assemble hordes of graduate students to do the actual work, producing reams of reports framed by the research plan, which are then analyzed by the principal investigator. That is not what happened in this case. For this report, Professor Darling-Hammond recruited two lead researcher-writers for each case study, both senior, one from the country being studied and one from another country, including top-level designers and implementers of the systems being studied and leading researchers. This combination of insiders and external observers, scholars and practitioner-policy makers, gives this study a depth, range, and authenticity that is highly unusual.

But this was not just an effort to produce first-class case studies. The aim was to understand what the leaders were doing to restructure the profession of teaching for top performance. The idea was to cast light on that by examining what was the same and what was different from country to country to see if there were common threads that could explain uncommon results. As the data-gathering proceeded, Professor Darling-Hammond brought her team together to exchange data, compare insights, and argue about what the data meant. Those conversations, taking place among a remarkable group of senior policy actors, practitioners, and university-based researchers from all over the world, give this work a richness rarely achieved in this sort of study.

The researchers examined all sorts of existing research literature on the systems they were studying, interviewed dozens of people at every level of the target systems, looked at everything from policy at the national level to practice in individual schools, and investigated not only the specific policies and practices directly related to teacher quality, but the larger economic, political, institutional, and cultural contexts in which policies on teacher quality are shaped.

Through it all, what emerges is a picture of a sea change taking place in the paradigm of mass education in the advanced industrial nations. When university graduates of any kind were scarce and most people had jobs requiring only modest academic skills, countries needed teachers who knew little more than the average high school graduate, perhaps less than that at the primary school level. It was not too hard to find capable people, typically women, to do that work, because the job opportunities for women with that level of education were limited.

But none of that is true anymore. Wage levels in the advanced industrial countries are typically higher than elsewhere in the world. Employers who can locate their manufacturing plants and offices anywhere in the world and who do not need highly skilled labor look for workers who have the basic skills they need in low-wage countries, so the work available to workers with only the basic skills in the high-wage countries is drying up. That process is being greatly accelerated by the rapid advance of automation. The jobs that are left in the high-wage countries mostly demand a higher level of more complex skills.

These developments have put enormous pressure on the governments of high-wage countries to find teachers who have more knowledge and a deeper command of complex skills. These are the people who can get into selective universities and go into occupations that have traditionally had higher status and are better compensated than school teaching. What distinguishes the countries with the best-performing education systems is that: 1) they have figured this out and focused hard on how to respond to these new realities; and 2) they have succeeded not just in coming up with promising designs for the systems they need but in implementing those systems well. The result is not only profound changes in the way they source, educate, train, and support a truly professional teaching force, but schools in which the work of teachers is very differently organized, the demands on school leaders is radically changed, teachers become not the recipient of a new set of instructions from the "center," but the people who are actually responsible for designing and carrying out the reforms that are lifting the performance of their students every day. Not least important, these systems offer real careers in teaching that enable teachers, like professionals in other fields, to gain more authority, responsibility, compensation, and status as they get better and better at the work, without leaving teaching.

This is an exciting story. It is the story that you are holding in your hand. The story is different in every country, province, and state. But the themes behind the stories are stunningly similar. If you find this work only half as compelling as I have, you will be glued to these pages.

MARC TUCKER, PRESIDENT
NATIONAL CENTER ON EDUCATION AND THE ECONOMY

ACKNOWLEDGMENTS

WE WISH TO ACKNOWLEDGE and thank the many individuals and organizations who contributed to the design, conduct, and reporting of the research presented in this book. In particular, we wish to thank the National Center on Education and the Economy (NCEE) who funded the overall International Teacher Policy Study and the members of their Center on International Education Benchmarking (CIEB) who reviewed and provided feedback on draft materials. We want to express our deepest thanks to Linda Darling-Hammond who was the overall principal investigator for the International Teacher Policy Study and who provided leadership, direction, and guidance to all case studies. We are indebted also to members of the Stanford Center for Opportunity Policy in Education (SCOPE), who provided advice and assistance throughout this study, particularly: Dion Burns, Maude Engstrom, Sonya Keller, and Jon Snyder.

We wish to thank and acknowledge our colleagues and coauthors who provided considerable research expertise and contributions to the conduct, writing, and completion of the Canada, Alberta, and Ontario case studies: Jesslyn Hollar, Ann Lieberman, Pamela Osmond-Johnson, Shane Pisani, and Jacqueline Sohn.

In addition, for the Alberta case study, we offer great thanks to those who provided us with information and materials related to policies and practices in Alberta: Mark Bevan, Paul MacLoud, and Karen Shipka of the Ministry of Education; Diane Wishart of the Ministry of Advanced Education; J. C. Coulture and Mark Yurick of the Alberta Teachers' Association; Jim Brandon of the University of Calgary; Jean Clandinin, Jim Parsons, and Randy Wimmer of the University of Alberta; Peter Grimmett of the University of British Columbia; Val Olekshy of the Edmonton Regional Learning Consortium; and the following Alberta teachers: Robert Gardner, Marion Brenner, Wayne LaVold, Katherine McReady, Katherine Macmillan, Tammy Thero-Soto, and another teacher who chose to remain anonymous.

For the Ontario case study, our deepest thanks go to the individuals who agreed to provide their expertise and time by being interviewed to inform our case study. Thank you to: Lindy Amato, Rob Andrews, Paul Anthony, Sandra Bickford, Megan Borner, Kathy Broad, Hanca Chang, Paul Charles, Camille Chenier, Suzette Clarke, Peter Edwards, Lori Foote, Richard Franz, Mary Jean Gallagher, Jacqueline Hammond, Rhonda Kimberley-Young, Wahid Khan, Judi Kokis, Ann Lopez, Judith Lyander, Pauline McNaughton, Dawn Merlino, Susan Perry, Demetra Saladaris, Michael Salvatori, Bruce Shaw, Tina Sidhu, Jim Strachan, Christina Terzic, and Sabir Thomas. We are grateful also to several teachers and principals who agreed to be interviewed but asked that we keep their identity confidential. Ontario's education system and students benefit tremendously from your individual expertise and collective professionalism. Thank you all! In addition, we wish to thank: Taddesse Haile and his team at the Education Statistics and Analysis Branch in the Ontario Ministry of Education and Barbara Gough and colleagues in the Ontario Ministry of Training, Colleges and Universities who provided advice and assistance with provincial data to inform our case study; Simon Young and Bill Powell from the Ontario College of Teachers who assisted with photographs; and Margaret Brennan who provided transcription services for the case study. We are grateful for all of the contributions that have benefited this case study. Any errors or omissions, however, are the responsibility of the authors.

CAROL CAMPBELL AND KEN ZEICHNER

ABOUT THE SPONSORING ORGANIZATIONS

THIS WORK IS MADE possible through a grant by the Center on International Education Benchmarking® of the National Center on Education and the Economy® and is part of a series of reports on teacher quality systems around the world. For a complete listing of the material produced by this research program, please visit www.ncee.org/cieb.

The Center on International Education Benchmarking®, a program of NCEE, funds and conducts research around the world on the most successful education systems to identify the strategies those countries have used to produce their superior performance. Through its books, reports, website, monthly newsletter, and a weekly update of education news around the world, CIEB provides up-to-date information and analysis on those countries whose students regularly top the PISA league tables. Visit www.ncee.org/cieb to learn more.

The National Center on Education and the Economy was created in 1988 to analyze the implications of changes in the international economy for American education, formulate an agenda for American education based on that analysis and seek wherever possible to accomplish that agenda through policy change and development of the resources educators would need to carry it out. For more information visit www.ncee.org.

Research for this volume was coordinated by the Stanford Center for Opportunity Policy in Education (SCOPE) at Stanford University. SCOPE was founded in 2008 to foster research, policy, and practice to advance high quality, equitable education systems in the United States and internationally.

ABOUT THE AUTHORS

 **Carol Campbell** is associate professor of Leadership and Educational Change and director of the Knowledge Network for Applied Education Research (KNAER) at the Ontario Institute for Studies in Education (OISE), University of Toronto. Carol is also an appointed education advisor to the Premier and the Minister of Education in Ontario, Canada. Her previous roles include: executive director of the Stanford Center for Opportunity Policy in Education (SCOPE) at Stanford University, USA; holding progressively senior leadership roles in the Ontario Ministry of Education including becoming the Ministry's first chief research officer; and academic, education, and policy roles in the UK. Carol is originally from Scotland and earned her PhD at the University of Strathclyde.

 **Jesslyn Hollar** is a doctoral candidate at the University of Washington and director of Central Washington University's alternative route to certification program. Her research interests include teacher education and policy, sociology of education and history of teacher education, teacher learning, and education reform. She is a member of the History of Education Society and the American Educational Research Association and serves on the editorial board for the Northwest Association of Teacher Educators.

 **Ann Lieberman** is currently a senior scholar at Stanford University. She is an emeritus professor from Teachers College, Columbia University. She is affiliated with two Stanford Centers: SCALE and SCOPE. Her major areas of research are: teacher knowledge, learning, and leadership, as well as school/university partnerships. She is

internationally known for her work on finding a way to get at teacher knowledge to go with research knowledge. She has written or edited over 18 books, scores of articles and chapters, all focused on the teacher, teacher leadership, and school reform. She has been on the forefront of arguing for policies that enable teacher learning and leadership that recognize the complexities of teaching and the critical importance of supporting teachers.

Pamela Osmond-Johnson is an assistant professor of Educational Administration with the Faculty of Education at the University of Regina. Pamela recently completed her doctorate in educational administration from the Ontario Institute for Studies in Education at the University of Toronto, with a focus on educational policy. Her research includes work around teacher leadership, teacher professionalism, teacher federations, and the professional growth of teachers. Prior to beginning her doctorate, Pamela was a high school science teacher and vice principal in Newfoundland.

Shane Pisani is a doctoral candidate in the University of Washington's Curriculum and Instruction Department. He is an instructor with the Seattle Teacher Residency and also teaches a number of courses for both the elementary and secondary teacher education programs at the University of Washington. His research interests include teacher perceptions of global education and the positioning of mentor teachers as teacher educators.

Jacqueline Sohn is a PhD candidate in Educational Policy at the Ontario Institute for Studies in Education, University of Toronto. Her current research focuses on the political influencers of evidence use for macro-level policy decisions in the area of child poverty. More broadly, she is interested in the use of interdisciplinary research and cross-sector collaborations for developing effective social policies. Prior to beginning her doctoral studies, she was employed at the Ontario Ministry of Health and Long-Term care in a provincial project coordination and policy role.

Ken Zeichner is the Boeing Professor of Teacher Education at the University of Washington, Seattle. Prior to moving to the University of Washington in 2009, Zeichner was the Hoefs-Bascom Professor of Teacher Education and association dean for Teacher Education and International Education. He was a member of the UW-Madison faculty for 34 years. He is an elected member of the National Academy of Education, a fellow in the American Educational Research Association (AERA), and a former vice president of AERA. His publications include *Teacher Education and the Struggle for Social Justice* (Routledge, 2009). His current work focuses on teacher education and professional learning, teacher education policy, and engaging local communities in teacher education.

ONLINE DOCUMENTS AND VIDEOS

Access online documents an videos at
http://ncee.org/empowered-educators

Link Number	Description	URL
2-1	Canada's Employment Equity Act	http://ncee.org/2017/01/canadas-employment-equity-act/
2-2	Inequality in Calgary	http://ncee.org/2017/01/inequality-in-calgary/
2-3	Closing the Aboriginal Non-Aboriginal Education Gaps	http://ncee.org/2017/01/closing-the-aboriginal-non-aboriginal-education-gaps/
2-4	Inspiring Education: A Dialogue with Albertans	http://ncee.org/2017/01/inspiring-education-a-dialogue-with-albertans/
2-5	Alberta Task Force for Teaching Excellence	http://ncee.org/2017/01/alberta-task-force-for-teaching-excellence/
2-6	Alberta Teaching Quality Standards	http://ncee.org/2016/12/alberta-teaching-quality-standards/
2-7	Education Funding in Alberta	http://ncee.org/2017/01/education-funding-in-alberta/
2-8	Alberta School Act	http://ncee.org/2017/01/alberta-school-act/
2-9	Canada's Approach to School Funding	http://ncee.org/wp-content/uploads/2016/12/Alb-non-AV-9-Herman-2013-Canadas-Approach-to-School-Funding.pdf
2-10	Alberta's Programs of Study (Curriculum)	https://education.alberta.ca/
2-11	Alberta Provincial Test Mathematics Grade 9 2013	http://ncee.org/2017/01/alberta-provincial-test-mathematics-grade-9-2013/

Link Number	Description	URL
2-12	Alberta Provincial Test Mathematics 30-1 2014	http://ncee.org/2017/01/alberta-provincial-test-mathematics-30-1-2014/
2-13	Alberta Provincial SLA Information Bulletin 2015-2016 Grade 3	http://ncee.org/2017/01/alberta-provincial-sla-information-bulletin-2015-2016-grade-3/
2-14	Performance of Alberta Students on National and International Assessments	http://ncee.org/2017/01/performance-of-alberta-students-on-national-and-international-assessments/
2-15	Randy Wimmer, Vice-Dean & Associate Dean (Academic) at the University of Alberta	http://ncee.org/2016/12/audio-randy-wimmer/
2-16	Collective Agreements	https://www.teachers.ab.ca/For Members/Salary Benefits and Pension/Collective Agreements/Pages/Collective Agreements.aspx
2-17	Alberta Education Sector Workforce Planning	http://ncee.org/2017/01/alberta-education-sector-workforce-planning/
2-18	Alberta: Teaching in the Early Years	http://ncee.org/2017/01/alberta-teaching-in-the-early-years/
2-19	Campus Alberta: A Framework for Action	http://ncee.org/2017/01/campus-alberta-a-framework-for-action/
2-20	Bridging Program for Foreign-Prepared Teachers Calgary Model	http://ncee.org/2017/01/bridging-program-for-foreign-prepared-teachers-calgary-model/
2-21	Mentoring Beginning Teachers	http://ncee.org/2017/01/mentoring-beginning-teachers/
2-22	2012 ATA Professional Development Survey	http://ncee.org/2017/01/2012-ata-professional-development-survey/
2-23	Alberta Professional Development Programs and Services Guide	http://ncee.org/2017/01/alberta-professional-development-programs-and-services-guide/
2-24	A Framework for Professional Development in Alberta	http://ncee.org/2016/12/a-framework-for-professional-development-in-alberta/
2-25	Alberta Teacher Growth Supervision and Evaluation Policy	http://ncee.org/2017/01/alberta-teacher-growth-supervision-and-evaluation-policy/

Link Number	Description	URL
3-1	Ontario PISA 2012 Highlights	http://ncee.org/2017/01/ontario-pisa-2012-highlights
3-2	Ontario Ministry of Finance 2015 – Ontario Fact Sheet	http://ncee.org/2017/01/ontario-mof-2015-ontario-fact-sheet/
3-3	Ontario Education Act 1990	http://ncee.org/2017/01/ontario-education-act-1990/
3-4	Audio: Ontario Governance, Policy, and Educational Goals	http://ncee.org/2017/01/audio-ontario-governance-policy-and-educational-goals/
3-5	Ontario Teaching Profession Act	http://ncee.org/2017/01/ontario-teaching-profession-act/
3-6	Public Education in Ontario: Who Does What	http://ncee.org/2017/01/public-education-in-ontario-who-does-what/
3-7	Ontario Guide to Funding for Student Needs	http://ncee.org/2016/12/ontario-guide-to-funding-for-student-needs/
3-8	Ontario Equity and Inclusive Education Strategy	http://ncee.org/2017/01/ontario-equity-and-inclusive-education-strategy/
3-9	Ontario FNMI Education Policy Framework	http://ncee.org/2017/01/ontario-fnmi-education-policy-framework/
3-10	Ontario Research and Evaluation Strategy brochure	http://ncee.org/2017/01/ontario-research-and-evaluation-strategy-brochure/
3-11	Ontario Education: Achieving Excellence	http://ncee.org/2017/01/ontario-education-achieving-excellence/
3-12	Ontario Report on Teacher Professional Learning	http://ncee.org/2017/01/ontario-report-on-teacher-professional-learning/
3-13	Ontario Bachelor of Education Course Descriptions 2015-2017	http://ncee.org/2017/01/ontario-bed-course-descriptions-2015-2017/
3-14	Ontario Transitions to Teaching Survey 2011	http://ncee.org/2017/01/ontario-transitions-to-teaching-survey-2011/
3-15	Audio: Initial Teacher Education	http://ncee.org/2017/01/audio-initial-teacher-education/
3-16	Ontario Standards of Practice	http://ncee.org/2016/12/ontario-standards-of-practice/

Link Number	Description	URL
3-17	Ontario Hiring Practices	http://ncee.org/2017/01/ontario-hiring-practices/
3-18	Ontario Putting Students First Act	http://ncee.org/2017/01/ontario-putting-students-first-act/
3-19	ETFO Teacher Workload and Professionalism Study	http://ncee.org/2017/01/etfo-teacher-workload-and-professionalism-study/
3-20	Audio: Ontario Recruitment, Induction, and Mentoring	http://ncee.org/2017/01/audio-ontario-recruitment-induction-and-mentoring/
3-21	Ontario New Teacher Induction Program Manual	http://ncee.org/2017/01/ontario-new-teacher-induction-program-manual/
3-22	Ontario School Effectiveness Framework	http://ncee.org/2017/01/ontario-school-effectiveness-framework/
3-23	Audio: Ontario Continual Professional Learning	http://ncee.org/2017/01/audio-ontario-continual-professional-learning/
3-24	Ontario Teacher Learning and Leadership Program Overview	http://ncee.org/2016/12/teacher-learning-and-leadership-program-overview/
3-25	Ontario Teacher Appraisal Manual	http://ncee.org/2017/01/ontario-teacher-appraisal-manual/
3-26	Ontario Annual Learning Plan	http://ncee.org/2017/01/ontario-annual-learning-plan/
3-27	Audio: Ontario Teacher and Leadership Development	http://ncee.org/2017/01/audio-ontario-teacher-and-leadership-development/
3-28	Ontario Leadership Strategy Quick Facts	http://ncee.org/2016/12/ontario-leadership-strategy-quick-facts/
3-29	Ontario Board Leadership Development Strategy Manual	http://ncee.org/2017/01/ontario-board-leadership-development-strategy-manual/
3-30	Ontario Principals Qualification Program	http://ncee.org/2017/01/ontario-principals-qualification-program/
3-31	Ontario Principal Performance Appraisal	http://ncee.org/2017/01/ontario-principal-performance-appraisal/

EDUCATION IN CANADA

Pamela Osmond-Johnson, Carol Campbell, and
Ken Zeichner

UNLIKE MOST INDUSTRIALIZED COUNTRIES around the world, there is no federal body of education in Canada; rather, education is under provincial or territorial authority, granted under Canada's *Constitution Act* of 1867. As highlighted in Figure 1–1, Canada is composed of ten provinces (Alberta, British Columbia, Manitoba, New Brunswick, Newfoundland and Labrador, Nova Scotia, Ontario, Prince Edward Island, Quebec, and Saskatchewan) and three territories (Nanavut, Northwest Territories, and Yukon). Thus, while there are many similarities across provincial and territorial education systems, there are significant policy variations in the areas of curriculum, assessment and accountability. These differences reflect the geography, history, language, culture, and corresponding specialized needs of the diverse populations served in each jurisdiction. All the education systems in Canada, however, are highly developed and widely accessible, reflecting a shared societal belief in the importance of education (CMEC, 2015). In this volume we begin by outlining the core commonalities that exist across the country while paying special attention to the localized nature of the systems—a hallmark of Canadian education. We then take a closer look at two of Canada's top performing jurisdictions, Alberta and Ontario, as exemplars of school systems that have developed strong supports around teacher development within their own unique policy contexts.

Overview of Canada

Canada is a multicultural society, with a foreign-born population of almost 20% (OECD, 2015). The Canadian constitution recognizes both English and French as its two official languages. According to 2011

Figure 1–1   Provinces and Territories of Canada

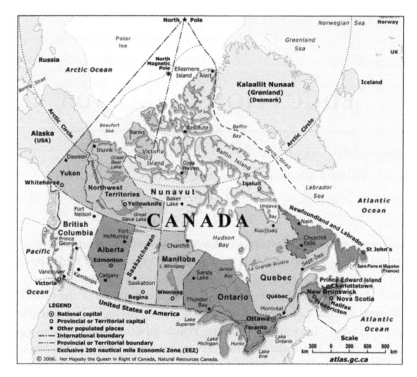

Source: Natural Resources Canada.

Statistics Canada census data, 5.8 million (17.5%) of Canadians speak both official languages. Nearly 7 million (21%) Canadians reported speaking French most often at home in 2011, although this is largely concentrated in the province of Quebec. In the rest of Canada, 74.1% of Canadians speak only English at home (CMEC, 2015). The minority language rights of French-speaking students living outside the province of Quebec and English-speaking students living in the province of Quebec are protected in the Canadian Charter of Rights and Freedoms. The Canadian Charter or Rights and Freedoms outlines the conditions under which Canadians have the right to access publicly funded education in either minority language. Each province and territory has established French-language school boards to manage the French-first-language schools. In the province of Quebec, the same structure applies to education in English-first-language schools.

All Canadians meeting age and residence requirements have access to free public education. In 2010–2011, there were 5,053,985 total students enrolled in public elementary and secondary schools in Canada (CMEC, 2015). Education is under provincial jurisdiction and there is no federal department of education. That being said, the federal government plays an important role in Canadian education, directly making provisions for First Nations schools on reserves and indirectly providing funding through intergovernmental transfers which aim to redistribute wealth across the country and "ensure a significant degree of equality across provinces in their ability to deliver social services such as education" (Parkin, 2015, p. 25). Although localized variations exist, the education systems within the ten provinces and three territories are based around a common belief in the importance of education, as evidenced by the significant proportion of budgets allocated to schooling (approximately 20% of total expenditures, depending on the jurisdiction).

In 2013, Canada's elementary and secondary school systems employed 397,122 educators (Statistics Canada, 2014), most of whom had four or five years of postsecondary study. The teaching profession is unionized in all jurisdictions; however, the scope of the work of teacher associations varies. National frameworks around teacher competencies, professionalism, and the work of teachers do not exist. Rather, teacher appraisal varies across jurisdictions and the establishment of professional standards and certification of the teaching profession are provincial/territorial responsibilities (OECD, 2015). To teach in Canada educators are required to obtain at least a bachelor of education from one of approximately 50 accredited teacher education programs at universities across the country. Some also offer postgraduate preparation for teaching. With large surpluses in teacher supply contrasted with available teaching jobs, Canadian teacher education programs and schools are selective in choosing candidates and teachers, which some analysts suggest is a contributor to high achievement (OECD, 2011). Positive learning environments and strong instructional leadership have also been identified as keys in Canada's continued school improvement efforts. Indicators from PISA 2012 showed that Canadian 15-year-olds viewed teacher-student relations at levels that are higher than the OECD average and school leaders reporter higher than average levels of instructional leadership (OCED, 2015).

Canada has a highly educated population, with 53% of 25–64-year-olds holding tertiary qualifications in 2012—ranking first among countries participating in the Organisation for Economic Co-operation and Development's (OECD) analyses, which collectively averaged 33% (OECD, 2014). In recent decades, Canada has consistently been ranked as a top performer on the OECD's Programme for International Student Assessment (PISA) (OECD, 2015). Across the ten provinces, Canadian 15-year-olds scored well above the OECD average in both mathematics and reading in the 2012 rankings and, of the 65 countries and economies participating in the assessment, only three OECD and six non-OECD countries outperformed Canada. As Parkin (2015) points outs, based on a variety of international assessments, "no country outside of East Asia performs better than Canada on a regular basis" (p. 6).

Complementing its focus on high quality education, Canada also has a strong focus on health and well-being, providing all residents with free health care and access to a host of social services dedicated to child, youth, and adult development. Since 2000, Canada has particularly focused on the provision of social programs and services in early childhood (birth to age 6) (Government of Canada, 2011). A national Universal Child Care Benefit (UCCB) issues a taxable monthly payment of $100 per child to families with children under the age of six (OECD, 2015). This funding is used at the discretion of parents to offset the costs of raising children. In late 2014, the federal government proposed increases to UCCB to $160 per child under the age of six and $60 per month for children aged 6–17. The increases took effect on January 1, 2015, and the first retroactive payment was made to families in July of 2015. Additional provincial baby bonuses and supplements for low-income families are also available to those who meet certain qualifications, with benefits and criteria varying between jurisdictions. While improvements in children's health have been made in a number of areas (such as infant mortality, teenage births, and bullying), when it comes to overall child well-being, UNICEF (2013) describes Canada as a country "stuck in the middle", achieving a middle ranking on their report card of 29 of the richest countries for the past decade. As such, key public education issues include a focus on diversity and equity with particular attention to social justice issues such as poverty, gender issues, mental health, racism, and violence prevention.

That being said, the impact of socioeconomic status on achievement in Canada is less than the OECD average, particularly in mathematics (9.4% compared with the OECD average of 14%). In fact, "in every OCED country except Finland, the socioeconomic status of the neighborhood a student is born in and of the local school they attend has more of an impact on their academic performance than in Canada" (Parkin, 2015, p. 24). Achievement among immigrant children is a particularly remarkable aspect of the nation's success as Canada is among only a few countries internationally where there is no significant achievement gap between its immigrant and nonimmigrant students on the PISA (OECD, 2015). It is also one of the few countries where there is no significant performance gap between students who speak the language of instruction at home and those who do not (OECD, 2011). These successes were recently highlighted by the Center on International Education Benchmarking (CIEB, 2015), who identified Canada as one of only three nations (with Finland and Estonia) whose education systems "are able to offer their students a quality education regardless of socioeconomic background at a low cost and still come out at the top of the international league tables for overall student performance."

Nevertheless, while Canada performs highly in international comparisons, there are some variations across provincial and territorial systems. For example, 2011 data for the upper secondary graduation indicates: "The proportion of students who completed their education in the expected time varied considerably across the country: from 12% in Nunavut to 84% in Nova Scotia" (Statistics Canada, 2015, p. 41). A Pan Canadian Assessment Program (PCAP) is administered to a sample of students across the ten provinces every three years. The average performance Canada is high; however, several provinces demonstrate performance at or above the Canadian average—Alberta in science and math; British Columbia in science; Newfoundland and Labrador in science; Ontario in math, reading, and science; and Quebec in math (CMEC, 2014). Within an overall high-performing system, it is important to remember that school education in Canada varies by province and territory.

Governance of School Systems

Provincial and territorial systems are centralized and schools have less autonomy regarding resource allocation, curriculum, and assessment than many of their OECD counterparts (OECD, 2015). In all 13 jurisdictions, departments or ministries of education are responsible for the organization, delivery, and assessment of education at elementary and secondary levels. A minister of education, who is almost always an elected member of the legislature, is appointed by the government leader to lead the department. Responsibility for the overall operation of the departments, however, is with the deputy ministers, who belong to the civil service. The provincial/territorial ministry or department provides education, administrative and financial management and school support functions. It also establishes the terms of the educational services to be provided, including the policy and legislative frameworks

(CMEC, 2015). The ministry or department of education typically lays out basic requirements around the assessment of students, with school boards and schools having the authority to establish their own assessment policies within the provincial/territorial framework. While format and structure vary across the country, students in most jurisdictions are required to participate in provincial or territorial summative examinations at key stages (typically grades 3, 6, and upper secondary) (OECD, 2015). The ministers of education collaborate through the Council of Ministers of Education, Canada (CMEC), with key pan-Canadian educational policies focused around evaluation and assessment (OECD, 2015).

Typically, school boards (also known as districts, divisions or district education councils in different provinces) are entrusted with local governance of education. Members are elected by public ballot, and the authority for operational and administrational (including financial) duties is delegated to local leaders at the discretion of the provincial and territorial governments. Local authorities oversee the group of schools within their board or division, and are responsible for curriculum implementation, personnel, student enrollment, and initiation of proposals for new construction or other major capital expenditures.

Organization of the System

Primary and Elementary Education (Grades K–8)

Operated by the local education authorities, one year of pregrade one (kindergarten) for five-year-olds is available in all provinces/territories. Preschool classes may also be available from age four or earlier, although there is substantial variation between jurisdictions in terms of provision and operation (OECD, 2015). Across Canada, 95 percent of five-year-olds attend pre-elementary or elementary school, and over 40 percent of four-year-olds are enrolled in junior kindergarten. Emphasized in the primary and elementary school curriculum are the basic subjects of language, mathematics, social studies, science, health and physical education, and introductory arts, with some jurisdictions including second-language learning. In general, schooling is compulsory from ages 5–18 but, in some provinces, can begin at age four and continue until graduation from secondary school or age 21. In 2012, the average hours per year of total compulsory instruction time for primary and elementary students in Canada was 919—higher than the OECD average of 794 hours (OECD, 2014).

Secondary Education (Grades 9–12)

Almost 98% of elementary students progress to the secondary level. Here, students are required to take primarily compulsory courses in the first years with access to specialized courses in later years to prepare for the job market or meet the entrance requirements of postsecondary institutions in specific areas of interest. Typically, vocational and academic programs are offered within the same secondary schools, but sometimes technical and vocational programs are offered in separate, dedicated vocational training centers. A number of jurisdictions also offer apprenticeship program at the secondary level that offer hands-on learning with a career focus (OECD, 2015). Students who complete the requisite number of compulsory and optional courses are awarded secondary school diplomas. In 2012, the average totally compulsory instruction time for lower secondary students in Canada was 924 hours—just above the OECD average of 905 hours (OECD, 2014). The upper secondary graduation rate for students below the age of 25 in 2011 was 81%, which was on par with the OECD average of 80% (OECD, 2014). In terms of the number of 25–34 year olds who have attained upper secondary qualifications, however, Canada ranks 10 percentage points higher than the OCED average at 92%. (OECD, 2015).

Separate and Private Schools

Legislation and practices concerning the establishment of separate educational systems and private educational institutions varies from jurisdiction to jurisdiction. In many jurisdictions separate school systems are publically funded and include both elementary and secondary education. These separate systems are public schools that reflect the constitutional right to religious education for Roman Catholics or Protestants, when either group is the religious minority in a community. Some jurisdictions also provide partial funding for private schools if certain criteria, which vary among jurisdictions, are met. In other jurisdictions, there is no public funding allocated to private schools, although they are still be regulated by the government. Government-funded school systems, both public and separate, however, serve about 93% of all students in Canada (CMEC, 2015), and the private system is relatively small in size.

Educational Funding

Funding for public education is overseen by each provincial/territorial government and sourced through a mix of government transfers and local taxes collected by either the government (in jurisdictions which have centralized funding) or by school boards themselves (in jurisdictions where school boards have retaining taxing rights). Revised annually, provincial/territorial regulations set out the grant structure that establishes the level of funding for each school board based on factors such as the number of students, special needs, and location. Provincial funding to districts is typically divided into three categories: block grants based on number of students; categorical grants—either for funding specific programmatic needs (for example, special education), or helping districts meet particular challenges in providing basic services (for example, funding transportation for more remote districts); as well as equalization funding for districts to equalize less wealthy districts (CMEC, 2015). The primary allocation of government transfers to school boards is based on a per-pupil funding level that is consistence across the jurisdiction. Some inequity in funding does exist in jurisdictions where school boards have retained the right to directly collect education tax. In these jurisdictions school boards in more affluent neighborhoods tend to generate higher revenues per capita than those based in less affluent communities. In most jurisdictions, however, governments often provide additional funding to smaller school boards and school boards with a large proportion of high needs students or students of minority languages in order to provide more equitable service.

Student Expenditure

The average per pupil expenditure in 2010 was $10,166US in secondary education—approximately 6% higher than per pupil expenditures in primary/elementary education ($9580US). This represented 6.7% of Canada's GDP and 13.2% of all public expenditures (up from 5.9% and 12.4% in 2000). This varies from province to province, however, partially influenced by the size of the school-age population and enrollment in education, as well as the provinces' relative wealth. The portion of expenditure per student allocated to core services represented 95% of the total expenditure per students. This is consistent with the proportion on core services in OECD countries (94%) in elementary through postsecondary nontertiary education (Canadian Education Statistics Council, 2014). The highest per-pupil spending typically occurs in the northern territories where remote locations make the delivery of quality education more costly. Outside of the territories, in 2010, the highest expenditure (across primary/elementary and secondary education) was Alberta ($10,423US) and the lowest was Nova Scotia ($8,719US).

Working Conditions

Teacher Pay

Teacher salaries in most jurisdictions are not based on the grade level at which a teacher teachers, with the exception of Ontario where primary teachers currently earn slightly less than their secondary counterparts (approximately 2% less). Salary scales in all jurisdictions, however, are influenced by a teachers' level of education and their years of experience. In 2009, teacher salaries in Canada represented 62.5% of overall expenditures in education—on par with the OECD average (Canadian Education Statistics Council, 2014). Canada and OECD averages also reveal similar relative differences between starting salaries and those at the top of the salary scales; however, Canada's teachers reached the top of their salary scales much faster than those of their OECD counterparts (11 years in Canada versus 24 years on average in the OECD countries). For example, in 2011, Canadian teachers at the beginning of their careers earned an average annual salary of $35,534US, compared to the OECD average of $28,854US. After 15 years of experience, however, teachers in Canada earned $56,349US—significantly higher than the OECD average of $38,136US (OECD, 2013a). Variations in starting and top-out salaries do exist across jurisdictions, however. Based on minimum training, in 2010/11, the North West Territories offered the highest salaries, regardless of career stage, at approximately $68,000CAN for beginning teachers and $97,000CAN for those at the top of the scale. This reflects the high cost of living in the far north and issues around teacher recruitment and retention in such remote locations. Among the provinces, Alberta teachers receive the highest compensation based on minimum training (approx. $55,000–$87,000CAN), with beginning teachers in Quebec ($42,000CAN) and top-of-the-scale teachers in British Columbia and Newfoundland ($65,000CAN) earning the lowest salaries based on minimum training (Canadian Education Statistics Council, 2014).

Teaching Time

The school year in most Canadian provinces consists of approximately 195 days of instruction. Teachers typically teach anywhere from four to five hours per day, depending on the allocation for preparation time, which varies both between and within the jurisdictions. In 2012, primary and elementary school teachers in Canada taught an average of 802 hours per year, compared with the OECD average of 782 hours. At the lower secondary level (generally Grades 7–9), the net annual teaching time was 747 hours and almost the same (751 hours) at the upper secondary level (generally grades 10–12). Overall, these figures are higher than the OECD averages: 20 hours higher in primary/elementary, 53 hours higher in lower secondary, and 96 hours higher at upper secondary (OECD, 2014).

Aboriginal Education

According to the Department of Aboriginal Affairs and Northern Development Canada (AANDC, 2015), in 2011–2012, there were approximately 110,597 First Nations students enrolled in Canada's K–12 education system. Approximately 60% of these students (66,388) attended on-reserve, band-operated schools (which are funded by the Federal government), while 37% (40,863) attended off-reserve schools operated by provinces/territories. The remaining three percent of students attended private schools or one of the seven federally operated reserve schools. While Canada has enjoyed much educational success, the education of First Nations students has historically been one of the countries more controversial and contentious issues. Bound to provide educational services to Canada's Indigenous peoples with the signing of treaties that gave the federal government control of the Aboriginal lands, for many years the governments answer to First Nations education was residential schools—educational institutions run by the churches that forced Native children to leave their homes to be educated at boarding schools. Students lived at the schools and were not permitted to speak their native tongue, engage in spiritual ceremonies, or dress in their traditional clothing in an attempt to assimilate them into the dominant culture. While the experiences of children at such schools varied, many students were subjected to years of abuse and mistreatment, which has contributed to intergenerational effects including family violence, substance abuse, and a deep mistrust of the education system as a whole. The last residential school in Canada closed in 1996, and in 2008 former Prime Minister Stephen Harper apologized to Canada's Indigenous peoples, acknowledging that "the consequences of the Indian Residential Schools policy were profoundly negative and that this policy has had a lasting and damaging impact on Aboriginal culture, heritage and language" (Government of Canada, 2008, ¶ 3). As part of the Indian Residential Schools Settlement Agreement (http://www.residentialschoolsettlement.ca/irs settlement agreement- english.pdf), the government also launched the Truth and Reconciliation Commission (TRC) (http://www.trc.ca/websites/trcinstitution/index.php?p=3) to investigate and document the injustices of the legacy of residential schooling in order to promote awareness among the general public and begin the momentous task of healing and moving forward together. However, Aboriginal education in Canada continues to be a challenge, with First Nations students typically achieving at levels that are below the Canadian average (CMEC, 2015b; Parkin, 2015). Issues include teacher training and retention, the recruitment of Aboriginal teachers, parental engagement, language instruction, lower per-pupil funding formulas, and the development of culturally relevant curriculum (Standing Senate Committee on Aboriginal Peoples, 2011). To support the diverse needs of these students, the federal government provided $1.55 billion to First Nations elementary and secondary education in 2010–2011. For construction and maintenance of education facilities on reserve, additional funding of approximately $200 million was provided. On a per capita basis, the federal government stated that $14,056 was allocated per full-time equivalent student in 2011–2012 for elementary and secondary education expenditure (AANDC, 2015), but this number has been questioned by the Assembly of First Nations who argue that only about 40% of this funding is provided to students on-reserves, with the remainder going to provincial school boards to pay the tuition fees for students living on reserves but attending public schools (Assembly of First Nations, 2011). According to AFN, a closer examination of this number reveals that, in 2011, students in First Nation schools were actually being funded at $7101—a gap of over $3500 less than students in provincial schools. Further to this, the inequities of the historical residential schooling system for Aboriginal peoples and continuing issues concerning supports for Aboriginal students in First Nation schools require further focused attention and resources. In this vein, the TRC issued their final report in June of 2015, which contained 94 calls to action including recommendations to eliminate the funding gap in education between First Nations children being education on and off reserves and to draft new Aboriginal education legislation with the full collaboration of Aboriginal peoples (Truth and Reconciliation Commission of Canada, 2015). According to the OECD (2015), improving the performance of Canada's Aboriginal students is a key issue in the continued betterment of equitable and quality education in the country.

Conclusion

Overall, Canada is a country that is proud of its education system and places a high value on—and participation in—publicly funded education. Teachers are highly qualified and, generally, a respected profession. The

Canadian population is, by international comparisons, well educated and inequities linked to socioeconomic status or immigrant status or lower than average compared to the OECD (OECD, 2015). Nevertheless, there remain national issues of concern, particularly recognition, reconciliation, and appropriate resources to support Aboriginal students and communities (Truth and Reconciliation Commission of Canada, 2015). Furthermore, while the values and practices of education are influenced by the national political, social and economic context and, particularly, by the Canadian Charter of Rights and Freedoms; school education is constitutionally the responsibility of provinces and territories. There is no one Canadian education system; instead there are local variations affecting teachers and teaching. In the following chapter, we provide in-depth case studies of two of Canada's highest performing provinces: Alberta and Ontario.

For more information on education in Canada and key policy initiatives, please see the OECD's recent Policy Outlook document on Canada (http://www.oecd.org/edu/EDUCATION POLICY OUTLOOK CANADA.pdf).

2

TEACHER POLICIES AND PRACTICES IN ALBERTA

Ken Zeichner, Jesslyn Hollar, and Shane Pisani

AS CANADA'S FOURTH MOST populated province, Alberta consistently ranks in the top 10 on the Programme for International Student Assessment (PISA) in science, numeracy, reading, and mathematics. Unlike some other high-performing education systems, Alberta has a diverse demographic; according to the National Household Survey administered in 2011, immigrants accounted for 18.1% of the total population in Alberta (Alberta Government, 2015). 12.4% of newcomers to Canada between 2006 and 2011 chose to settle in Alberta, with the majority living in and around the Calgary region. With its historically conservative government and progressive social ideologies, Alberta has managed to maintain a delicate balance between top-down policy directives and teacher agency (Alberta Government, 2015). Much of this balance is the result of a long-standing mutual trust among the teaching profession, school administration, and the government. As one Ministry official explained:

> We've created a community that has come together collectively and collaboratively on issues in the education sector workforce. So where many jurisdictions might struggle because they're battling with the union or they're battling with the Home School Association . . . We have built relationships where we have all of the education sector stakeholder partners working together to address shared challenges and opportunities. . . That's huge. That allows us to do things that we might not have been able to do.
>
> (Ministry Official, Mark Bevan, p.18)

Alberta's sociopolitical and historical context, governance structure, and education system will be explored in this report to (1) better understand how this highly developed system supports teaching quality; (2) understand the ways in which the province's policies and practices emerge and function in the system and cultural context; and (3) create a window into the work of Alberta's teachers. Our hope is that by investigating this consistently high-performing and highly developed education system, policy makers can draw valuable lessons from Alberta when crafting policy in their home countries.

Geography

The province of Alberta is geographically similar to Montana and Colorado in the United States. With the Rocky Mountains in the western half of the province and prairies in the eastern half, Alberta's topography is highly varied. This topographical variation reflects Alberta's education system. While holding common ideals, or in the case of Alberta's geography, common boundaries, variety exists to meet the diverse needs of Albertans.

Alberta also boasts plentiful natural and nonrenewable resources, including large oil and oil sand deposits, gas, bountiful forests, and agriculture (see Figure 2–1). Alberta's natural resources include more than 60% of Canada's conventional crude oil reserves and all of its heavy oil and oil sands reserves (Alberta Canada, 2014). Other key industries in the province include petrochemicals, agriculture, nanotechnology, forestry, biotechnology, and information and health technologies. Nonrenewable resource revenues comprise 21% of Alberta's general revenue (Horner, 2014). Due to the fluctuating nature of oil prices, however, the revenues obtained on an annual basis can be unpredictable. Even so, Alberta's revenue from oil plays a large role in Alberta's education budget. For example, Alberta's general revenue funded 68% of the 2014–2015 budget ("Education Funding in Alberta," 2014). As such, the education system in Alberta is affected by the price of oil and gas (in what is referred to as a "boom and bust economy"), and funding for schools varies with the condition of the economy.

Demographics

Alberta is a multilingual and ethnically diverse province with dramatic population growth. As of April 2014, Alberta's population stood at 4.1 million people, with three times the national average growth rate (Hansen, 2014). Interprovincial and international migrants have fueled this population growth rate more than birth rates. Alberta's large migrant population also makes it a multilingual society. According to the 2011

Figure 2–1 Province of Alberta

Source: Natural Resources Canada.

Census of Canada, while Canada recognizes both English and French as official national languages, German, Tagalog (Philipino/Filipino), Ukrainian, and Cree are also popular languages spoken by Albertans (Hansen, 2012). Despite this multilingual society, English remains the sole home language for nearly nine out of ten Albertans (ibid).

Most of Alberta's population is concentrated in its cities and their surrounding suburbs. The southern half of the province contains the vast majority of the population. North of Edmonton, the province remains largely rural, and includes many First Nation communities. Alberta is home to two of Canada's largest and most diverse cities, Calgary and Edmonton. Calgary is the third most diverse city in Canada and the fourth largest with a population of 1,195,194 in 2014 ("Civic Census Results," 2014). It is also considered to be wealthier than Edmonton in part because it houses the head offices of the major oil and gas companies. Calgary has the fourth highest immigrant population after Toronto, Vancouver, and Montreal. The Philippines, India, and China are lead source countries for immigrants to Calgary. Among young people 15–24 years of age, almost 14% are immigrants and 23% are members of visible minority groups ("Calgary at a Glance," 2013). The influx of immigrants into Calgary has been associated with increased economic disparity in the city.

Edmonton is Alberta's second largest city with a population of 877,926 in the 2014 census and Canada's fifth largest city (Dyck, 2014). Edmonton is a staging point for northern Alberta's oil sands and diamond-mining operations. Additionally, there are a number of postsecondary institutions operating in Edmonton including the University of Alberta. The large presence of the provincial government in Edmonton combined with the highly educated population that government infrastructure brings impacts the culture of Edmonton.

As a consequence of being an entry point to industry and higher education within Alberta, Edmonton is also the sixth most popular city for all immigrants to Canada. The number of immigrants residing in Edmonton more than doubled from 2000 to 2010, prompted primarily by an economic boom, an increasing foreign student population, and humanitarian immigrants. According to a report released by the Edmonton Social Planning Council in 2013, with respect to immigration, the fastest growing immigrant population comes from East and Southeast Asia (41.8%) (Neilson et al., 2013). The University of Alberta also attracts a considerable number of Asian students who contribute to the immigrant population.

Inequity for Racial (Visible Minorities) and Aboriginal Populations

Within Alberta as is the case throughout much of Canada, visible minorities are defined as "persons, other than Aboriginal peoples, who are non-Caucasian in race or non-white in color" (Employment Equity Act, 1995) (Link 2-1). Visible minorities and immigrant populations face significant economic challenges even during periods of robust local growth. There is an overrepresentation of Aboriginal people living in poverty in Calgary, and Aboriginal people are more frequently employed in low-paying and low-status positions. Calgary has also witnessed increasing income disparity between minority and nonminority populations. According to a report on inequality in Calgary authored by Pruegger et al. (2009) (Link 2-2), it is estimated that within 30 communities in Calgary, 60–80% of the low-income population is what the authors define as "racialized"—that is, any number of superficial physical characteristics in population groups that lead to a systematized and institutionalized hierarchy that creates social and economic inequities, power differentials, and discrimination against population groups viewed as undesirable due to perceived racial origin. Within seven communities in the city limits, 80% of the low-income population is considered by the authors to be "racialized"—and typically, visible minorities, recent immigrants, and Aboriginal people fall into this category.

Similar to Calgary, Edmonton's Aboriginal population suffers high unemployment at around 13% compared with 5.6% for the overall population (Neilson et. al., 2013). Most of the Aboriginal population (First Nations, Metis, and Inuit [FNMI]) lives in Edmonton and north of Edmonton. Consequently, schools in these areas contain the highest concentrations of FNMI students.

In 2011, 10.6% of Edmontonians lived in families below the low-income cut off, after taxes (LICO) (Neilson et al., 2013). In Canada, families are considered to be low income if they spend 63% or more of their after-tax take home income on food, shelter, and clothing. At present, one out of every seven Albertan children lives in poverty. This is lower than the United States' child poverty rate of 22%, or about one in five American children (National Center for Children in Poverty, 2014). In Alberta, for unattached individuals, the poverty rate is nearly double that of one parent family units. Nearly one in four single parent households, particularly those with female heads of households, are also living below the poverty line, as over two thirds of low-wage workers in Alberta are women, and women reportedly earn less than men, which contributes to the higher number of single-parent households below the Low-Income Cut Off (LICO) (Neilson et al., 2013).

Students in Alberta

Student Population and Demographics

According to Alberta Education, as of September 30, 2013, 657,811 students attend Alberta's 2,189 schools (Alberta Education, 2014a,

2014b). Province-wide, the ESL student population comprises about 10% of the total student population though this percentage is higher in large metropolitan areas (Alberta Education, 2013, p. 10). In the larger metropolitan areas of Calgary and Edmonton, the ESL population comprises almost 25% of the total student population (p. 10). Aboriginal populations comprise another part of Alberta's 5- to 19-year-old school-aged population. First Nations, Metis, and Inuit (FNMI) students make up about 9% of Alberta's school-aged population (p. 10).

To accommodate the diversity of students enrolled in Alberta's schools and to allow for some school choice, there are Alberta public schools, separate schools (separate schools created by a religious minority, either Protestant or Roman Catholic), charter schools, private schools, and band schools for FNMI students. Albertan families also have a relatively broad range of options available to them in terms of school choice. Families can choose to have their children attend public, Catholic, Francophone, private, or charter schools. They can also access home education, online/virtual schools, outreach programs, and alternative programs. Despite having many options, roughly 67% of the student population is enrolled in the public education. For a breakdown of the school types, total schools within Alberta, and students attending each type of school as of September 18, 2014, see Table 2–1.

Table 2–1 Breakdown of Alberta Student Population 2013/2014

Type of School	Number of School Type in AL	Students in Attendance
Public	1,461	443,713
Separate	379	152,628
Francophone	38	6,801
Charter	21	8,732
Private	171	28,076
Private ECS operators	119	5,062
Other ECS to grade 12 education providers		12,799
Total student population and schools	2,189	657,811

Sources: "Breakdown of Alberta Student Population 2013/2014"; "Number of Alberta Schools and Authorities," 2014.

ESL and FNMI Students

Alberta has had to address a range of issues to ensure equitable education and student success for First Nations, Metis, and Inuit (FNMI) students. Much research has been conducted at both the provincial and national levels to examine the need for education reform that would lead to greater educational attainment by FNMI students. For Alberta, secondary education completion rates among self-identified Aboriginal students are about 64%. The graduation rate drops even more for those who live on reserves with only a 32% completion rate (Richards, 2008) (Link 2-3). The literature on Canadian Aboriginal education suggests many reasons for this problem, including feelings of marginalization in schools; lack of caring; poor relationships with other students and teachers; and a history of government sponsored residential schools whose goal was to eliminate Aboriginal culture (Gunn et al., 2011). This has been a subject of considerable attention, as described later.

Social Welfare

With the number of low-income families, a variety of safety nets are well established within Alberta to support them. For example, there are a variety of childcare subsidies for eligible parents available through Alberta's Department of Human Services ("Child Care Subsidy," 2014). These safety nets and subsidies likely help maintain an overall low child poverty rate and enable maximum learning opportunities for LICO students in the schools. Consequently, Alberta has the lowest child poverty rate among the provinces at 11.2 percent. Additionally, residents of Alberta are eligible to register for the Alberta Health Care Insurance Plan (AHCIP) coverage to receive insured hospital and physician services, which insures a number of basic health care services. Many employers also provide supplementary health insurance to their employees. Rent support subsidies and affordable housing are available for low-income families as well.

Although the overall child poverty rate is relatively low, the Early Childhood Development Mapping Project that was conducted by the University of Alberta from 2009–2013 (ECMP, 2014)[1] indicates that there is variation across the province in a number of indicators of healthy early childhood development. Additionally, although over three quarters of young children are developing appropriately in physical health and well-being, social competence, emotional maturity, and language and thinking skills, nearly one-third are experiencing difficulty in communication skills and general knowledge.

In an effort to investigate the various factors that lead to this high-performing education system, policies and practices related to teaching and teacher education are explored in the rest of the case study. We focus first on an educational policy context with respect to Albertan governance, the Alberta Teachers' Association, curriculum and curricular decisions, and the social and political historical contexts. From there, we move to the students in Alberta's education system, including student demographics, student performance, and student assessment. Then we move to gain an understanding of teachers in Alberta at their various points of development. We focus on teacher preparation, evaluation and supervision, induction, retention, professional development, compensation, and what is expected of teachers within a typical workday.

Student Learning in Alberta

In the past, Alberta had consistently outperformed other countries and Canadian provinces in science on the PISA. In 2006, Alberta was second only to Finland in science (Stewart 2012). Alberta also outperformed the other provinces in reading and science on the 2010 PISA. However, the 2012 PISA indicates a slight downward trend in performance for Alberta with an uptick in performance by British Columbia. Despite this, Alberta still had a strong showing on the 2012 PISA results overall. The drop in 2012 PISA scores in Alberta possibly reflects shifting demographics in the province due to increased immigration.

Alberta had the highest dispersion among the Canadian provinces between low and high achievers on the 2012 PISA (Brochu et al., 2013). This dispersion index does not factor in poverty levels of individuals or immigrant status but simply takes into account performance on the test. As we describe below, reducing this dispersion between low and high achievers, particularly with respect to First Nations students and immigrants, has been an object of considerable professional effort in Alberta. Despite this relatively high within Canada dispersion rate between high and low achievers in Alberta, the overall rate of equity in achievement in Alberta is still above the OECD average as will be discussed below in the section on educational equity concerns.

Governance, Sociopolitical, and Historical Context in Alberta

Alberta had four decades of leadership of Progressive Conservative government. The preceding five decades of governance by the Social Credit Party were also politically conservative. Thus, until the beginning of a

New Democratic government in May 2015, Alberta had seen more than 90 years of conservative governance. Despite this right of center political climate, policymakers in Alberta have been largely supportive of public education and teachers. Historically, teachers have been respected throughout the province, and a high value has been placed on education. Even with 90 years of conservative government under two parties, the public has maintained its respect for teachers and belief that they should be supported. Its conservative governments recognized that the public continued to hold the public education system in relatively high esteem.

In interviews conducted March 19 and 20, 2014, when asked what is most responsible for Alberta's success as an educational system, all of the 10 interviewees from the Ministry of Education, Teachers' Association, the University of Alberta, and schools talked about the level of trust and cooperation that exists across the different sectors in education (government, teachers, administrators, universities) and that how despite political differences over specific issues, such as class size and teacher workload, the parties have been able to come together to support a strong public education system.

One aspect of this strong level of collaboration is the stability of the government. Instead of shifting educational policies according to differing governing administrations ideologies (i.e., cut funding with this administration, restore it with the next one), the stability of four decades of conservative government in Alberta has allowed for continued, sustained commitment to education and educational progress. There also appears to be a lot of temporary, lateral movement of staff across schools, districts, administration, the union, and the Ministry that has given individuals experience in different parts of the education infrastructure and has contributed to the culture of collaboration among different education stakeholders. According to an Alberta Teachers' Association official:

> A true culture of trust exists between the (teacher) organization and government. This political stability has resulted in the tendency of both government and the association, the Alberta Teachers' Association, not to jump too quickly to solutions. So we don't have the initiative fatigue that many jurisdictions have fallen into. When we do move, the ocean liner called education reform in Alberta tends to take quite a while. But when it does turn its course, it goes in a decisive and sustained way with everybody steering more or less in the same direction.

> (Couture, Alberta Teachers' Association 3/14)

Education is seen as an important public good and worthy of investment. Because of this broad-reaching belief in the value of strong education, unions and government have generally maintained a united front.

In fact, the Inspiring Education (Link 2-4) project resulted in an aspirational document with much citizen and educator input to define the direction of education for the future in Alberta. It was initiated in 2009 and has the support of both the government and the teachers' association ("Inspiring Education," 2010). With increasing fiscal cuts and shielding of taxpayer revenue, however, this favorable climate toward education and investment in the public good might be shifting somewhat. There were noticeable tensions two years ago when we began this case study between the Alberta Teachers' Association (ATA) and government over

a number of issues, including the Task Force on Teaching Excellence (Alberta Education, 2014c) (Link 2-5). The ATA felt that teachers were not adequately involved in this effort, which was charged with operationalizing policy shifts in education previously outlined in the Inspiring Education document (Alberta Education, 2010).

Alberta Education (Ministry of Education)

The Ministry[2] is responsible for developing curriculum and setting standards; evaluating curriculum and assessing outcomes; developing and certifying teachers; supporting special needs responsibilities; funding and supporting school boards; overseeing Aboriginal and francophone education; and overseeing basic education policy and regulations (https://education.alberta.ca/alberta-education-fr/).

The Alberta Teachers' Association

There is one teacher's organization in Alberta. Created in 1918 as the Alberta Teachers' Alliance, the name was changed to the Alberta Teachers' Association in 1936. All teachers employed by a school board in Alberta are required to become active members of the association. Interestingly enough, principals and other leaders within the education system also belong to the Alberta Teachers' Association and consider themselves to be teachers first.[3] This unusual situation where teachers and administrators belong to the same professional association is widely believed to be an important factor in the high level of trust that exists among educators in Alberta and a contributor to some of the policies that reflect this trust, such as the separation that exists between the supervision and evaluation of teachers. It is also believed that the suggestion in the report of the Teaching Commission to remove principals from the Alberta Teachers' Association as one of several elements suggested to further empower them to do their work was one of the recommendations in the commission's report that led to increased tensions between the teachers' association and the government.

Historically, Alberta Education (the name given to the Ministry of Education of Alberta) and the Alberta Teachers' Association have generally gotten on well. During Jeff Johnson's years as minister (2012–2014), however, and most notably with the Alberta Education Task Force on Teaching Report's recommendation that oversight for evaluation of teacher competency be removed from hands of the ATA and ceded to a College of Teaching as in British Columbia and Ontario, tensions increased between the union and the Education Ministry. Another example of these proposed changes was a recommendation in the Taskforce on Teaching Report to introduce the formal evaluation of teachers every five years.

In addition to the inclusion of both administrators and teachers in membership, the majority of Alberta Teachers' Association revenues derived from members' fees go toward the support of educator professional development. Couture (2012) contrasts this with the figure of under 5%, which he claims is allocated by most U.S. teacher associations.

Alberta Ministry of Innovation and Advanced Education

The Ministry of Innovation and Advanced Education[4] is involved with teacher education in the province because of its role in overseeing postsecondary education (Figure 2–2). This Ministry approves all new postsecondary programs including teacher education programs. In addition to approving new programs, it provides periodic evaluations of approved degree programs. It is also the Ministry that provides funding in the form of block grants to campuses to support the implementation of approved programs. The Professional Standards and Certification branch in the Ministry of Education monitors the quality of teacher education programs after they are approved in relation to the Teaching Quality Standard Ministerial Order (Link 2-6) that states the knowledge, skills, and attributes that all teachers are supposed to have.

Funding for Education

Funding for the education system in Alberta comes from two sources within the government: general government revenues, which make up 68% of the funding, and education property taxes, which comprise around one third of the $6.4 billion dollars of operational funding in the 2014 K–12 education budget ("Education Funding in Alberta," 2014) (Link 2-7).

Figure 2–2   Alberta Education Governance Structure

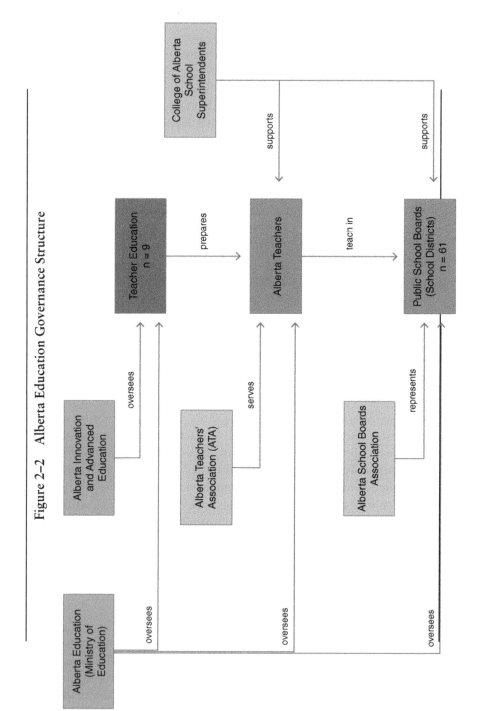

Money collected through education property taxes can be used only to fund the public education system, including public and Catholic schools (Figure 2–3). Private school funding comes from provincial general revenues, tuition, or instruction fees paid by parents, and private fundraising (ibid). The province funds all schools except the band schools on the First Nation Reserve. The federal government funds education in band schools (on the reserves) and in the cities for FNMI students.

The Ministry of Education in Alberta allocates all funding to local school boards, but the local school boards and school district authorities have considerable flexibility in determining how to best use these funds—up to 98% of funding (other than funds for staffing) is flexible. Local school boards can get approval to levy a special school tax. The School Act (Link 2-8) limits the amount raised to at most 3% of the board's budget for the applicable year. This ensures that if a board does choose to raise money locally, the amount does not significantly undermine the broader equality and equity principles of the funding system ("The School Act," 2000).

According to a report published in May 2013 by the Center for American Progress, "Professors Dean Neu of the University of Calgary and Alison Taylor of the University of Alberta have noted that the impact of Alberta's new, more equitable provincial-level funding system was not the same for all school boards. After the system was reformed in 1994, some boards such as Calgary's saw a disproportionally greater reduction in per-pupil funding relative to the province as a whole" (Herman, 2013) (Link 2-9).

There are four different types of funding: base, differential, targeted, and capital. Base funding is determined in kindergarten through grade 9 on a per-student basis. In grades 10 through 12, funding is based on the number and type of high school credits taken. Beyond base funding is differential funding. Differential funding is based on the unique characteristics and circumstances of each school authority. Components of differential funding include funding for severe disabilities, English as a Second Language instruction, French language and enculturation (Francisation), First Nations, socioeconomic status, Northern (geographic reach) funding, learning resources, transportation, and plant operations and maintenance funding. Targeted funding is provided for specific province initiatives. Targeted funding has included Alberta Initiative for School Improvement (AISI) funding, student health funding, children and youth with complex needs funding, and high-speed networking services funding. Capital funding for school construction and infrastructure maintenance and renewal is also allocated for approved projects. With the funding provided, school authorities must ensure that they provide access to education programs

Figure 2–3   2014–2015 Educational Funding Allocations

Budget 2014
Total Operational Funding K-12 Education in Alberta
over $6.4 Billion Total

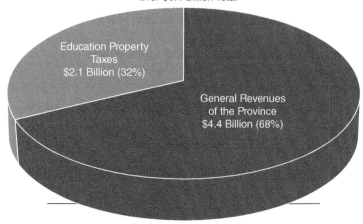

Alberta Education

Budget 2014 Breakdown - $7.4 Billion
Includes $204 million in education property taxes for opted-out boards

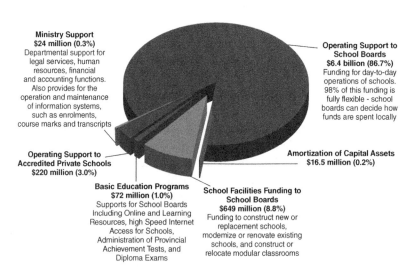

Source: Alberta Education, Education Funding in Alberta 2014–2015, Funding Booklet.

for their students that follow Alberta's Programs of Study (Curriculum) (Link 2-10), employ certificated teachers, provide students with the required hours of instruction each school year, provide the education minister with audited financial statements, and provide transportation services for students who reside more than 2.4 kilometers from their school.

Curriculum and Curricular Decision Making

Alberta Education develops and designs the scope and sequence for Alberta's Early Childhood Services (ECS) to Grade 12 curriculum. Curricula are outlined in provincial programs of study, which identify what students are expected to learn and do in all subjects and grades. Alberta Education also provides resources for teachers to aid them in designing or adapting lesson plans aligned to standards for different programs of study. At present, Alberta Education is adapting its curriculum to the 21st century through an initiative called Curriculum Redesign. Through Curriculum Redesign, Alberta Education reviews and revises standards and guidelines for curriculum, which include programs of study, assessments, and learning and teaching resources, as well as processes for developing curriculum.

Stewart (2012) has stated that the Alberta curriculum, which exists in every K–12 subject is considerably more detailed than the typical curriculum in the U.S. She uses the example of the grades 7–9 science curriculum in Alberta which is 73 pages long in comparison with the comparable curriculum in Iowa, a local control state, which is 4 pages (p. 46). Stewart writes favorably about this detailed curriculum as providing for greater consistency of instruction across the province. There is however some evidence in the Alberta Teachers' Association literature that some have seen this detailed curriculum as too prescriptive. One of the stated goals in the current curriculum redesign is to reduce the detail in the curriculum to provide teachers with more flexibility in making curricular decisions.

> Teachers have always said that we had too much content and they had challenges in covering the content. So if we can reduce the content and give teachers more autonomy to engage with the curriculum and to plan for learning in different ways, to go deeper into learning for kids, and to differentiate instruction for kids, then that will benefit the kids in the system so that it's a more personalized approach to education.

(Ministry of Education official Karen Shipka, p. 3)

Prior to the development of the current very detailed curriculum, there was more flexibility for school-designed courses to meet local needs. Because of some push back on the relatively rigid curriculum, there are new efforts to try and bring some of this flexibility back by reducing the curriculum (Alberta Education, 2014b).

Focus on the Whole Child

Based on various interviews that we conducted in the spring of 2014, there appears to be a focus on the whole child ingrained in much of the vision, teaching, and curricular decisions in the schools. Rather than cutting funding for the arts, music, and athletics, as has been the case in many school districts in the United States, these components beyond traditional academic learning are encouraged. In fact, one elementary teacher we interviewed facilitates learning around play. Additionally, the teaching quality standards that all teachers must meet use language that suggests a more holistic approach to education than in the U.S. For example, one of the teaching quality standards states:

> Teachers strive to involve parents in their children's schooling. Partnerships with the home are characterized by the candid sharing of information and ideas to influence how teachers and parents, independently and cooperatively, contribute to students' learning.

(Teaching Quality Standards 1997)

The Teaching Quality Standards were approved by the Minister of Education in 1997. They apply to teacher certification, professional development, supervision and evaluation, and provide descriptors of selected knowledge, skills, and attributes for teachers throughout their career. Understanding contextual factors and variables and using context in adaptive decision making seem to be key threads running throughout the standards in addition to content knowledge, pedagogy, and viewing children holistically. The Teaching Quality Standards in Alberta are discussed in more detail in the "Teaching in Alberta" section and are also provided in Appendix 2–A.

Student Assessment

On the whole, Albertans place an emphasis on assessment for learning rather than on the punitive assessment of teachers that exists in the United States. The Fraser Institute (an independent think tank) ranks schools according to student test scores, and this has some impact on the public perception of schools, but the main emphasis in the province is on creating the conditions for teacher and student learning rather than on identifying and punishing schools and teachers with poor test results.

Students are assessed at the provincial level four times throughout their tenure in the school system. These assessments occur during grades 3, 6, 9, and 12 and are called the Provincial Achievement Tests (PATs, Link 2-11) for grades 3, 6, and 9 and the Diploma Exams (Link 2-12) for grade 12, respectively. The PATs combine multiple-choice, numerical-response, and written-response questions. It is important to note that new Student Learning Assessments (SLAs, Link 2-13) will replace the Provincial Achievement Tests (PATs) and incorporate these kinds of questions with the possible addition of more developmentally appropriate question types. Alberta Education is developing the new Student Learning Assessments in consultation with the Alberta School Boards Association (ASBA), Alberta School Councils' Association (ASCA), Alberta Teachers' Association (ATA), College of Alberta School Superintendents (CASS), and Alberta Assessment Consortium (AAC).

Additionally, Alberta Education's FAQ document on the new Student Learning Assessments notes that these new assessments will neither be used to rank schools nor evaluate teachers. Piloting of the computer-based SLAs began with grade 3 students in September 2014 with almost all students participating ("Student Learning Assessments," 2014). Instead of assessing students at the end of the school year, information will be collected via this assessment at the beginning of the school year with the hope of better informing student learning.

Diploma exams are offered in particular diploma examination courses and are taken by students enrolled in those examination courses, mature students (19 or older), or students who would like to improve their examination score ("Diploma General Information Bulletin," 2014). The results of the examinations contribute to a student's final score in the course: 50% is the score on the diploma exam; 50% is their class score. The closest thing to compare diploma exams to at this point seems like New York State Regents Exams or the exams in the Australian States.

Alberta Education does not support ranking and comparison of schools or authorities based on achievement test scores even as it participates in nationwide and international assessments. At the national level, students have been involved in the School Achievement Indicators Program (SAIP) ("National and International Testing," 2014). SAIP was replaced by the Pan-Canadian Assessment Program (PCAP) in 2007. According to the Council of Ministers of Education, Canada (CMEC) website, "a new pan-Canadian assessment program was needed to reflect changes in curriculum, integrate the increased jurisdictional emphasis on international assessments, and allow for the testing of the core subjects of mathematics, reading, and science. [. . .] During each test one subject is the focus of the assessment and the majority of the students write the test on this subject. However, the other two subjects are also tested, with a smaller number of students writing the tests in those subjects. In this way, PCAP provides results in all three subjects. Sample sizes have permitted results to be calculated at both a pan-Canadian and jurisdictional level. PCAP, and SAIP before it, is not intended to replace provincial and territorial assessments, but rather to complement them. Given the random sampling and the nature of the PCAP assessment, it is also not a measure of individual student achievement."

As alluded to earlier by the Council of Ministers of Education, in Canada, international assessments have received stronger emphasis lately among the provinces. Alberta also participates in international studies of achievement, along with other provinces and countries. These include: Programme for International Student Assessment (PISA), Progress in International Reading Literacy Study (PIRLS), and Trends in International Mathematics and Science Study (TIMSS) (Link 2-14).

Educational Equity Concerns

Even with the safety nets and social welfare supports available in Alberta, certain populations and groups of students—FNMI, refugee, and some immigrant children in particular—often exist on the margins of Albertan education. They have higher drop out rates, and there is a lot of concern about these students.

Mirroring the inequities in the broader society (e.g., in access to jobs that pay a living wage), there are some inequities within the education system between FNMI students, some immigrant and refugee populations, and the rest of the student population. One aspect of these inequities is the inequitable access to experienced teachers in the rural northern part of the province. Although the Ministry is engaged in several initiatives to increase teacher retention in the rural north (e.g., in band schools), there continues to be a serious problem in attracting teachers to teach and then stay in these remote schools. The government is focusing on preparing more people who live in these communities to be teachers (e.g., it funds the aboriginal teacher education program at the University of Alberta as described below). The government also funds a rural practicum for teacher candidates to experience the rural north, and it provides financial incentives to teachers who agree to teach for a specified number of years in some northern districts.

Overall however, Alberta has achieved equity for students in the 2012 PISA above the OECD average and student performance levels above the OECD average. The better than OECD average equity for students in Canada is evidenced by the strength of the association between student performance in mathematics and socioeconomic status. Alberta's better than OECD average student equity specifically, is evidenced by the spread between the 90th and 10th percentiles in student test scores in mathematics.

Another provincial initiative that is focused on teacher preparation for teachers in FNMI schools is the Aboriginal Teacher Education Program (ATEP) (Link 2-15). This program is organized by the University of Alberta and is funded by the Ministry. It runs one to two cohorts a year in the northern parts of the province. Teacher candidates in these cohorts tend to have been working as support staff (in one case, there was a bus driver) at schools in the First Nation communities and are then selected for recruitment into the cohorts. By offering a blended model of instructional delivery, the University of Alberta prepares these individuals to become teachers. Some of the course work is offered online by university faculty and other aspects of the course work are offered closer to the teacher candidate's communities at partner institutions. Much of the focus of the ATEP program remains on educating teachers who are already members of these communities to remain in and find success in teaching students in these communities. A four-year pilot of this program that graduated 27 new teachers for northern FNMI communities was completed in June 2014.

In addition to the ATEP program, the University of Calgary and University of Lethbridge both offer First Nations courses that are specific to the bands in their areas. Considering that there are 46 different First Nations communities in Alberta alone, a generic FNMI approach would be insufficient in meeting the needs of the diversity within the First Nations communities.

Teachers in Alberta

According to a document by the Alberta Government published in 2013 entitled *A Transformation in Progress,* there were approximately 35,000 FTE teachers and 42,000 certified teachers working in Alberta's elementary and secondary schools in 2011/2012. This teaching force has a high ratio of females (71%) to males (29%), and this ratio is increasing with men comprising only 23% of the teacher candidate enrolled in teacher education programs (p. 15). Approximately 3% of teachers graduating from bachelor of education programs in Alberta self-identify as FNMI (p. 16). These numbers, unfortunately, do not mirror Alberta's student population. Efforts to diversify the teaching force other than the targeted recruitment of FNMI teachers in the Aboriginal Teacher Education Program (see below) are not readily apparent. There does seem though to be more efforts in recent years to prepare teacher candidates to teach students who are different from themselves, including course work around aboriginal history, cultural awareness, and cultural competence.

Despite efforts to criticize teachers in a number of education systems internationally that have led to the lowering of teacher morale, an erosion of teacher autonomy, and to the deregulation of teacher education (e.g., Weiner & Compton, 2008), teachers in Alberta seem to feel valued and respected. For example, in the 2013 survey conducted by the ATA of a 10% random sample of its membership, about 89% of teachers agree or strongly agree that they are very committed to teaching as a profession and that in public they are proud to say that they are teachers. In this same survey, about two-thirds of teachers reported that they experience no or low stress because of the lack of control over their professional practice. In the 2013 Teaching and Learning International Survey (TALIS) conducted by the Organisation for Economic Co-operation and Development (OECD) however, only 49% of lower secondary teachers report that teaching is a valued profession in society (OECD, 2014). The bulk of the evidence that we have examined, including the elementary and high school teachers interviewed for this case study, and the relatively high levels of teacher compensation seem to support the view that teaching is a valued profession in Alberta.

Teacher Compensation

The province of Alberta pays its teacher well when compared to the other Canadian provinces and territories. On average, Alberta has the highest teacher salaries among the 10 provinces ("Questions about . . .Teacher Salaries," 2014). When the teacher salaries of the four additional Canadian territories are included for comparison, teacher salaries in Alberta drop to fourth place (ibid). As a whole, Canadian territories pay their teachers more, on average, than the 10 provinces—most likely because of difficulty in recruitment and retention of teachers in the territories. Since Stewart (2012) compares the size of Alberta to Iowa, consider the following comparisons in teacher salaries between Iowa and Alberta. For the 2012–2013 school year, an average total teacher salary among all districts in the state of Iowa was between $36,000 and $63,000 ("2012–2013

Table 2–2 Average Teacher FTE Earnings

Length of Schooling	FT Average Teacher Earnings	FT Veteran Teacher Earnings
(10+ yrs)		
4 (B.Ed.)	$58,500	$92,300
5 (Combined-Degree)	$61,800	$95,600
6 (2 yr. After-Degree)	$65,400	$99,300

Iowa Public School and AEA Teacher Salary," 2013). This includes first year teachers and teachers with 10+ years of experience.

In Alberta, the average first year full-time teacher with four years of university earns approximately $58,500 (all dollars referenced in this paragraph are in Canadian dollars), indicating that Alberta teacher salaries are by and large much higher than teacher salaries in Iowa ("Questions about. . .Teacher Salaries," 2014). Table 2–2 provides average teacher salaries in Alberta. The average Alberta teacher with 10 years of experience makes over $92,000 per year; this is the highest among all Canadian provinces. Over the last decade, the average salary of teachers with at least 10 years of experience has increased by 41%, from $65,203 in 2001/02 to $92,261 in 2013/14 ("Putting Students First," 2014). Alberta teachers with five years of education are the highest paid across all provinces. Teacher salaries make up over 53% of the total operating budget for education. A beginning teacher with a four-year degree will earn about $58,500 and a beginning teacher with a master's degree will earn about $65,400.

For additional information about Alberta teacher salaries, Table 2–3 provides the salaries of teachers in eight focus districts according to collective bargaining agreements. The eight focus districts, which constitute a representative sample in terms of size and geography across Alberta, have competitive salaries. For example, Fort McMurray, in Northern Alberta, has a higher entry-level salary than more popular geographical areas such as Calgary and Edmonton; after five years, however, the salaries between Calgary and Edmonton differ by only a few hundred dollars suggesting that the initial discrepancy in entry level pay is a function of recruiting teachers for a more remote region of Alberta.

In addition to teacher salaries, teachers in Alberta have a generous pension and benefits plan. In fact, in 2012/2013 alone, operating support to school boards included $353 million for current service payments for teachers' pensions, with a further $455 million budgeted in the Ministry of Finance to provide for the costs of the pre-1992 teachers' pension

Table 2–3 Salary Schedules for Eight Focus Districts

With four years of university training effective September 1, 2011 (in Canadian Dollars)

	Calgary RCSSD	Calgary Public	Edmonton CSSD	Edmonton Public	Fort McMurray RCSSD	Fort McMurray Public	Red Deer CRD	Red Deer Public
Entry	57,725	57,660	58,411	58,158	61,090	61,928	57,017	58,387
Year 5	74,450	71,179	75,069	74,740	74,408	77,907	73,917	73,506
Year 10	88,120	88,093	88,396	92,020	91,063	94,295	90,817	92,405

(In U.S. dollars exchange rate $1 Canadian = $0.92 U.S.)

	Calgary RCSSD	Calgary Public	Edmonton CSSD	Edmonton Public	Fort McMurray RCSSD	Fort McMurray Public	Red Deer CRD	Red Deer Public
Entry	53,107	53,047	53,728	53,505	56,202	56,973	52,455	53,716
Year 5	68,494	65,484	69,063	66,000	68,455	71,674	68,003	67,625
Year 10	81,070	81,045	81,324	84,658	83,777	86,751	83,551	85,012

With six years of university training effective September 1, 2011 (in Canadian Dollars)

	Calgary RCSSD	Calgary Public	Edmonton CSSD	Edmonton Public	Fort McMurray RCSSD	Fort McMurray Public	Red Deer CRD	Red Deer Public
Entry	65,267	64,905	65,537	65,256	68,212	68,164	64,060	65,451
Year 5	81,994	78,423	78,865	78,521	81,534	81,446	77,580	80,570
Year 10	95,158	95,336	95,521	99,119	98,186	98,052	103,380	99,468

(In U.S. dollars exchange rate $1 Canadian = $.92 U.S.)

	Calgary RCSSD	Calgary Public	Edmonton CSSD	Edmonton Public	Fort McMurray RCSSD	Fort McMurray Public	Red Deer CRD	Red Deer Public
Entry	60,045	59,712	60,294	57,275	62,755	62,710	58,916	60,214
Year 5	75,434	72,149	72,555	72,239	77,771	74,930	71,373	74,124
Year 10	87,545	87,709	87,879	91,189	90,331	90,207	95,109	91,510

Source: Averages are also listed here: http://education.alberta.ca/admin/workforce/faq/teachers/teachersalaries.aspx.

liability ("Putting Students First," 2014). Benefits for full-time teachers are approximately worth $7,500 and typically include life insurance, disability benefits, dental care, extended health care, and vision; but this varies from school authority to school authority. There are always exceptions to these generalizations and so individual collective agreements must be consulted to determine specific pay-rates for each jurisdiction in Alberta. The salary grids for each school authority are usually listed near the end of each collective agreement (Link 2-16) between the individual school boards and the Alberta Teachers' Association (ATA).

In Alberta, a teacher's salary is determined by the teacher's education and experience. The Teacher Qualifications Service (TQS) evaluates a teacher's education. All public, separate, and francophone school authorities in Alberta, as well as some private boards, accept evaluation statements from the TQS to help determine a teacher's salary. The employing school authority does the evaluation of a teacher's experience. A combination of the TQS assessment and the school authority's assessment will determine a teacher's placement on the salary grid.

Teachers' salaries in Alberta compare well with salaries paid in other professional fields. Our focal teacher, an experienced social studies teacher with over 25 years of experience, thinks that he is among the top 5% of wage earners in the province. When compared with other professions, teachers rank toward the top. Educator salaries are on par with public administration and professional, scientific, and technical sectors ("2013 AWSS Wages by Industry and Region," 2013). The average educational services wage is $36.74. Utilities and oil and gas extraction are the only two industries with significantly higher average wages than educational services. See Table 2–4 for a chart detailing average industry wages.

The Work of Alberta's Teachers

An analysis of the work of Alberta's teachers shows that recent reductions in teaching positions and budget have led to an increased workload for the remaining teachers. ATA-sponsored surveys of teachers in 2005 and 2011 indicate that teachers reported worsened conditions of support for teachers of students with special needs. The percentage of teachers indicating this rises from 25 in 2005 to 50% in 2011 (Couture, 2012). A study sponsored by the Alberta Teachers' Association of the work lives of 20 beginning teachers in Calgary randomly selected from those who attended an orientation workshop for beginning teachers has shown an intensification in teachers' work ("The New Work of Teaching," 2012). This is perhaps a result of cuts in government funding due to decreased

Table 2–4   Average Industry Wages

Industry	Athabasca-Grande Prairie	Banff-Jasper Rocky Mountain House	Calgary	Camrose-Drumheller	Edmonton	Lethbridge-Medicine Hat	Red Deer	Wood Buffalo-Cold Lake	ALL REGIONS
1 Agriculture	$21.62	NA	$22.27	$20.75	$16.91	$19.41	$16.38	$25.72	$19.73
2 Forestry, logging, fishing, and hunting	$25.62	$28.83	NA	NA	NA	NA	NA	$28.15	$26.03
3 Oil and gas extraction	$33.30	$31.81	$49.98	$32.79	$37.86	$21.52	$33.77	$48.55	$42.91
4 Utilities	$39.78	$37.55	$53.18	$38.17	$47.30	$33.77	$31.56	NA	$45.30
5 Construction	$28.81	$29.19	$31.24	$28.40	$32.16	$25.44	$28.83	$35.67	$31.22
6 Manufacturing	$28.37	$26.35	$26.83	$26.63	$27.49	$23.58	$34.09	$28.81	$27.31
7 Wholesale trade	$25.10	$25.60	$26.97	$26.66	$24.94	$25.63	$27.11	$27.12	$25.95
8 Retail trade	$19.08	$18.19	$18.92	$17.96	$19.67	$17.42	$19.24	$18.83	$18.99
9 Transportation and warehousing	$31.89	$28.72	$25.60	$27.40	$24.94	$30.72	$27.32	$29.70	$26.93
10 Information, culture, recreation	$18.30	$14.23	$17.84	$16.57	$19.09	$17.18	$17.28	$20.64	$17.92
11 Finance, insurance, real estate, leasing	$25.88	$26.07	$28.79	$24.86	$29.84	$24.53	$25.26	$27.39	$28.40

12 Professional, scientific, and technical services	$30.40	34.13	$36.16	$30.09	$36.00	$28.26	$31.80	$30.28	$35.05
13 Business, building, and other support services	$26.50	25.38	$19.64	$19.39	18.97	$16.74	$18.83	$26.01	$19.86
14 Educational services	$31.41	28.96	$37.26	$32.44	$39.74	$31.99	$24.87	$28.41	$36.74
15 Health care and social assistance	$28.15	26.67	$32.11	$25.56	$30.10	$27.56	$28.57	$29.76	$29.94
16 Accommodation and food services	$13.02	13.36	$13.08	$12.05	$12.41	$11.57	$12.55	$15.22	$12.76
17 Other services (repair, personal services, and related)	$25.67	21.82	$28.34	$21.07	$26.72	$19.37	$22.35	$29.17	$26.14
18 Public administration	$31.24	30.11	$40.17	$30.57	$38.71	$31.80	$33.43	$32.12	$36.93
19 Mining and quarrying	NA	NA	$39.49	$26.75	$28.19	$22.01	NA	NA	$35.53
20 All industries	$25.95	21.93	$27.64	$23.86	$26.68	$22.74	$24.87	$31.63	$26.58

Source: 2013 AWSS Wages by Industry and Region, 2013.

oil revenues and the subsequent elimination of certain teaching positions, which have been subsumed by other teachers. Cuts to education funding appear to be continuing with a 9% budget cut in the 2015 budget across the board due to low oil revenues and a slowing economy ("Budget Cuts," 2015). This study indicates that teachers in Alberta work between 50 and 55 hour per week. Of these, approximately 80% are dedicated to such core instructional activities as teaching, planning, assessing, and reporting. The ATA report places the workload of Alberta's teachers alongside that of teachers in the U.K. and U.S. and other countries where the workload is considered high.

In the ATA report, a breakdown of the average time spent on specific activities as indicated by the responses of 20 beginning teachers states that teachers spend, on average, 19 hours per week on instruction, 3.1 hours per week on assessment, 3 hours per week on planning, and 2.7 hours per week on reporting/communication (entering grades and comments, preparing curriculum newsletters, assembling report cards, writing e-mails or making calls related to reporting, carrying out parent-teacher interviews, preparing for student-led interviews, and producing parent newsletters). Supervision of students, clerical work, and meetings take on another five to six hours each week. It is likely that some of these areas are tougher to delineate and multitasking occurs across all areas. Consequently, those work hours reported might significantly underestimate the actual number of hours worked in an average week. An ATA survey of a random sample of 10% of its members in 2013 shows that 86% of the 1,012 respondents indicated that the lack of preparation time caused a high or moderate amount of stress in their lives (personal communication with JC Couture, September, 2014).

In the 2013 TALIS survey, lower secondary teachers in Alberta report working 48.2 hours per week, nearly the highest in the survey, just behind Japan, in first place at 53.9 hours. The average number of total working hours in a week for the 35 participating countries was 38.44. The total working hours per week for teachers in the U.S. is 44.8 and in the U.K. it is 45.9. Of the 48.2 working hours per week reported by Alberta teachers, the teachers reported that 26.4 hours is spent on classroom instruction, 7.5 hours on individual planning or preparation of lessons at home or at school, and 3.0 hours on team work and dialogues with colleagues within the school.

The teachers that we interviewed in March and June 2014 generally confirmed the intense nature of their workday and the lack of time for collaboration with colleagues.

The reality is that the vast majority of our time in school is spent with kids. There is not very much prep time given. When it comes to collaboration time, there is very little that is built in, very little. We do have PD days that are built into the year.

(teacher, Wayne Lavold, p. 3)

I would say that in the 8am-4pm day there is not a moment that I am not doing something school related or curriculum related. There's no amount on any given day. . . I would say that whatever the closest thing to nothing would be what I would view as collaboration time.

(teacher, Kelsey McCready, pp. 3–4)

Teacher Attrition and Retention

In some jurisdictions, attrition rates are as high as 50% within the first five years. Exceptionally high rates tend to occur in schools in low-income areas and geographically isolated areas in schools having very high needs. Otherwise stated attrition rates vary from lows of about 15% to highs of 50%. According to Alberta Education Sector Workforce Planning Framework for Action (2010) (Link 2-17), early career attrition is about 25% (Alberta Teachers' Association, 2011, p. 4).[5]

As a result of Alberta's compliance with the Agreement on International Trade in 2009 (Grimmett & Young, 2011), there is a trend toward greater labor mobility in the Canadian teaching force. Since this agreement was signed, Alberta relies more on employing teachers who were prepared elsewhere along with preparing teachers to work outside the provincial boundaries. At present there is a greater in-province migration of teachers than out of province. For example, in 2008, just over 50% of Alberta's teaching workforce was prepared for teaching in other Canadian provinces, the U.S., and other countries.

The 2012–2013 Educator Workforce planning document for Alberta entitled *A Transformation in Progress* states "that a relatively high number of teachers leave the Alberta education system during the first four years of their career" (p 18). It goes on to say "on average, approximately 10% of early career attrition happens in the first year. An additional 6.4% of the base year new hires leave in year two, and additional 5.9% the next year" (p. 18). The conclusion is that "a trend toward a five-year early career attrition rate above 25% is evident" (p. 18). In an Alberta Teachers' Association document in June 2013, the authors make a point of stating that accurate attrition data is difficult to establish due to the many variables affecting early-career decisions of teachers. Some teachers are "pulled" out of teaching for more attractive or lucrative opportunities while others are "pushed" out of teaching by unfavorable working conditions or failure to obtain continuing contracts. They go on to say that there are a variety of factors affecting hiring and retention, and attrition cannot be considered in isolation from those other factors ("Teaching in the Early Years of Practice," 2013) (Link 2-18).

Teacher attrition is indeed a problem in some jurisdictions and in some subject areas despite relatively high salaries and respect for the profession of teaching. About 25% of those who graduate from Alberta's teacher education institutions do not teach in Alberta. According to one study of teacher attrition and retention conducted by Jean Clandinin at the University of Alberta and others, of the beginning teachers who do teach in Alberta, the fourth year is the highest year for departures with no distinct answers as to why (Clandinin et al., 2012). A study conducted by the Alberta Teachers' Association followed 135 first-year teachers for five years beginning in 2008 and found that 17% of the teachers had left teaching by the end of the fifth year (Alberta Teachers' Association, 2013). Both of these studies conclude that teacher attrition is a problem. As discussed elsewhere in this report, attrition is clearly a very significant problem in the rural north of Alberta.

Some of the reasons for teacher attrition might be linked to the volatile economy and funding for education tied to the successes of the oil and gas industries (Clandinin et al., 2012). Because schools cannot guarantee funding, many end up awarding temporary (two-year) contracts to teachers. As such, these teachers are left with a lack of job security and plenty of uncertainty, leading many to seek other careers. Additionally, lack of transparent hiring policies and practices leave a number of teachers in the dark about how to go about securing permanent contracts instead of flitting from position to position. The difficulty of securing a permanent contract seemed to be more pronounced for those teachers who had recently started a family and were looking to return to teaching after a maternity leave, especially when those teachers did not have a continuing contract at the start of their career. Another reason for attrition that was brought up in several interviews is the difficulty in balancing work and life demands by new teachers.

According to an analysis by the Alberta Teachers' Association, entitled *The New Work of Teaching* (2012), the average teacher works about 56 hours a week.[6] Seventy-two percent report high levels of conflict between their working life and personal time. More flexible employment practices such as part-time continuing contracts or job shares might help to allow those pushed out of teacher for family reasons to reenter the workforce.

With regard to the issue of work-life balance, many teachers in their first five years seemingly underestimate the difficulty of teachers' daily work lives and consequently struggle to maintain a comfortable work-life balance as teachers.

> Many of the teachers in the intentions study, and those who left teaching questioned what teaching was. Many spoke of loving their work with the students, but found that "much more" was expected. They were often not prepared in teacher education, or by what was said about teaching in the public discourse, to take on the "much more," and often did not consider anything other than being with children as teaching. (Alberta Teachers' Association, 2012, p. 6)

Another factor contributing to teacher attrition in some cases is the failure of existing teacher induction programs to provide them with the support they felt they needed. As discussed elsewhere in this report, although teacher induction programs are encouraged in the province,[7] school jurisdictions are not required to provide them. Even when they are provided though, they do not necessarily meet the needs of beginning teachers. Clandinin et al. (2012) concluded that "mentoring and induction programs were often not seen as safe places to explore their more authentic concerns" (p. 6).

In conclusion, the problem of teacher attrition varies across different school jurisdictions and subject areas.[8] In some areas such as the rural north, there is a very serious retention problem, while in the large urban areas like Calgary and Edmonton the problem is much smaller. A variety of factors have been identified in the various studies on the issue that contribute to teacher attrition such as the lack of availability of a fulltime contract, the quality of mentoring and induction support, unrealistic expectations of the work of teaching, failure to achieve a satisfactory work-life balance, and natural teaching mobility related to raising children and other family issues.

Teacher Preparation

Alberta typically produces the fourth largest number of teachers in Canada. Canada graduates about 21,000 teachers a year from 56 college and universities that have initial (preservice) teacher education programs. Of the approximately 2,000 teachers produced by Alberta's nine teacher education institutions each year, around 75% become teachers in Alberta's classrooms.

> According to an Alberta Education official: We graduate about 2,000 teachers per year and of that number about 1,500 get jobs. We have

about 2,200 openings each year. So there's a gap of about 750 teachers that get jobs from outside the province or outside the country.

(Alberta Education official, Mark Bevan, p. 6).

Funding

The provincial government does not set supply and demand targets for the teacher education universities based on projections of supply and demand. Instead, the number of slots in university teacher education programs is decided by the teacher education universities and is based on block grants provided to the institutions by the provincial government. According to Diane Wishart of the Ministry of Innovation and Advanced Education,[9] funds are provided to postsecondary institutions that include the funds that are eventually allocated by institutions to support teacher education programs. These funds are allocated in the form of block grants (Campus Alberta Grants, Link 2-19) on the basis of political considerations and do not take into account the number of teachers needed. Individual campuses ultimately make the decisions about how to distribute the funds.

In 2013, there were cuts in the Campus Alberta Grants, and the cuts in teacher education funding at some campuses such as the University of Alberta reflect internal campus decisions about how to absorb these cuts. Additionally Alberta currently prepares more teachers than there are open teaching positions although there are still serious teaching shortages in the rural north of the province. While the Faculty of Education at the University of Alberta asked the central administration to reduce their teacher enrollment target by about 300 per year over the last two years, the oversupply of teachers was not the motivation for doing so. Instead, the Faculty of Education was concerned about an imbalance in the professor-student ratio—the result of a dramatic decrease in faculty and a substantial increase in student enrollment. While provincial funding of teacher education does not take labor market projections into account, the Ministry of Innovation and Advanced Education considers teacher labor market needs when it reviews proposals for new teacher education programs.

Tuition costs for students in teacher education programs are much lower than teacher education programs in the United States. The Association of Universities and Colleges in Canada reports tuition fees for the University of Alberta to be $5,321—listed in Canadian dollars. In contrast, the University of Wisconsin's tuition is $14,213—listed in Canadian dollars as of January 18, 2015 (Parsons, 2015). Teacher education students can apply for government loans through Student Aid Alberta to support their education. Scholarships and need-based grants are also used to assist with tuition costs.

Teacher Preparation Programs

Alberta's teachers are well educated. Individuals wanting to become teachers in Alberta first need to have a bachelor of education degree from a postsecondary institution, or possess a recognized degree supplemented by an approved postgraduate teacher preparation program.

Alberta has nine approved teacher preparation institutions: Ambrose University, the University of Alberta, the University of Calgary, the University of Lethbridge, Concordia University College of Alberta, The King's University, Canadian University College,[10] St. Mary's University College, and Mount Royal University. Table 2–5 provides more information about individual teacher education institutions.

The majority of institutions, with the exception of Mount Royal University, offer two-year after-degree programs (post-baccalaureate programs leading to a bachelor of education degree and teaching license). Most institutions offer five-year dual or combined degree programs resulting in a bachelor of arts, science, fine arts, music, and bachelor of education degree. Four-year bachelor of education degree programs are also offered. Bachelor of education programs require 120 semester credits; combined-degree programs are 150 credits; and two-year after-degree programs require 60 credits on top of 90 completed undergraduate credits. With respect to the different program options and requirements toward degree, teacher preparation programs in Alberta are pretty similar.

Beyond four-year, five-year, and two-year after-degree programs, a master of education degree (graduate program) takes around three years to complete. Also, several postsecondary institutions provide transfer programs for bachelor of education degrees. While there has been genuine collegiality between Alberta Education and the universities that prepare teachers, with the new additional universities now entering teacher preparation (including several nonresident universities from the U.S.),[11] there is some question as to what effect this expanded group of preparers will have on the long-standing collegial relations between the Ministry and Alberta's university teacher educators.

Admission to teacher certification programs in Alberta is somewhat competitive. For Fall 2013, there were 5,363 applicants for spots in teacher education programs in the nine teacher education institutions, 3,453 were qualified for admission, 2,695 were offered spots, and 2,123 accepted and enrolled in a program.[12] Although minimum requirements

Table 2-5 Teacher Education Program Offerings

IHE	B.Ed.	B.Ed. (combined degree)	B.Ed. (after-degree)
Ambrose University College			X (elementary focus)
Canadian University College (now Burman University)	X		X
Concordia University College			X
The King's University College			X
Mount Royal University	X (elementary only)		
St. Mary's University			X
University of Alberta	X (elementary and secondary)	X B.A./B.S. (in only certain areas)	X
University of Alberta Campus Saint-Jean	X (elementary and secondary)	X B.Ed./B.Sc (in only certain areas)	X (elementary and secondary)
University of Calgary	X (launching Fall 2015)	X B.A./B.F.A./B.Mus./B.Kin./ B.Sc. (elementary and secondary in select areas) 3 years (years 1, 2, and 4) with nonteaching degree area and 2 years (years 3 and 5) with education degree	X (elementary and secondary in select areas)
University of Lethbridge		X B.A./B.S./B.F.A.	X

for program admission and program completion are the responsibility of the postsecondary institutions with teacher education programs, admission requirements to teacher preparation programs are similar across teacher preparation programs. Most programs require at minimum a 2.3 GPA (published minimum GPAs for entry range from 2.3–2.7), previous documented experience working with students and/or children, a teaching philosophy statement, and an interview with the faculty of education.

Additionally, various documented checkpoints along the way must be completed satisfactorily in order to continue on in the program. In undergraduate and combined-degree programs (concurrent), prospective candidates are required to take an orientation to teaching course or series of courses around the teaching profession with or without a field experience in the schools before applying to the teacher preparation program. Admission requirements in Alberta's institutions for teacher preparation are not particularly noteworthy, especially when held up against admissions requirements for teacher candidates in countries like Finland, South Korea, and Singapore. However, admission requirements (particularly the interview component), combined with checkpoints along the way to counsel students out of the program if needed, may be strong suits in Alberta's teacher preparation programs.

Secondary education programs require both a major and a minor specialization where teacher candidates complete between 32 to 36 credits of course work in the major specializations and 18 credits of course work in the minor specialization area. In some smaller schools though, teachers are sometimes required to assume more cross-subject assignments such as physics/math, or English/social studies. So although teaching certificates in Alberta do not include subject area specializations, the preparation of secondary teachers in the province and teaching positions reflect a specialization focus. Per the Ministry of Education, secondary teachers are required to present a minimum of 24 semester hour credits in a teachable subject area, and six-semester hour credits in English/ French Literature and Composition.

The preparation and work of elementary teachers are broad and interdisciplinary. Like most elementary teacher preparation programs in the U.S., elementary teacher preparation programs in Alberta require a broad liberal arts foundation. As a requirement for certification per the Ministry of Education, elementary teachers are required to present 24-semester hours of credits in academic course work including six semester hour credits in English/French Literature and Composition and three-semester hour credits each in Canadian Studies, mathematics, and science. The additional nine credits of academic courses for elementary teachers are determined at the institutional level. Table 2–6 provides

Table 2–6 Teacher Education Program Admission Req., Course Work and Field Experience Requirements

IHE	GPA	Gen. Ed. Credit	Content Area Credit	Education Credits	Total Length of Clinical Experience
Ambrose University College	2.7 GPA	n/a	n/a	60 credits	25 weeks over four semesters
Canadian University College	2.5 GPA	42 credits +/- 9 Elective Credits (for elementary track)	32 credits of Major Specialization Area 18 credits in Minor Specialization Area		100 hours of field experience + 16 weeks of practicum (student teaching), over 2 semesters
Concordia University College	2.3 GPA on last 30 credits	n/a	n/a	60 credits	14 weeks over three semesters, 1wk-4wks-9wks
The King's University College	2.5 GPA	Documented Completed Course work; 90 credits with broad liberal arts course work For elementary track	Documented Completed Course work; 90 credits of which 33 cr in teaching major, 18 cr. in teaching minor for secondary track	60 credits	17–18 weeks, over 2 semesters, 5/6wks-12wks
Mount Royal University (elementary only)	"B" or higher to continue	24 gen. ed. req.	30 in minor specialization	60 credits	14 weeks, over 2 semesters 5wks-9wks
St. Mary's University	2.7 GPA on last 60 credits	BA degree with strong liberal arts component		60 credits	24 weeks, over 2 semesters 6wks-8wks-10wks

University					
University of Alberta	2.0–2.3 GPA B.Ed. Program Req. 120 Credits Combined Degree Programs Req. 150 credits, 90 cr. in BA Area; 60 cr. in Education Area	51 Credits for Elementary Track, B.Ed.	36 in Major Specialization 18 in Minor Specialization Secondary Track B.Ed. 90 cr. in BA area	69 credits for Elementary Track; 66 credits for Secondary Track; 54–60 credits for After-Degree Elementary Track; 48–54 credits for After-Degree Secondary Track 60 cr. of education course work with combined-degree program	14 weeks total; 2 field experiences in years 3 and 4. 5wks–9wks
University of Alberta Campus Saint-Jean	2.7 for admission, 2.0 for graduation	n/a	36 in Major Specialization 15 in Minor Specialization	n/a	15 weeks total 3 field experiences I. 10 visits to the schools, II and III combine for a total of 13 weeks
University of Calgary	2.5 GPA		90 credits in undergraduate course work for after-degree program; for secondary track, must have degree in major specialization or an equivalent for after-degree program		20 weeks, over 4 semesters, 2wks-4wks-6wks-8wks
University of Lethbridge	2.5 GPA	90 Credits (30 courses)		60 Credits (20 courses)	21–28 weeks, over 3 semesters 5wks-6wks-12–17weeks

information on teacher education programs' admission requirements, course work, and field experience requirements.

If completing a B.Ed. or concurrent combined-degree program of study, teacher candidates spend their first two years completing content area course work and general education requirements. While a few education courses may be required in some programs over the first couple of years, the bulk of education course work and clinical experience occurs in years three and four (and possibly five if completing a combined-degree program). In the majority of cases, education course work begins with foundational education courses such as Child Development and orientation to the teaching. Advanced course work focuses on courses in content-specific methods, assessment, and planning. After-degree programs, typically 60 credits, focus entirely on education course work as the candidate's complete content course work (either via a broad liberal arts focus for the elementary track candidate or major and minor specializations for the secondary track candidate) in his/her previous degree program.

Beyond these programmatic requirements the Ministry of Education has set a number of certification requirements, some of which differ for elementary and secondary teachers. To become certified, individuals must provide evidence of at least four years of university education, the completion of at minimum 48 semester hour credits in professional teacher education course work, and minimum of 10 weeks of field experience.

To meet certification requirements, elementary teachers need to provide documentation of semester hour credits related to their broad-field and general education course work. Elementary teachers are required to present 24-semester hours of credits in academic course work and three-semester hour credits each in Canadian Studies, mathematics, and science and six semester-hour credits in English/French Literature and Composition. Secondary teachers are required to present a minimum of 24 semester hour credits in a teachable subject area, and six-semester hour credits in English/French Literature and Composition.

Despite the minimum 10-week practicum requirement, the director of the Professional Standards Branch in the Ministry explained to us that the actual length of student teaching in Alberta's programs is at least 14 weeks. For transfer teachers trained in other provinces, there is an agreement among the Canadian provinces that 10 weeks of student teaching is acceptable. The director also noted that many teacher education programs are moving toward a 23-week practicum.

The length and structure of clinical experiences in teacher preparation programs in Alberta differ according to the institution of higher education and the program type. Three institutions, the University of Alberta, Mount Royal University, and Concordia University College require candidates to complete 14 weeks of field experiences over two or three semesters, whereas the University of Lethbridge and St. Mary's University require more than 21 weeks of clinical experience. After-degree (consecutive) programs also have more innovation in the structure, delivery, and relationship of pedagogical content to clinical practice (e.g., The King's University College and the University of Lethbridge have a spiraling curriculum of pedagogical content tied to clinical experience; Ambrose University College links field experiences and course work every semester). In the United States, there is a push to increase the duration and intensity of clinical field experiences. In Alberta, there does not appear to be anything noteworthy about the length or intensity of the clinical field experience that differentiates Alberta's programs from university programs in other OECD countries. Vignettes for teacher preparation program can be found in Appendix 2–B.

From an interview with Paul Macleod, the former director of the Professional Standards Branch, it is clear that Alberta values a strong foundation in course work and clinical experience before individuals become teachers of record. This is in stark contrast to the United States, where the proportion of early-entry teachers continues to grow.

> We often talk about cardiologists. I really prefer he [complete] his program before he opens me up. I would prefer he's not learning on the job. We know there's an internship process. We know he's going to be going through that but we prefer the [degree is] in place before he actually decides to split me open. Same with teachers. We know that they're going to grow. We know that you never stop learning professionally, but you've got to have that degree or some form of meeting a certification standard.

> (Paul MacLeod, June 2014)

Alternative certification, specifically emergency or conditional certification, is something that does not, with two exceptions, happen in Alberta. Alberta currently has two "bridging programs" (Link 2-20): one for career and technical education and the other for foreign-prepared teachers. These programs offer teacher candidates some credit for their expertise and then require that candidates to complete a program (about one year in duration) where they receive additional credit hours. Essentially, by combining the candidate's work experience and a year of schooling, the candidate has completed half of his/her teacher education requirements. At that point, a letter of authority is issued stipulating the particular content area the candidate can teach. This is different from the fully fledged Interim Professional Certificate, which, when granted, gives the teacher the ability to teach in any area in the K–12 system approved by the Minister of Education. In other words, in this alternative bridging program, an individual can begin teaching prior to completing his/her teacher education program and without an Interim Professional Certificate if he/she has expertise in an area and has made substantial progress on his/her teacher education course work.

There is also a new Teach for Canada initiative to supply teachers who will stay over time in schools serving FNMI students. Teach for Canada intends to provide teachers beginning in the summer of 2015 with extensive cultural training and cultural awareness in First Nations communities in an effort to prepare them to be successful and stay teaching in these communities. Teach for Canada only accepts individuals who have already completed a B.Ed. or other certification program. The director of the Professional Standards Branch in the Ministry confirmed this assumption. He said clearly to us that in Alberta, Teach for Canada teachers will not be able to teach in their own classrooms unless they've completed a teacher education program that meets Alberta's standards. He said that if they have not achieved certification in Alberta, they'll be able to serve as an "instructor" with a supervised teacher in the room until they do. "Teach for" programs in other countries that allow teachers to begin teaching as teachers of record after only five-weeks of training are not looked upon favorably by most stakeholders in Albertan education. Unlike in other countries like the U.S. and the U.K. where the government has endorsed "Teach for" programs and even provided them with funding, the Alberta Ministry of Education has not lent support in any way to Teach for Canada and has instead focused its efforts on improving the quality of education in indigenous communities by supporting indigenous teacher education programs.

Teacher Certification

After completing an approved teacher preparation program, all teachers in Alberta must obtain the authority to teach, which is granted through a certification process similar to that of Departments of Education or Offices of Public Instruction in the United States. Alberta has two levels of teacher certification: the Interim and Permanent Professional Certificate ("Teacher Certification in Alberta," 2014). The Interim Professional Certificate is the initial certificate issued to all applicants who meet the requirements as outlined in the regulation. The Interim Professional Certificate is valid for a period of three years (ibid). Once expired, Interim

Professional Certificates may be reissued upon recommendation from a school authority. The Permanent Professional Certificate is issued upon receipt of a recommendation from a school authority attesting that the teacher has completed two years of successful teaching and has had two evaluations based on the knowledge, skills, and attributes for permanent certification outlined in the Teaching Quality Standard.

Teachers who hold certifications elsewhere and plan to teach in Alberta must provide documentation of a valid certification resulting from their initial teacher preparation. Teachers in Alberta also need to demonstrate proficiency in either English or French.

Unlike the current move in the United States toward online teacher certification programs and narrowly defined skill-based programs (Zeichner, 2014), teacher preparation programs in Alberta offered entirely through self-directed study are not accepted for certification, and graduates of distance delivery (e.g., online programs) would undergo a full transcript review to ensure minimum requirements for certification are met. Furthermore, school-based or employment-based teacher training programs are also not recognized for certification purposes.

Instead of maintaining an "iron fist" of control over teacher preparation program, Alberta Education is careful to note that it does not preapprove teacher preparation programs. According to the Registrar/Director for the Professional Standards Branch with Alberta Education, Paul McLeod, the Ministry of Innovation and Advanced Education looks after the universities, approving their teacher education programs. That being said, the Professional Standards Branch in the Ministry of Education holds memorandums of agreement with nine teacher preparation institutions. In so doing, the Professional Standards Branch meets with the deans of the institutions on a fairly regular basis and receives annual updates from the deans regarding any programmatic changes to the teacher preparation program(s). Then, every five years the Professional Standards Branch completes an efficacy report, similar to an audit of the program, ensuring that the institution meets the Teaching Quality Standard. This process includes surveys of current students, alumni, and employers of program graduates.

Teacher candidates who complete their teacher preparation course work, therefore, based on the dean's attestation, meet the teaching quality standard. Rather than many requirements for specific courses and credits, the emphasis is on ensuring that the program is aligned with the knowledge, skills, and attributes that are outlined in the Teaching Quality Standard. In the interview with the director of the Professional Standards Branch, it appears as though there is not a hierarchical relationship between the Professional Standards Branch and the Teacher Education Programs.

While the Professional Standards Branch may encourage and recommend that teacher education programs make some adjustments to their programs, such as more closely aligning parts of their programs to Inspiring Education for example, they do not issue mandates. There appears to be a high degree of mutual trust between the governance system and the teacher education system.

Teacher Induction

> We don't fund it right now. It's not required, but every school, every jurisdiction will offer something to beginning teachers, whether it's the teacher in the next classroom or one in the same grade that will support them. Many of our school authorities are offering formalized programs.

(Ministry of Education staff, Karen Shipka, p. 5)

According to the 2013 TALIS study, informal induction programs are available for more than 80% of lower secondary teachers for teachers new to a school, while formal programs are available to 50% of lower secondary teachers new to a school and 80% for teachers new to teaching.

In 1998, a teacher growth, supervision, and evaluation policy was developed to support the Teaching Quality Standard. This policy mandated the creation of an annual teacher professional growth plan. Included in these plans could be a mentoring and/or student teacher supervision component. As a response to this policy, and in collaboration with the Red Deer School District, the ATA worked to develop a comprehensive mentor-training pilot program between 1996 and 1998. Grounded in a relational component, this program pilot was seen as a success, and funding was set aside for its continued support. As a result of the pilot program, a document entitled *Mentoring Beginning Teachers* (Link 2-21) was developed and published in 2003. The document includes information on the purposes of mentoring; the stages of new teacher development; projections of how a successful program should operate; the complex role a mentor plays; the responsibilities that accompany a mentor and the specific roles of mentor and protégé; areas of caution and how to appropriately assist the protégé; a program evaluation; specific information for the protégé about their needs and areas for support; the administrators' role; the mentor-protégé plan outline; resources; and references to literature on mentorship (Alberta Teachers' Association, 2003). It is accessible from the ATA website and outlines provisions for mentor teacher training and district-level development of high-quality mentoring program.

According to an editorial written by Dana Garvey, of the Alberta Teachers' Association, "What makes the ATA's mentoring program model unique is the partnership between the school district and the ATA local. School districts and locals were invited to establish partnerships and invited to have at least two representatives of the partnership attend the information and training session offered by the ATA" (Garvey, 2003–2004). These training sessions have since resulted in 43 mentoring programs throughout the province as of 2004. The first training session held in 1999 was attended by nine districts and ATA locals; a second training session was held in 2000. As a result, 32 beginning mentoring programs were established across the province; that number has since grown to 43.

Despite the expansion of these mentoring programs across the province, in a subsequent investigation of the Red Deer Public School's website, it is unclear whether the mentoring program has continued (Garvey, 2000). Today, there are jurisdictional induction programs that involve matching new teachers with mentors to assist with development of the professional growth plan and transition into the profession. While the initial intent was that the provincial government would fund induction programs, that did not happen, so induction programs are funded by jurisdictions.

While teacher induction is encouraged, it is not required in all districts. Some districts like Edmonton require participation in a program. Some have told us in interviews that teacher attrition is a function of the volatile economy and temporary contracts as well as the younger generation discovering in their beginning years of teaching that they want more of a balance between their work lives and personal lives than they see teaching offering them. Districts are somewhat reticent to invest in induction for teachers on temporary contracts when they lack assurance that they will be staying in the district.

According to the Alberta Teachers' Association's 2012 Professional Development Survey, there are some positive trends toward providing formal and longer teacher induction. These mentorship programs are designed by local jurisdictions and appear to be collaborative. In the survey, respondents reported frequent examples of mentoring beyond the first year. That being said, it seems that there is a lack of professional development for substitute teachers, including new teachers working as substitutes who are looking for full-time teaching positions. New teachers in Alberta tend to be increasingly trained outside of the province and/or

country, and there is a need to induct these teachers new to the province
or country not only to the profession, but also to the province. "During a one-year period between 2011 and 2012, 46 percent of all first-
time applicants to the Teacher Qualifications Service had taken some or
part of their studies outside of Alberta, an increase from 43 percent in
 2010" (ATA Professional Development Survey, 2012, p. 25) (Link 2-22).
At present, 32% of respondents in the survey reported no professional
development support structure for this unique subset of teachers.

In a report also published by ATA entitled *Teaching in the Early
Years: A Longitudinal Study,* new teachers reported that mentoring initiatives tend to vary in consistency and efficacy. Assigned mentor teachers often do not have the training or skillset required of them to mentor
the new teachers. Additionally, smaller schools do not always have the
staff resources to provide mentors aligned with the beginning teachers' content areas or grade levels. For those new teachers who were not
assigned a mentor teacher, they sought out informal mentors. Even when
formal mentors were assigned, new teachers often found themselves not
benefitting from the help of informal mentors when the formal mentor
teacher was not a good fit.

All in all, the mentoring of new teachers appears to be haphazard despite
attempts to make it more formal. When funding for the Alberta Initiative
for School Improvement (AISI) was cut, much of the funding for formal
mentorship programs went by the wayside. Consequently, mentoring of
new teachers tends to default to informal networking, collegial collaboration, quick hallway conversations or common planning time, or relationships cultivated over the course of a teaching career. We were not able to
locate a source that has an accurate picture of the specific kinds of induction programs available to teachers in each jurisdiction within Alberta.

Professional Learning/School Improvement

There is a considerable percentage of professional development offered
and supported by the Alberta Teachers' Association. The ATA publishes
a listing of professional development workshops for individuals, administrators, and schools in a document entitled *Professional Development
 Programs and Services Guide* (Link 2-23). Professional development
opportunities are also provided within school catchment areas for teachers in the schools in an area, by the school jurisdictions, and within individual schools. There are also regional centers that offer professional
development for K–12 educators within their regions. School districts
usually provide a certain number of days of professional development

when the students do not come to school. According to the 2012 survey of teacher professional development conducted by ATA, "the prevalence of site-based management and budgeting practices has resulted in a fragmented array of professional development supports even within jurisdictions" (p. 13).

Teachers clearly have some opportunities to choose what professional development opportunities they want to engage in, but in other cases they are told what to attend. Although there have been some criticisms that teacher professional development has been increasingly determined by those other than the teachers themselves, the teachers that we interviewed in March and June 2014, while acknowledging that there seems to have been an increase in others asking teachers to attend particular professional development activities, generally felt that teachers have much control over their own professional development.

> It's very much teacher driven, the PD. You won't see very many experts anymore leading sessions where teachers sit back and listen and take it in. So a lot of development is you get to choose. You get to pick what you want... There are many opportunities online and at the district level and at the school level where you can become more informed about literacy or assessment or feedback. I'm very happy with our PD because I can choose how I want to learn and where I want to learn and I kind of go about it at my own pace.

> (teacher, Tammy Thero-Soto, p. 3)

A survey conducted in 2013 by the ATA of a 10% sample of its membership indicated that when asked if they control their own professional development, about one-third of the teachers disagreed or strongly disagreed and two-thirds of the teachers agreed (Personal communication, J. C. Couture, September 2014).

The Professional Development Survey undertaken by the Alberta Teachers' Association (ATA) in 2012 indicates that conditions for professional learning have declined. Professional development opportunities for individual teachers based on their unique teaching contexts and goals established in their professional growth plans now compete frequently with demands on teachers' time, including external professional development mandates. This trend toward system-directed professional learning has come at the expense of individuals' learning goals (ATA, 2012).

While spending on professional development has remained relatively stable, 15.2% of respondents in the ATA 2012 Professional Development Survey reported a decrease in access to professional development compared with 0% of respondents in the 2009 survey (p. 4). This apparent erosion of professional development access is noticeable when one considers the reality behind the professional leave clauses written into many of the school districts' collective agreements. Dedicated professional development days at the district level also vary widely across jurisdictions. Seventy-five percent of respondents report having eight or more days for professional development, while 25% of respondents reported having less than seven days for professional development (p. 4). Contextual job-embedded professional development also appears to be on the decline: 23% of respondents claimed in 2012 that job-embedded PD was nonexistent compared with 0% of respondents in 2010 (p. 5).

Professional development in Alberta appears to be largely up to the discretion of the district, school, and individual teachers. While some collective agreements stipulate a certain number of paid professional development days, the majority of collective bargaining agreements for our focus districts allow professional leaves for the purposes of professional development. Individual teachers are also provided with some monetary assistance to partake in professional development conferences, workshops, seminars, etc. aligned with their individualized professional growth plan. It appears that a significant number of teachers who work within a district that offers professional leave options do not benefit from this option, either because the financial incentives are not high enough or because their proposals to take leave have been denied. The individually constructed professional growth plan is the main driver behind professional development, but increasingly system-directed professional development is competing with self-identified goals for PD. There are also increasing demands to align individual professional growth goals with the school's goals. To get a sense of the number of allocated professional development days stated in the collective bargaining agreements of our eight focal districts, a list of allocated professional development opportunities as stipulated by the focal districts' collective bargaining agreements is provided in Table 2–7.

When we asked teachers about the quality of their professional development opportunities in our interviews in June 2014, we came away with the impression that the quality of PD as perceived by teachers is quite varied. In some cases, because of the initiatives of particular principals, teachers seemed very pleased with their PD opportunities. In other cases, principals' initiatives generated a negative reaction from teachers such as in the following example:

> The communication and collaboration have taken such a nosedive this year that it is starting to have an impact on the staff. We're put in grade level groups and we're told what to do. It's not terribly

collaborative. There is a misconception that people can be told what to collaborate on. If you're told what to collaborate on, it's inherently not collaborative.

(teacher, p. 3)

The comments of one teacher captured the sense of teachers' perceptions of variation in quality that we heard in our interviews:

It ends up being a mix. I don't know that I could draw a conclusion. I'd say that there is some stuff that is crappy; there's no doubt about it.

Table 2–7 Allocated Professional Development Time Noted in Collective Agreements

Calgary School District No 19 (2007–2012)	Two nonteaching organizational days to be determined by school staff and three nonteaching professional activity days to be determined by school staff.
Calgary RCSSD No 1 (2007–2012)	None specified in CBA.
Edmonton School District	Professional Improvement Leaves may be granted to individual teachers. A maximum of two professional development days per school year for activities such as local professional development, in-service program planning, and budgeting.
Edmonton CSSD No 7 (2007–2012)	Professional Improvement Leaves may be granted to individual teachers but no specific designation for PD days in the CBA.
Fort McMurray School District No 2833 (2007–2012)	None specified in CBA.
Fort McMurray RCSSD No 32 (2007–2012)	The CBA indicates that there are district-wide professional development days, but doesn't stipulate number of days.
Red Deer School District No 104 (2007–2012)	Professional Improvement Leaves may be granted to individual teachers. There is a fund established to assist with PD, but no specific number of days specified.
Red Deer CRD No 39 (2004–2012)	Teachers can receive a $500.00 subsidy to partake in personal professional development. Teachers are given two days per year to take as PD days and the PD must adhere to the Professional Growth Plan.

There is also some stuff that is very useful and one of the biggest issues that we face is trying to sort through the crappy stuff and get the good stuff, but our time is sometimes wasted when we don't have a choice.

(teacher, p. 12)

Despite all of the different professional development opportunities for teachers, they don't always take advantage of what is available because of the intensity of their work lives.

To be completely honest, most teachers don't take advantage of them because they don't have the time. They are so swamped with marking and prepping and then the fact that they have this outside life with families and kids.

(teacher, p. 11)

Regardless of the issues raised in the 2012 ATA survey about the nature and quality of professional development opportunities for teachers, there is still much more of an emphasis in this province on supporting teacher professional learning than on teacher evaluation. The teacher evaluation that exists, with the professional growth plan as its basis (see below) focuses on teacher learning and development. There seems to be the belief that investing in teacher learning carries with it a form of internal and informal teacher evaluation and accountability and that the kind of formal teacher evaluation practices that are growing in popularity in the U.S. and some other countries are unnecessary in Alberta. As one teacher put it:

Once you gain tenure, you are evaluated on an informal basis. There is a constant evaluation of you informally. Your principal will pop into your class and see what's going on. Your department head will be watching what's happening and will sit in on your classes and will listen to what students have to say so forth and so on. There's no formal review process. It's being suggested by the task force board. My personal opinion is that it's not necessary. It's a mountain being made out of a molehill.

(teacher, p. 7)

One arena where teacher-centric professional development and locally driven teacher and district innovation seems to have flourished was with The Alberta Initiative for School Improvement (AISI).

The Alberta Initiative for School Improvement (AISI) was a multi-stakeholder project that encouraged teachers and local communities to collaborate and develop projects aimed at improving student learning across the province. Beginning in the 2000–2001 school year, the AISI was envisioned as a 12-year project divided into three-year cycles with each cycle having its own defining theme. AISI eventually lasted for four three-year cycles plus another two years. With a $75 million budget per year, or approximately $75 per student, teachers were encouraged to develop school-based action research projects that would address local needs and lead to improved student learning (Parsons and Beauchamp, 2012). Teachers were responsible for all aspects of their projects including design, collection and analysis of data, sharing of findings as well as fiscal accountability.

Sumera and Davis (2009) identify both collaboration and connection as core values of AISI that extended through each project. Partners in AISI included:

- ○ Alberta universities;
- ○ Government of Alberta—Alberta Education;
- ○ Alberta Teachers' Association (ATA);
- ○ College of Alberta School Superintendents (CASS);
- ○ Alberta School Boards Association (ASBA);
- ○ Association of School Business Officials of Alberta (ASBOA);
- ○ Alberta School Councils Association (ASCA)

With such broad support across the province, AISI was able to support over 1,800 projects that were guided by the values of collaboration and connection. Each three-year cycle was meant to build upon the successes of the previous cycle. The initial cycle of the project was meant to highlight the diversity of local projects and encourage teacher activism in the goals of AISI. Cycles 2 and 3 made a concerted effort to link projects and their goals. Each project approved by school boards/districts was started and completed with the span of the three-year cycle. As a result, new projects were encouraged to build upon previous projects and successes in cycles 2 and 3. Cycle 4 furthered the values of collaboration and connection with a focus on leadership capacity building and the networking of schools and projects across the province. With AISI having a 95% participation rate of Alberta's schools, Sahlberg (2009, p. 87) believes that globally it is "difficult to find anywhere a comparable change effort that would be of the scale and overall magnitude of AISI." Further recognition of the impact of AISI on education practice and teacher development comes from Hargreaves and Shirley (2009, p. 4) who states AISI's "commitment to school-based and district-based initiatives with targeted funding includes almost all schools in the province in a concerted effort at systematic change. It encourages local initiative and expresses high degrees of professional trust within what are nonetheless some of the most stringent systems of external accountability and achievement testing in the nation and the world."

The success and global recognition of the AISI as a leader in education innovation and change can be attributed to a number of factors, most notably the encouragement of teachers as researchers at their local sites. AISI at its core was a variety of teacher-led action-research projects aimed at improving student learning at the local level. What Hargreaves (2009) described as professional trust earlier, Shirley and McEwen (2009) take this further describing the active trust between Alberta Education, school districts, and teachers to engage in risk-taking with these projects in order to explore strategies of student learning and improved teaching. It is this movement away from a conservative and traditional route of professional growth through individualism and engaging in a "more collective understanding of peer learning" that had Alberta teachers supporting the AISI model (Shirley & McEwen, 2009, p. 55). One identified example of the above was the shift in Alberta schools to recognize the importance of formative assessments in student learning and its role in teacher planning.

Another area where AISI made a substantial contribution was in the education of First Nations, Metis, and Inuit students. Much research has been conducted at both the provincial and national levels to examine the need for education reform that would lead to greater educational attainment for FNMI students. The literature on Canadian Aboriginal education suggests many reasons for low achievement and attainment rates, including feelings of marginalization in schools, lack of caring, poor relationships with other students and teachers, and a history with government-sponsored residential schools whose goal was to eliminate Aboriginal culture (Gunn et al., 2011).

With such an obvious need for reform in the approach to education for FNMI students, a wide range of projects focused on FNMI students were initiated by teachers through AISI. Gunn et al. (2011) examined 16 AISI projects that focused on Aboriginal learning and identified a number of common themes that they addressed. These themes included improving the academic potential of FNMI students; increasing the involvement of and communication with FNMI parent/guardians; creating a more inclusive sense of belonging for FNMI students within cooperating schools and districts; and enhancing cultural awareness within cooperating schools and districts (p. 332).

One of the projects studied identified a number of broad goals over its three-year lifespan. The need to educate all teachers about Aboriginal culture/traditions and curriculum reform plus increased attendance and improved grades for FNMI students were to be accomplished through professional development sessions for teachers and administrators revolving around Aboriginal culture; initiating partnerships that would bring Aboriginal agencies, postsecondary institutions, and Elders into the district; identifying positive Aboriginal role models in the region; and the hiring of an Aboriginal coordinator to facilitate greater collaboration and understanding between the school and community (Gunn et al., 2011). While most AISI projects measured student learning to gauge success, this particular project identified the hiring of the Aboriginal coordinator as the key piece to meeting all the identified goals, including the creation of the Aboriginal Parent Advisory Council to liaison the various Aboriginal education stakeholders. The position was so successful and instrumental in helping this particular school reach its projected goals that the Aboriginal coordinator position was made permanent after the AISI three-year cycle with continued funding from the district.

AISI and its partners have measured success in their projects from a number of perspectives. One obvious measure was based on student achievement. Based on collected data throughout the three-year cycles, student achievement increased across the province, most notably with the students considered at risk (Parsons et al., 2006). Other initiatives that had a notable impact on student achievement included early literacy interventions, transitions programs from middle to secondary school, and increased technology into the classroom. Many projects developed under AISI used student learning as one of the measurable outcomes. Crock (2009), using data from cycles 2 and 3, cautiously stated that "positive change has, indeed occurred over time and across AISI projects and measures" (p. 27) while Shirley and McEwen (2009) identified a shift in rethinking the types of assessments Alberta teachers used as a factor for greater student achievement.

School Improvement

Parsons et al. (2006) suggest the success of AISI can be examined through school improvement. Using a framework developed by Fullan (2001), three areas of change were identified that can measure school improvement: (a) a change in institutional resources; (b) a change in teaching approaches and/or strategies; and (c) an alteration of beliefs or pedagogical assumptions or theories related to innovation.

Change in Institutional Resources

A continuous goal throughout the project cycles was to produce tangible and sustainable resources for education in Alberta. The development of curricular websites, classroom resources, the creation of a common report card across the province, and teacher generated action research reports have all contributed to the improved understanding of effective pedagogy and teaching strategies in Alberta's classrooms. Perhaps the largest impact that AISI has had would be the diffusion of Information and Communication Technology (ICT) across the province's schools. Contrary to the common idea that purchasing more computers for schools equates to a technology policy, most of the successful AISI technology-driven projects focused on "teachers learning how to use to technology for enhancing core curriculum" (Parson et al., 2006, p. 103). The idea of teacher technology knowledge as an institutional resource is prevalent throughout the AISI professional development projects and led to greater acceptance of technology and its use in Alberta's classrooms.

Change in Teaching Approaches and Strategies

While numerous individual school strategies for improved teaching were developed throughout the various projects, the growth and success of two approaches, Problem-Based Learning and Professional Learning Communities, can be attributed to AISI. The teaching community in Alberta realized the value of Problem-Based Learning (PBL) and many of the projects throughout the four cycles focused on combining technology and PBL strategies to improve student learning. Parsons et al. (2006) define problem- or project-based learning and teaching as being "grounded in an extended pedagogical relationship that combines the social and educative in a natural way" (p. 42). The goal of PBL is for students to have an authentic experience with the problem or issue being examined, and to work in groups to collaboratively discuss to develop a deeper understanding. Students now take the lead in the PBL model with teachers acting as facilitators throughout the process. PBL in AISI projects, while in all subject areas, were notably successful in how math and science were taught. Through the increased use of technology, Alberta's math and science teachers were able to create PBL lessons and units that were self-identified as more engaging for students and moved past pen and paper activities (Parsons et al., 2006).

Early in cycles 1 and 2, those participating in AISI projects began to recognize the role that professional learning communities (PLC's) could have in changing how curriculum was taught in Alberta. PLCs encouraged greater collaboration among stakeholders such as teachers and administration to address specific goals and issues in their schools and districts. Teaching historically is often seen as a solitary endeavor with teachers working by themselves to plan and deliver curriculum. However, many of the AISI projects identified community building among school staff as key outcomes in their proposals. Consider the following from a final report of an AISI project, "Teachers morale, skills, and sense of professionalism improved as they worked in teams to plan lessons, integrate technology into curriculum, develop assessment tools, share teaching strategies, and implement school improvement initiatives" (University of Alberta, 2004, p. 12).

Alteration of Pedagogical Assumptions or Theories Related to Innovation

When examining the reviews and assessments of AISI after its completion, it is obvious that the culture of teaching has changed: changes in resources and how technology is utilized, the role of PBLs and student-driven knowledge creation, the importance of action research in classrooms and schools, and the emergence of teachers as leaders in Alberta's education system (Alberta Education, 2010; Gunn et al., 2011; Hargreaves et al., 2009; Parsons & Beauchamp, 2012; Parsons et al., 2006). While each could be further discussed individually, their collective sum has changed pedagogical thinking in Alberta and how professional development (PD) is conceived and delivered to its teachers (Alberta Education, 2012). Professional development for Alberta's teachers has become more structured and incorporates many lessons learned over the 12 years and four cycles of AISI. Teachers are now recognized more as leaders and experts in their fields and are now asked to deliver PD to their colleagues—a shift from previously bringing in external experts. This fosters greater collaborative sharing and knowledge building and continues to reinforce the effectiveness of professional learning communities. "Collaboration and sharing between the teachers across divisions through lead teacher meetings and projects. Having a collaborative leader makes sharing the positives and negatives a safe, supportive endeavor" (Alberta Education, 2012, p. 3).

After a series of budget cuts to education and a belief that the three-year cyclical model of AISI served as an obstacle to the scaling up of individual innovations and to more systemic impact, money to support the AISI was ended. Many of the commitments and ideas that were associated with this project, however, live on in the current system in other ways. For example, The Alberta Teachers' Association (ATA) has developed a framework for professional development (Link 2-24) that acknowledges the insights gained from AISI to help both teacher and student learning. With the goal of student learning as the end result, the Alberta Teachers' Association (2010) identifies three components that should be present in all PD opportunities:

1. Process—professional development should encourage teachers to explore, reflect critically on their practice, and take risks in the planning and delivery of curriculum.

2. Content—utilize current research highlighting effective teaching and learning strategies.

3. Context—regardless of the PD activity, a teacher's professionalism is recognized as well as their judgment in determining their needs.

To achieve the above, professional development in Alberta takes many forms: the continued growth of professional learning communities; a structured approach to coaching, training, and mentoring of teachers in Alberta; and traditional PD events such as conferences and workshops. Critical to the success of PD in Alberta is the follow-up after the session. Teachers are expected to initially apply what was learned during their PD in conjunction with professional reflection and sharing with their peers. After this, teachers engage in what the ATA terms full implementation where the strategy is adjusted and used in the classroom not only based on teacher reflection and peer feedback but also student performance (2010). This approach to professional development and knowledge mobilization ensures that the three components of the PD framework—process, content, and context—are engaged and that theory, reflection, and practice work together to improve teacher and student learning. According to an Alberta Teachers' Association official:

> We started seeing what became known in the province as "projectitis" where projects would start over a three-year cycle, that was the funding formula. Money was released over the three years. The initiatives would start and then they would stop after three years and then we would start running into difficulties because it was difficult not only to scale the work across the province, but also because it became difficult to sustain the initiatives after the funding was moved to another project or another focus area. And so over time we had a number of key school leaders who became frustrated and thought it would be far better just to have the money, the AISI money, rolled into general operating funds and that way there would be more local flexibility to do the work. (ATA staff, J. C Couture, p. 15)

Teacher Evaluation/Supervision/Teacher Growth

Since 1998–1999 teachers in Alberta have been responsible for completing an annual professional growth plan that: (a) reflects goals and objectives based on an assessment of learning needs by the individual teacher; (b) shows a demonstrable relationship to the teaching quality standard; and (c) takes into consideration the education plans of the school, the school authority, and the government. This annual plan must be submitted for review or approval to either the principal or a group of teachers delegated by the principal. Unless the teacher agrees, this plan may not be a part of the teacher evaluation process.

In reality, the ideal situation where a teacher sits down with his or her supervisor and discusses the plan at the beginning and the end of the year does not always happen according to what several teachers told us. For example,

> The only opportunity for evaluation is when we have our own professional growth plans. We submit our professional growth plans to our department head and my department head's exact words to me were, she's new this year: "I don't know what to do with these things, no one ever comes and asks for them." So she just files them in a drawer and we don't have a conversation. There's been two years where I have had conversations with my department head about the professional growth plan, but not in the last two and one half to three years.

(teacher, June 2014, pp. 10–11)

A principal may evaluate a teacher (a) upon written request of the teacher; (b) for purposes of gathering information related to a specific employment decision; or (c) when, on the basis of information received through supervision, the principal has reason to believe that the teaching of the teacher may not meet the teaching quality standard. Additionally, principals are responsible for supervising teachers on an ongoing basis to provide support and guidance to teachers: observe and receive information from any source about the quality of teaching a teacher provides to students, and identify the behaviors or practices of a teacher that for any reason may require an evaluation ("Teacher Growth, Supervision and Evaluation Policy," 2014) (Link 2-25).

It seems from this policy that formal teacher evaluation is not done unless there is a reason to do so, such as when a teacher is being considered for a new teaching certificate or there is a specific concern. The emphasis here on the professional growth plan and with the Alberta Initiative for School Improvement is on professional development and learning.

After you receive your permanent certificate, the only time that you receive an evaluation is if you're moving into leadership or if you request it. Otherwise, the process is around growth, so I would create my professional growth plan and I would meet with my principal. I would set my targets and goals for the year. I would go about my learning for the year. That is reviewed twice through the year and then you have a conversation about the results of your plan.

(Ministry official, Karen Shipka, p. 17)

Conclusion

In this closing section of the case study, we summarize the main takeaways about what factors we think are responsible for Alberta's success as an education system. One of our main conclusions is that the success of Alberta's education system is a result of a variety of cultural, economic, and political factors and policies both inside and outside the education sector and that it would be a mistake to point at educational policies and practices alone to draw conclusions about success. Merely transplanting particular education policies and practices from Alberta to other systems will not necessarily address educational problems including problems of inequity.

One of the factors in educational success in Alberta is the set of social safety supports that are provided for students and their families. Alberta, unlike some other high-performing systems, has many immigrants and refugees and a significant indigenous population and, despite some problems in early childhood development identified in a recent provincial mapping study, the social supports that exist for children and families better provide for the social preconditions for learning than in some education systems.

A second factor in Alberta's success is the political stability that has existed in the province with over 90 years of Progressive Conservative leadership that has prevented some of the shifting and turning that is associated with constant changes with party leadership in some other systems. Even though this stable leadership has been relatively conservative on a number of issues until May 2015, it has provided strong support for both public education and teachers. This strong public and government support has translated into very generous salaries and benefits for teachers, more generous overall than the compensation of teachers anywhere else in North America.

A third factor supporting Alberta's educational success has been the unusual degree of trust and collaboration that has existed across the various education stakeholder groups such as the Ministry of Education, Teachers' Association, and school administrators. The fact that school principals belong to the same professional association as teachers has supported a collaborative rather than adversarial relationship between teachers and principals. Also the common practice of individuals being seconded for periods of time from one sector of education to another (e.g., teachers who spend time working at the Ministry or Teachers' Association) has also supported the culture of trust and collaboration that has existed. This may also support coherence and strong knowledge of practice in the Ministry.

One consequence of the trust and collaboration across education stakeholder groups that has been interrupted only or brief periods of time under various governments is the emphasis on teachers' professional learning rather than on teacher evaluation. One notable example of this emphasis is the Alberta School Improvement Initiative that resulted in a huge investment in teacher-led learning over a 14-year period following the rejection of a teacher pay-for-performance plan that was proposed by a staff member in the Ministry. Although we found some evidence that the availability of professional learning opportunities for teachers and their control over its nature and substance have been eroded some in recent years, the emphasis is still on teacher learning rather than on teacher evaluation and there are many opportunities for teacher learning.

Alberta is currently operating in a climate of funding cuts due to decreased oil revenues and an economic slowdown. This has put pressure on teachers to do more with less. Despite the clear evidence that the work of teaching has intensified in Alberta and teachers overall spend a relatively high number of hours per week teaching and grading and meeting with students and have relatively little time during the school day for collaboration with their colleagues, Alberta's teachers generally feel respected and valued by the public and government.

Another important factor in Alberta's education success is the insistence, with two minor exceptions, that teachers must complete a provincially approved preservice teacher education program before they are permitted to assume full responsibility for a classroom of students. The two exceptions to this are bridging programs for people with journeyman licenses in certain vocational/technical fields and individuals who are certified as teachers in other countries. Nothing exists in Alberta like the early entry programs that are expanding in a growing number of education systems where individuals are permitted to assume full classroom responsibility with a few weeks of preparation and where they complete their certification on the job while they are responsible for classrooms.

Even the Teach for Canada program that is now emerging in the country and will begin operating first in Ontario will require those admitted to be already licensed as teachers. This is in sharp contrast to the many other "Teach for" national programs that allow individuals to be teachers of record with no more than a few weeks of preservice preparation. A strong university system of teacher preparation is certainly a significant factor in Alberta's educational successes.

It is too early to tell in this early stage of the New Democratic Party government what changes in policies and practices might develop. It is likely though under this new more politically liberal government that the strong support for public education, teachers, and teacher education and professional learning that are evident in this case study will continue and be strengthened.

NOTES

1. This project's findings were based on a sample of approximately 70,000 kindergarten children between 2009 and 2013.
2. From May 2012 until September 2014, the Minister of Education was Jeff Johnson, who had previously worked as the Minister of Infrastructure. During our first visit to Edmonton on March 19 and 20, 2014, the Premier of Alberta resigned, and a new Education Minister, Gordon Dirks, was appointed in September 2014 by the newly elected Progressive Conservative Premier, Jim Prentice. In May 2015, David Eggen became the new Minister of Education when the New Democratic Party took control of the government.
3. AERA Educational Change Special Interest Group. J. C. Couture. Issue No. 22 November 2012.
4. The name of this Ministry has recently been changed to the Ministry of Advanced Education.
5. Attrition in this context refers to attrition from teaching rather than from a particular school or district.
6. It was pointed out above that the 2013 TALIS survey of lower secondary teachers concluded that teachers reported working 48.2 hours per week.
7. Alberta Education (2013) has implemented pilot teacher induction programs in 11 school districts in northern Alberta including Medicine Hat, Chinook's Edge, and Red Deer.
8. Some subject areas where there have been teacher shortages include ESL, mathematics, science, FNMI education, special education, and career and technology studies.
9. Personal communication 9/23/14.
10. Per a vote by the CUC Board of Trustees in December 2014, Canadian University College officially changed its name to Burman University.
11. For example, City University of Seattle, Gonzaga University, and University of Portland.
12. Provided by an Innovation and Advanced Education staff member.

Interviews

- Mark Bevan, Ministry of Education
- Jim Brandon, Professor of Education, University of Calgary
- Marion Brenner, Teacher
- D. Jean Clandinin, Professor of Education, University of Alberta
- J. C. Couture, Alberta Teachers' Association
- Robert Gardner, Teacher
- Peter Grimmett, Professor of Education, University of British Columbia
- Wayne LaVold, Teacher
- Paul MacLoud, Ministry of Education
- Katherine Macmillan, Teacher
- Kelsey McReady, Teacher
- Val Olekshy, Edmonton Regional Learning Consortium
- Jim Parsons, Professor of Education, University of Alberta
- Karen Shipka, Ministry of Education
- Randy Wimmer, Professor of Education and Associate
- Dean, University of Alberta
- David Stawn, Teacher
- Tammy Thero-Soto, Teacher
- Diane Wishart, Ministry of Innovation and Advancement
- Mark Yurick, Alberta Teachers' Association

Appendix 2–A Teaching Quality Standards

TEACHING QUALITY STANDARD APPLICABLE TO THE PROVISION OF BASIC EDUCATION IN ALBERTA

MINISTERIAL ORDER (#016/97)

1 Pursuant to Section 39(1)(f) of the School Act, I approve the following as the Teaching Quality Standard which shall apply to teacher certification, professional development, supervision and evaluation, and which is supported by descriptors of selected knowledge, skills and attributes appropriate to teachers at different stages of their careers:

(1) Teaching Quality Standard

Quality teaching occurs when the teacher's ongoing analysis of the context, and the teacher's decisions about which pedagogical knowledge and abilities to apply result in optimum learning by students.

All teachers are expected to meet the Teaching Quality Standard throughout their careers.

However, teaching practices will vary because each teaching situation is different and in constant change. Reasoned judgment must be used to determine whether the Teaching Quality Standard is being met in a given context.

(2) Descriptors of Knowledge, Skills and Attributes Related to Interim Certification

Teachers who hold an Interim Professional Certificate must possess the Knowledge, Skills and Attributes Related to Interim Certification (Interim KSAs), and apply them appropriately toward student learning. During their first two years of teaching, teachers should use the Interim KSAs to guide their teaching, reflect on their practice, and direct their professional development in collaboration with their supervisors and evaluators.

As situations warrant, teachers who hold an Interim Professional Certificate are expected to demonstrate consistently that they understand:

a) contextual variables affect teaching and learning. They know how to analyse many variables at one time, and how to respond by making reasoned decisions about their teaching practice and students' learning;

b) the structure of the Alberta education system. They know the different roles in the system, and how responsibilities and accountabilities are determined, communicated and enforced, including the expectations held of them under the Certification of Teachers Regulation, A.R.3/1999 as amended and their school authority's teacher's evaluation policy;

c) the purposes of the Guide to Education and programs of study germane to the specialization or subject disciplines they are prepared to teach. They know how to use these documents to inform and direct their planning, instruction and assessment of student progress;

d) the subject disciplines they teach. They have completed a structured program of studies through which they acquired the knowledge, concepts, methodologies and assumptions in one or more areas of specialization or subject disciplines taught in Alberta schools;

e) all students can learn, albeit at different rates and in different ways. They know how (including when and how to engage others) to identify students' different learning styles and ways students learn. They understand the need to respond to differences by creating multiple paths to learning for individuals and groups of students, including students with special learning needs;

f) the purposes of short, medium and long term range planning. They know how to translate curriculum and desired outcomes into reasoned, meaningful and incrementally progressive learning opportunities for students. They also understand the need to vary their plans to accommodate individuals and groups of students;

g) students' needs for physical, social, cultural and psychological security. They know how to engage students in creating effective classroom routines. They know how and when to apply a variety of management strategies that are in keeping with the situation, and that provide for minimal disruptions to students' learning;

h) the importance of respecting students' human dignity. They know how to establish, with different students, professional relationships that are characterized by mutual respect, trust and harmony;

i) there are many approaches to teaching and learning. They know a broad range of instructional strategies appropriate to their area of specialization and the subject discipline they teach, and know which strategies are appropriate to help different students achieve different outcomes;

j) the functions of traditional and electronic teaching/learning technologies. They know how to use and how to engage students in using these technologies to present and deliver content, communicate effectively with others, find and secure information, research, word process, manage information, and keep records;

k) the purposes of student assessment. They know how to assess the range of learning objectives by selecting and developing a variety of classroom and large scale assessment techniques and instruments. They know how to analyse the results of classroom and large scale assessment instruments including provincial assessment instruments, and how to use the results for the ultimate benefit of students;

l) the importance of engaging parents, purposefully and meaningfully, in all aspects of teaching and learning. They know how to develop and implement strategies that create and enhance partnerships among teachers, parents and students;

m) student learning is enhanced through the use of home and community resources. They know how to identify resources relevant to teaching and learning objectives, and how to incorporate these resources into their teaching and students' learning;

n) the importance of contributing, independently and collegially, to the quality of their school. They know the strategies whereby they can, independently and collegially, enhance and maintain the quality of their schools to the benefit of students, parents, community and colleagues;

o) the importance of career-long learning. They know how to assess their own teaching and how to work with others responsible for supervising and evaluating teachers. They know how to use the findings of assessments, supervision and evaluations to select,

develop and implement their own professional development activities;

p) the importance of guiding their actions with a personal, overall vision of the purpose of teaching. They are able to communicate their vision, including how it has changed as a result of new knowledge, understanding and experience; and

q) they are expected to achieve the Teaching Quality Standard.

(3) Descriptors of Knowledge, Skills and Attributes Related to Permanent Certification

Teachers who hold a Permanent Professional Certificate must demonstrate, in their practice, professional repertoires that are expanded beyond the Interim KSAs.

The following descriptors comprise a repertoire of selected knowledge, skills and attributes from which teachers who hold a Permanent Professional Certificate should be able to draw, as situations warrant, in order to meet the Teaching Quality Standard. Teachers, staffs, supervisors and evaluators should use the descriptors to guide professional development, supervision, evaluation and remediation strategies in order that teachers can meet the Teaching Quality Standard consistently throughout their careers.

a) Teachers' application of pedagogical knowledge, skills and attributes is based in their ongoing analysis of contextual variables.

Teachers' analysis of contextual variables underlies their reasoned judgments and decisions about which specific pedagogical skills and abilities to apply in order that students can achieve optimum learning. Selected variables are outlined below.

STUDENT VARIABLES
demographic variables, e.g. age, gender
maturation
abilities and talents
relationships among students
subject area of study
prior learning
socio-economic status
cultural background

linguistic variables
mental and emotional states and
conditions
resource availability and allocation
teaching assignment
class size and composition
collegial and administrator support
physical plant

TEACHER VARIABLES
teaching experience
learning experiences

REGULATORY VARIABLES
Government Organization Act
School Act and provincial regulations,
policies and Ministerial Orders
Child, Youth and Family Enhancement Act
*Canadian Charter of Rights and
Freedoms*
school authority policies
Guide to Education
Program of Studies

PARENT AND SOCIETAL VARIABLES
parental support
parental involvement in children's
learning
socio-economic variables
community support for education
multiculturalism
cultural pluralism
inter-agency collaboration
provincial, national and global
influences

b) Teachers understand the legislated,
moral and ethical frameworks within
which they work.

Teachers function within a policy-based
and results oriented education system
authorized under the School Act and
other legislation.

Teachers also function within policy
frameworks established by school
authorities.

This includes policies which require: a
commitment to teaching practices that
meet their school authority's teaching
quality standard(s); and that teachers
engage in ongoing, individualized
professional development.

Teachers recognize they are bound by
standards of conduct expected of a
caring, knowledgeable and reasonable
adult who is entrusted with the
custody, care or education

of students or children. Teachers
recognize their actions are bound in
moral, ethical and legal considerations
regarding their obligations to students,
parents, administrators, school
authorities, communities and society
at large. Teachers acknowledge these
obligations and act accordingly.

c) Teachers understand the subject
disciplines they teach.

Teachers understand the knowledge,
concepts, methodologies and
assumptions of the subject disciplines
they teach. This includes an
understanding of how knowledge
in each discipline is created and
organized, and that subject disciplines
are more than bodies of static facts
and techniques - they are complex and
evolving. Their understanding extends
to relevant technologies, the linkages
among subject disciplines, and their
relevance and importance in everyday
life at the personal, local, national and
international levels.

Teachers understand that students
typically bring preconceptions and
understandings to a subject. They
know strategies and materials that are
of assistance in furthering students'
understanding.

d) Teachers know there are many
approaches to teaching and learning.

Teachers appreciate individual
differences and believe all students
can learn, albeit at different rates
and in different ways. They recognize
students' different learning styles
and the different ways they learn,
and accommodate these differences
in individuals and groups of students
including students with special learning
needs.

Teachers understand the fluidity of
teaching and learning. They constantly
monitor the effectiveness and
appropriateness of their practices and
students' activities, and change them
as needed.

e) Teachers engage in a range of planning
activities.

Teachers' plans are founded in their
understanding of contextual variables

and are a record of their decisions on
what teaching and learning strategies
to apply. Plans outline a reasoned and
incremental progression toward the
attainment of desired outcomes, for
both teachers and students. Teachers
monitor the context, their instruction,
and monitor and assess students'
learning on an ongoing basis, and
modify their plans accordingly.

Teachers strive to establish
candid, open and ongoing lines of
communication with students, parents,
colleagues and other professionals, and
incorporate information gained into
their planning.

f) Teachers create and maintain
environments that are conducive to
student learning.

Teachers establish learning
environments wherein students feel
physically, psychologically, socially and
culturally secure. They are respectful
of students' human dignity, and seek
to establish a positive professional
relationship with students that is
characterized by mutual respect, trust
and harmony. They model the beliefs,
principles, values, and intellectual
characteristics outlined in the Guide to
Education and programs of study, and
guide students to do the same.

Teachers work, independently
and cooperatively, to make their
classrooms and schools stimulating
learning environments. They maintain
acceptable levels of student conduct,
and use discipline strategies that result
in a positive environment conducive
to student learning. They work with
students to establish classroom
routines that enhance and increase
students' involvement in meaningful
learning activities. They organize
facilities, materials, equipment and
space to provide students equitable
opportunities to learn, and to provide
for students' safety.

Where community members work
with students either on-campus or
off-campus and where students are
engaged in school-sponsored off-
campus activities, teachers strive to
ensure these situations also are secure

and positive environments conducive to students' learning.

g) Teachers translate curriculum content and objectives into meaningful learning activities.

Teachers clearly communicate short and long range learning expectations to students, and how the expectations are to be achieved and assessed. They engage students in meaningful activities that motivate and challenge them to achieve those expectations. They integrate current learning with prior learning, and provide opportunities for students to relate their learning to the home, community and broader environment.

Teachers apply a broad range and variety of instructional and learning strategies.

The strategies vary in keeping with contextual variables, subject content, desired objectives, and the learning needs of individuals and groups of students. The strategies are selected and used to achieve desired outcomes, primarily the expectations outlined in the Guide to Education, programs of study and other approved programs.

h) Teachers apply a variety of technologies to meet students' learning needs.

Teachers use teaching/learning resources such as the chalkboard, texts, computers and other auditory, print and visual media, and maintain an awareness of emerging technological resources. They keep abreast of advances in teaching/learning technologies and how they can be incorporated into instruction and learning. As new technologies prove useful and become available in schools, teachers develop their own and their students' proficiencies in using the technologies purposefully, which may include content presentation, delivery and research applications, as well as word processing, information management and record keeping.

Teachers use electronic networks and other telecommunication media to enhance their own knowledge and abilities, and to communicate more effectively with others.

i) Teachers gather and use information about students' learning needs and progress.

Teachers monitor students' actions on an ongoing basis to determine and respond to their learning needs. They use a variety of diagnostic methods that include observing students' activities, analysing students' learning difficulties and strengths, and interpreting the results of assessments and information provided by students, their parents, colleagues and other professionals.

Teachers select and develop a variety of classroom assessment strategies and instruments to assess the full range of learning objectives. They differentiate between classroom and large-scale instruments such as provincial achievement tests, administer both and use the results for the ultimate benefit of students. They record, interpret and use the results of their assessments to modify their teaching practices and students' learning activities.

Teachers help students, parents and other educators interpret and understand the results of diagnoses and assessments, and the implications for students. They also help students develop the ability to diagnose their own learning needs and to assess their progress toward learning goals.

Teachers use their interpretations of diagnoses and assessments as well as students' work and results to guide their own professional growth. They assist school councils and members of the community to understand the purposes, meanings, outcomes and implications of assessments.

j) Teachers establish and maintain partnerships among school, home and community, and within their own schools.

Teachers engage in activities that contribute to the quality of the school as a learning environment. They work with others to develop, coordinate and implement programs and activities that characterize effective schools. They

also work cooperatively with school councils.

Teachers strive to involve parents in their children's schooling. Partnerships with the home are characterized by the candid sharing of information and ideas to influence how teachers and parents, independently and cooperatively, contribute to students' learning.

Teachers seek out and incorporate community resources into their instruction, and encourage students to use home and community resources in their learning. Teachers make connections between school, home and community in order to enhance the relevance and meaning of learning. Home and community resources are utilized to make learning meaningful and relevant, and so students can gain an increased understanding of the knowledge, skills and attitudes needed to participate in and contribute positively to society.

k) Teachers are career-long learners.

Teachers engage in ongoing professional development to enhance their: understanding of and ability to analyze the context of teaching; ability to make reasoned judgments and decisions; and, pedagogical knowledge and abilities. They recognize their own professional needs and work with others to meet those needs. They share their professional expertise to the benefit of others in their schools, communities and profession.

Teachers guide their actions by their overall visions of the purpose of teaching.

They actively refine and redefine their visions in light of the ever-changing context, new knowledge and understandings, and their experiences. While these visions are dynamic and grow in depth and breadth over teachers' careers, the visions maintain at their core a commitment to teaching practices through which students can achieve optimum learning.

Appendix 2–B Vignettes of Teacher Preparation Programs

Ambrose University

Ambrose University offers a 60-credit, two-year after-degree bachelors of education (B.Ed.) degree. The program focuses on elementary education and has a partnership with the Rocky View School Division.

Course work revolves around 10 competencies that are tightly articulated with the Teaching Quality Standards. Courses integrate these competencies in a spiraling fashion beginning with "foundations" during the first semester of the program, "understanding" in the second semester, "application" in the third semester, and "reflection" in the fourth semester. Field experiences are included each semester for a total of 25 weeks, making field experiences at Ambrose University the longest in duration of all of the teacher preparation institutions.

The competency-based program includes four components: 12 credits of field experience over the duration of three semesters, 18 credits of course work in curriculum design and program development, 18 credits of course work in learning theory and application, and 12 credits of what is termed Society and Culture: Methodologies and Practices. According to correspondence from Dr. Bernie Potvin, associate professor and chair at Ambrose University, "each component consists of three distinct but not separate courses, each integrating with the other courses in the component in a developmental and graduated way. For example, in the curriculum design and program development component's three courses, students will learn how to apply theories of curriculum, learning, and assessment to the development of school programs over the two years of the program. In addition, this important competency will receive ongoing, systematic and graduated attention in the three other components of the program, from within each component's perspective. Students will learn how to apply theories of curriculum, learning, and assessment over the two years of courses in the Society and Culture: Methodologies and Practices component. And, perhaps most importantly, students will be given planned opportunities, in developmental and graduated ways, to apply this competency in their field experiences. As well, each student will be afforded opportunity to apply this competency not as mere technique but through deliberate reflection with the guidance of classroom teachers, university professors, mentors, and the research story and vision of education for all children found in the most important writing and practices of our profession" (email correspondence, Dr. Bernie Potvin).

For admission to the after-degree program, candidates must have completed a bachelor's degree with a strong liberal arts component and hold a minimum of 90 credits. The required cumulative GPA for admission is 2.7. As part of the admissions process, candidates must do the following: (a) provide documentation that they have worked with children, (b) submit a written philosophy of education statement, and (c) complete an interview.

Canadian University College

Canadian University College, now Burman University, does not offer a combined degree program option. Instead, teacher candidates earn a bachelor's of education degree. Canadian University College also offers a two-year after-degree program for candidates to obtain a B.Ed. as post-baccalaureate students. For the purposes of comparison, we are choosing to focus on the undergraduate B.Ed. degree program requirements.

Canadian University College (CUC) appears to have a lengthy admission process for prospective teacher candidates. First, candidates must apply and be admitted to CUC. After their first year of course work, candidates must apply for initial admission to the B.Ed. program. Admission requirements include a minimum cumulative GPA of 2.5, reference letters, security clearance, an autobiographical sketch with a statement of goals, and an essay indicating why the candidate wants to be a teacher. After initial admission to the B.Ed. program, within two years and typically before entering their third year of university, students must apply full admission to the B.Ed. program. The full admission process involves an interview with two faculty members from within the school of education, who recommend the student for admission. If a student is not offered full admission, he/she must wait a full year before applying for full admission again. Full admission to the B.Ed. program allows the student to complete the next two years (years three and four). Both the elementary education and secondary education tracks require a minimum of 120 credits and a minimum 2.5 grade point average for graduation.

The elementary education track requires students to complete 42 credits of what are termed "breadth requirements," 69 credits of "professional education requirements" and an additional 9 credits of elective course work. Breadth requirements include courses in health and fitness, humanities and social sciences, English composition, science and mathematics, Canadian history, and religious studies.

Professional education requirements include course work in two categories: basic education and curriculum and instruction. Required basic education courses include Philosophy of Education, Multicultural Education, Educational Technology, Child Development and Learning Theories, Assessment, Classroom Management, Orientation to Teaching, and two practicum courses. Curriculum and instruction courses are more specific to teaching elementary school and include course work in methods for teaching music, language arts, art, readings, physical education, religion, health and science, mathematics, children's literature, exceptional learners, remediation of mathematics and reading, and multigrade methods.

Students completing their B.Ed. degree in Elementary Education spend their first year of school completing predominantly breadth requirements and then gradually move to completing their professional education requirements in years two through four.

The secondary education track is similar to the elementary track in that the secondary education track also has breadth requirements and professional education requirements. However, in addition to these two requirements, the secondary track has specialization and minor requirements as well. Consequently, only 18 credits of breadth requirements are required compared to 42 credits in the elementary track. The professional education requirements in the secondary education track total 46 credits. Specialization requirements, or content specific course work, total to 36 credits and the minor requirements total 18 credits. While professional education requirements are layered on more heavily in years 2–4, course work in years 1–3 is spread relatively evenly between specialization, minor, and breadth requirements.

For students completing a B.Ed. in secondary education, breadth requirements include religious studies course work, English composition, and health and fitness course work. Specialization requirements delve into content area requirements. For example, to satisfy specialization requirement for an English focus, candidates take twelve English courses with courses in literature, theory and criticism, Shakespeare, American and/or Canadian literature, composition and/or creative writing.

Professional education requirements, similar to the elementary education track, are further divided into two areas: basic education and curriculum and instruction. Required basic education courses are the same as the elementary education track. Curriculum and instruction requirements include content specific methods courses, exceptional learners, reading and writing in the content areas, and curriculum and instruction courses in the area of specialization and minor.

Unlike the University of Lethbridge with its three semesters of clinical fieldwork, Canadian University College only requires two clinical experiences in years three and four of the course sequence.

Concordia University College of Alberta

Concordia University College of Alberta offers a 60-credit, two-year after-degree bachelor of education program in Elementary Education.

For admission into the program, candidates must have complete a three- or four-year baccalaureate degree and have a minimum of a 2.3 GPA on their 30 credits. Additionally, candidates must have completed 12 credits of course work in English language/literature and two areas of discipline study from the following topics: archeology, anthropology, classics, computing science, economics, fine arts, history, languages other than English, mathematics, philosophy, physical education and sports studies, political sciences, psychology, religious studies, sciences, and sociology. When applying, candidates include a philosophy of teaching statement, two letters of reference attesting to the candidate's ability to work with children, and a volunteer or work experience record. Interviews are scheduled with qualified candidates after receipt of application materials.

Course work in the program is designed around the knowledge, skills, and attributes as defined in Alberta Education's Teaching Quality Standard. Each semester of course work confers 15 credits. The first semester of year one, candidates take "foundation" course work entitled the Organizational Framework of Teaching, Teaching and Schooling in Western Culture, Learning, Instructional Psychology and Educational Practice, Introduction to Planning in Elementary School, and their first field experience. The second semester of year one, termed Instruction I, includes courses on curriculum design and instructional methods in the elementary school (designed for core subject areas and elective subject areas), the second field experience, and reflections on the first two field experiences with a focus on inclusive education. The first semester of the third year extends candidates' knowledge of instruction with course work in advanced planning in the elementary school, in addition to the nine-week field experience, and reflections on field experience three. The final semester of the program, termed the "integration" semester, candidates complete another course in advanced planning in the elementary school, and subject-specific methods courses in literature and literacy, mathematics, science, and social studies for elementary school.

There are three primary field experiences in the program. The first field experience features 10 half-day observations and occurs in the first semester of year one. The second field experience, termed the intermediate field experience, lasts for four weeks with the expectation that the teacher candidates teach half of the day. The final "senior" field experience occurs in the first half of year two, is nine weeks in duration, and includes the first week of the school year. During the latter half of year two in the program, teacher candidates complete reflections on their teaching practice, take online modules to assist in reflective practice, and develop professional growth plans.

To assist candidates in preparing for the teaching profession and securing employment, in the second year of their program, teacher candidates can participate in a service called the Employment Processes Program. This program is designed to help students understand the diversity of school authorities. Components of the Employment Processes Program include career fairs, employment mentorship, employment preparation seminars, the development of a professional employment portfolio (a requirement for teacher candidates in the program), and a bridging program toward employment with school authority partnership. The Bridges Bursary Program, as it is called, funds volunteer time in the schools by recent graduates of the program. While not an additional practicum, this program is designed to aid in the transition to full-time teaching positions. The Bursary Bridges Program appears to be unique among the teacher preparation program in Alberta.

The King's University

Like Ambrose University, The King's University offers a two-year, 60-credit B.Ed. after-degree program with a focus on elementary education and secondary education. Admission to the after-degree program is nearly identical to Ambrose University with the main difference between a 2.5 GPA to 2.7 GPA requirement, respectively. Admission to the after-degree program at The King's University requires a B.A. degree of a minimum of 90 credits with broad liberal arts course work. Candidates applying for admissions must hold a minimum of a 2.5 cumulative GPA, have had previous experience working with children or adolescents, write an essay on their philosophy of education, and complete an interview with education faculty.

Candidates completing the after-degree program can obtain a B.Ed. in Elementary or Secondary Education. Candidates progress through the program by completing a series of four themed semesters, moving through preparation, integration, extension, and completion.

In Elementary Education, the fall semester of year one (or preparation semester) features course work in learning theory, curriculum planning, language arts methods, mathematics methods, and one choice elective. In the second semester of year one, candidates complete the integration semester by taking a series of nine, one-week modules taught by master teachers and completing a practicum in the schools. This first practicum in the schools features five weeks of field experience and one week of debriefing.

Year two of the elementary education focus kicks off the extension semester. In this semester, candidates take course work in children's literature, exceptional children, educational administration (or school law), advanced curriculum planning, and one choice elective. In addition, candidates complete a course called Elementary Classroom Startup where they participate in and experience the start of the school year within actual classroom. The second semester of year two (or completion semester) features a 12-week-long practicum with one week of debriefing.

For candidates on the secondary education track, admission requirements differ somewhat in that candidates must have a documented undergraduate course work in acceptable major and minor areas for specialization. Applicants need 33 credits of course work in a teaching major and 18 credits in a teaching minor. Acceptable major/minor areas offered at The King's University include: biology/environmental studies; chemistry; CTS: business; CTS: computing science; drama; English language arts; general physical sciences; general sciences; mathematics; music; physical education; and social studies.

Course work also differs somewhat from the elementary track. During year one semester one (preparation), candidates complete many of the same foundation courses as the elementary education students. They complete courses in learning theory and curriculum planning. In addition to those two courses, candidates take a required education course entitled Strategies for Teaching and Learning and two choice electives. The second semester of the first year, secondary education students complete three, one-week modules taught by a master teacher (note that this is different from the nine, one-week modules at the elementary education level), course work in curriculum and instruction in the teaching major/minor, sociocultural influences, which appears to be similar to multicultural education courses in the U.S. During the second semester, like the elementary education candidates, secondary education students also complete a practicum in the schools though theirs lasts for six weeks with an additional week for debriefing.

Year two features course work in exceptional children and educational administration, cross-curricular literacy, two choice electives, another course on curriculum and instruction in the teaching major/minor, and a 12-week field experience with one week of debriefing.

University of Alberta

The University of Alberta offers a bachelor's of education degree in both Elementary and Secondary Education. In addition to the B.Ed. degree, combined degree programs lasting five years are offered with Native studies, physical education, human ecology, drama, and science. For students already holding a bachelor's degree, after-degree B.Ed. programs are also available. In addition to these programs toward teacher certification, the University of Alberta also offers graduate degrees in education. For the sake of comparison across universities, we focus on two B.Ed. programs leading to licensure in elementary education and secondary education with a major specialization in English, respectively.

Both the elementary and secondary tracks for the bachelors of education degree begin with two years of preliminary course work, which frontloads content-specific courses. Candidates register with the Faculty of Education leading into their third year. In the elementary route, 42 of 51 required noneducation course work credits must be completed prior to registering for year three.

To make sure education is a field of interest for all education candidates, nine credits of preliminary education course work are completed within the first two years of study. These nine credits include three required three-credit courses in Contexts of Education, Educational Technology, and a course entitled Aboriginal Education and Contexts for Professional and Personal Engagement.

While completing the required three-credit education courses, elementary education majors must also take required noneducation courses in aboriginal and indigenous histories and cultures (3 cr), fine arts (6 cr), language and literature (9 cr), mathematics (6 cr), natural science (6 cr), physical education and health (6 cr), social science (6 cr)—three credits of which must include course work in Canadian history, and nine elective credits. In year three, elementary education majors begin completing the bulk of their education course work. Course work includes learning and development in childhood, introduction to language arts, two education electives, educational assessment, and three courses from a block of courses on curriculum and instruction in mathematics, music, social studies, science, and physical education. In the second half of year three, elementary education majors complete their first field experience. This field experience consists of three weeks of on-campus course work, three days of in-school observation, and five weeks of student teaching with a mentor teacher. The second field experience occurs during the fourth year of study and includes nine weeks of student teaching. In addition to the second field experience, in their fourth year of study, elementary education majors take another course from the block of curriculum and instruction courses, an inclusive education course, and ethics and law in teaching courses, and then two additional education courses of the candidate's choosing, one education elective, and one free choice elective.

Secondary education teaching candidates also take the three, three-credit required education courses in years one and two, but rather than taking the noneducation survey courses required for elementary education majors, secondary education majors must take six credits of English or French language and composition. Then, students must take 36 credits worth of major specialization requirements and 18 credits of minor specialization courses. Some of the course work toward an English major specialization includes English, Writing, Canadian Literature, Literature Pre-1900, and Film and Media Studies.

In their third and fourth year, secondary education candidates begin education course work in earnest. Required education course work for secondary route candidates includes some of the same course work required of elementary education majors and a few courses tailored specifically to the secondary level. Courses include Ethics and Law in Teaching; Inclusive Education; Adolescent Development and Learning; Assessment, Integrated Theory, and Classroom Practice in the Advanced Professional Term; Language, Literacy, and Society in Educational Contexts; two courses of curriculum and instruction for secondary school in the major specialization area; and one course of curriculum and instruction for secondary school in the minor specialization area. In addition to course work, secondary education students also complete an introductory field experience in year three and an advanced field experience in year four.

Faculté Saint-Jean

Campus Saint-Jean in Edmonton, which was incorporated by the University of Alberta in 1976, offers B.Ed., combined degree B.Ed/B.Sc., and B.Ed. after-degree programs for teacher candidates through its Faculté Saint-Jean (Cammarata, Cavanagh, & d'Entremont, 2015, p. 25). Faculté Saint-Jean trains teachers specifically to teach in a Francophone minority setting or in French immersion programs. The program is entirely in French. General admission requires a 2.7 GPA and demonstration of French language proficiency. One particularly unique component about the education programs at Campus Saint-Jean is a French proficiency test requirement for admission.

B.Ed. program offers an elementary and secondary track. The elementary track leads to a generalist specialization. Candidates completing the elementary track must also select a minor area of specialization in arts, music education, physical education, humanities, or inclusive education—the last of which features course work in psychology and educational psychology. The majority of course work for the generalist focus occurs in the first year, with education course work added in the last three years of the program. The secondary track, similar to all of the other secondary track programs, requires major and minor specialization areas. Specializations offered at Faculté Saint-Jean within the secondary track include French, general science, mathematics, music, and social studies. Secondary track students must complete a minimum of 36 credits in their major specialization area and 15 credits in their minor specialization area. In addition, they need to take 9 credits of French Canadian.

The undergraduate B.Ed. programs confer 120 credits. The combined degree program leads to a bachelor's of education and a bachelor's of science with available specializations in biological sciences, mathematical sciences, and physical sciences.

Like other after-degree programs offered throughout the province, Faculté Saint-Jean's B.Ed. after-degree program is two additional years and requires 60 credits of study. These 60 credits of study are education-related courses within both the elementary and secondary B.Ed. tracks.

Within the education programs, there are three required practica. The first practica requires 10 visits to the schools. The second and third field experiences add an additional 13 weeks of experience in the schools.

To continue through the program, candidates must maintain a 2.0 GPA.

The University of Calgary

The University of Calgary currently offers a five-year combined (concurrent) B.Ed./B.A./B.Sc./B.Kin. degree and a two-year B.Ed. after-degree (consecutive) program. Beginning Fall 2015, however, a new four-year B.Ed. program, entitled a Community-Based B.Ed. Pathway Program is being launched. This program will allow rural and remote students to remain in their community while completing the program. Like Campus Saint-Jean, the University of Calgary also offers French as a teachable subject area. This program of study prepares teachers to teach in Francophone schools and French immersion schools.

For the concurrent five-year programs, applications to the program apply to and are admitted to both departments (education and either arts, science, or kinesiology) at the same time. Admission decisions are based on high school courses. Also, as part of their application, candidates must decide on a particular track (elementary or secondary), a teachable subject area, and a program major. Students completing the concurrent program take course work during years 1, 2, and 4 in their program major area (arts, science, or kinesiology) and then take course work during years 3 and 5 in the school of education.

The two-year after-degree program offers an elementary and secondary track. Admission to the program requires a minimum of a 2.5 GPA, one completed course in English or French literature, and a degree with at least 15 transferable full course equivalents from an accredited post-secondary institution recognized by the University of Calgary. For candidates hoping to complete the elementary track, approved undergraduate degrees normally have degrees in the humanities, social sciences, natural science, fine arts, communication, or cultural studies but course work should be sufficiently broad. Secondary track after-degree candidates need to have a degree in the subject area in which they intend to teach.

English language proficiency is a requirement for admission to the University of Calgary B.Ed. programs, but candidates have a number of options available to them to demonstrate proficiency, including satisfactorily complete English courses in high school.

Since the concurrent (five-year) and consecutive (two-year after-degree) programs are each comprised of two years of course within the School of Education, the progression of education courses is straightforward and the same for both programs. Each semester is organized around a theme. The first semester's theme is Introduction to Teaching and Learning. Teacher candidates take a lecture entitled Issues in Teaching and Learning, three seminars, one of which is unique to teaching route and specialization, and two which are entitled The Pragmatics of Teaching and Learning, and Literacy, Language, and Culture. Beyond that, in the first semester, students also complete their first field experience. It is a two-week field experience "focused as an ethnographic research inquiry into the culture of schools (University of Calgary School of Education Handbook, 2015–2016, p. 8).

The second semester's theme is Principles of Individual Learning and Development. Again, the semester is structured around one lecture, three seminars, and a second field experience, this time lasting four weeks. The lecture is entitled Individual Learning: Theories and Applications. One of the seminars is specialization focused, yet this time on pedagogy and methods. Another seminar focuses on diversity in learning. The third seminar is entitled Professional Development and Lifelong Learning and focuses on how to encourage, understand, and reflect on teachers' own learning.

The third semester follows the same format as the first two and has the theme of Principles of Social and Cultural Engagement. Courses for this semester have names like Interdisciplinary Learning, Ethics and Law in Education, and FNMI History, Education, and Leadership. Additionally, there is a specialization-focused seminar aimed to strengthen teacher candidates' pedagogical content knowledge. This semester's field experience is six weeks in duration, and considered a team-blocked practicum focused on principles of collaborative learning.

The fourth semester is entitled Extending Teaching and Curriculum. In this semester, teacher candidates take courses with the same titles as the previous semester but specific to their track and specialization area. The final field experience lasts eight weeks and is the formal, student teaching field experience.

Students must maintain a 2.5 GPA each semester in order to continue on to the next semester. Candidates not successfully completing the requirements of each semester will have to repeat the semester in order to continue on.

The University of Lethbridge

The University of Lethbridge offers two programs of study for one to obtain an interim teaching certificate: a combined degree program or an after-degree program. The after-degree program is, as the name suggests, for degree holders and operates in a similar fashion to college-recommending programs in the United States. To compare university teacher preparation program across Alberta, however, we have chosen to focus on undergraduate degree programs. For the University of Lethbridge, students hoping to become teachers seek to obtain a dual degree with bachelor's degree in the arts (BA), in the sciences (BS), or in fine arts (BFA) with a bachelor's of education degree (B.Ed.).

To complete the combined degree program BA/BS/FA and B.Ed. takes five years but course work toward both degrees is integrated throughout all five years. Students must take 30 courses in their arts, sciences, or fine arts area and then also complete 20 courses within the faculty (department) of education. The first year as a matriculated student, the student completes general liberal education requirements and course work toward the major program of study (arts, science, or fine arts). Beginning in the second year, students interested in pursuing the combined degree complete an introductory Orientation to Teaching course which places students in schools for six hours a week during the semester. During this period of time, students observe and reflect on their experience. This course allows students to learn about the profession of teaching and decide if education is the appropriate path for them. It also allows teacher educators within the faculty of education to determine if the student is a good fit for the profession. The rest of year two is dedicated to completing course work toward the content area focus.

Students planning to complete the combined degree program can apply for admission to the faculty of education after completing twenty semester courses, the orientation to teaching practicum, and maintaining a 2.50 cumulative GPA. Typically, these requirements have been satisfied at the end of year two.

In the fall semester of year three, students who have decided to pursue the combined degree, and who have been admitted to the faculty of education combined degree program, begin the first of three of what are termed "professional semesters." These professional semesters combine field experience—with gradually increasing student responsibility—and education course work.

Professional Semester I features six education courses of two credits each with a five-week, 125-hour field experience. The six education courses are generic and not content-area specific and feature topics on curriculum and instruction, educational technology, teaching as a profession, assessment, educational psychology, and language. The expectation for the field experience is that the teacher candidate will spend one-third of the time teaching, one-third observing/preparation, and one-third assisting.

The next two semesters (year 3: spring and year 4: fall) are focused once again on content area mastery and elective course work. Professional Semester II occurs in the spring semester of the fourth year. This second of the professional semester series features 11.5 credits or course work and a six-week clinical field experience. This time, course work includes content-specific methods courses and additional courses on classroom management, curriculum planning, exceptional learners, and the social context of schooling. The 150 hours of field experience feature one week where the teacher candidate takes over half of the classroom teaching load and then five weeks where the candidate takes over two-thirds of the classroom teaching responsibility.

Depending on the grade level (whether elementary or secondary education), candidates complete their third and final Professional Semester in the fall or spring quarter of their fifth year. Professional Semester III is the equivalent of the U.S. "student teaching" field experience; however, although teacher candidates are required to complete a semester (12–17 weeks) of teaching, candidates are only expected to take over one half of their mentor teacher's teaching load. In addition to completing their final clinical field experience, this semester is dedicated to work on a professional portfolio, professional development, and reflective practice under the direction of their university field supervisor. Depending on the semester in which Professional Semester III is completed, teacher candidates, before graduating, are also expected to take an additional four courses (for a total of 12 credit hours), one of which must be an educational foundations course and three education elective courses.

3

TEACHER POLICIES AND PRACTICES IN ONTARIO

Carol Campbell, Pamela Osmond-Johnson,
Ann Lieberman, and Jacqueline Sohn

THIS CHAPTER DOCUMENTS AND DISCUSSES the policies and practices
that support teachers' development and teaching quality in the province
of Ontario, Canada. Consistent with Canada's overall performance in
international assessments, Ontario is recognized as a province that has
high levels of both academic achievement and equity, with a lower than
average impact of socioeconomic status on educational outcomes compared to countries across the Organisation for Economic Co-operation
and Development (OECD, 2013). For example, in the 2012 Programme
for International Student Assessment (PISA), Ontario's scores were
considerably above the OECD average results; specifically, Ontario's
score in Reading was 528 (contrasted with an OECD average of 496);
Ontario's score in Science was 527 (contrasted with an OECD average of 501); and Ontario's score in Mathematics was 514 (contrasted
with an OECD average of 494) (Education Quality and Accountability
Office, 2013) (Link 3-1). Ontario's strong performance in Reading in
PISA is reflected also in Ontario being the highest performing province
for Reading results in the latest national Pan-Canadian Assessment Program (PCAP). In the 2013 PCAP results, Ontario is the only province to
have results above the Canadian average in all assessments—coming in
first in Reading, second (to Alberta) in science, and second (to Quebec) in
mathematics (Education Quality and Accountability Office, 2014a). As
will be discussed in this chapter, Ontario's education performance takes
place in a context of public support for the value of publically funded
education and political attention to educational improvement with a

priority focus on supporting the development of teachers and teaching quality to enable all students to learn and succeed.

System Improvement and Ontario's Theory of Action

Consistent with the above results in international and national testing, Ontario has been noted for its relatively high-performing and equitable education system. For example, in the OECD's study of Ontario as part of their Strong Performers and Successful Reformers in Education series, the OECD concluded: "The Ontario strategy is perhaps the world's leading example of professionally driven system change" (2010, p. 75). Similarly, Mourshed, Chijioke, and Barber (2010) included Ontario in their study of *How the World's Most Improved School Systems Keep Getting Better*. There has been considerable commentary on the nature of the Ontario education reforms and factors contributing to their successes (and challenges).

Michael Fullan—a key advisor and architect of Ontario's change strategies—emphasizes the importance of "whole system education improvement" (e.g., Fullan & Rincón-Gallardo, 2016) involving the tri-level combination of capacity building, focus, and results at the provincial level (government and Ministry of Education), school district level, and in schools (Fullan, 2010). Recently, Fullan and Rincón-Gallardo (2016) have characterized the fundamental components of Ontario's educational change strategies as involving:

ɔ Focus on a small number of ambitious goals (raise the bar in literacy, numeracy and high school graduation, and increase public confidence in education);

ɔ Pursue a high trust "peace and stability" partnership with the school districts and the unions;

ɔ Invest in capacity building at all levels with a focus on instructional practices linked to results;

ɔ Foster learning from implementation laterally (across schools and districts), and vertically (between schools and districts) and

ɔ Build the capacity of the Ministry to work in partnership with the sector.

The balance of power, responsibilities, and roles involved in the tri-level of government/province, school district, and school/teachers has been subject of debate and evolution over time. The OECD (2010,

p. 76), for example, identified six key elements associated with Ontario's system reform:

1. **Commitment to education and to children**: A strong cultural commitment in Canada to the welfare of children and to support public education.

2. **Cultural support for universal high achievement**: Families and educators who believe in supporting all children to achieve educationally.

3. **System coherence and alignment**: The development of a shared purpose among government, provincial stakeholders, and educators to develop a systemic strategy for educational improvement.

4. **Teacher and principal quality**: High confidence in the capacity of teachers and administrators coupled with further development of educator's leadership and instructional practices.

5. **A single capable center with authority and legitimacy to act**: "The Ontario story is very much one of strong central leadership coupled with a major investment in capacity building and trust building in the field." At the government level, prolonged political leadership focused on educational improvement combined with the development of the Ministry of Education's professional leadership and capacity is important.

6. **Professional responsibility**: The Ontario strategy blends use of formal accountability and testing with support for the development of professional responsibility.

However, for some commentators, such Andy Hargreaves (also a contributor and advisor to Ontario's education system) and Dennis Shirley, there are concerns about too much emphasis on central direction to drive and deliver reform. Instead they emphasize the importance for Ontario—and for other jurisdictions—of prioritizing professionally led change (Hargreaves & Shirley, 2009, 2012). Based on research with Ontario school districts, Hargreaves and Braun (2012) have called for an emphasis on "leading from the middle," enabling school district and school leaders to develop, champion, and lead educational improvement. Furthermore, there has been increasing attention to school leaders (Leithwood, 2012) and teachers (Campbell, 2015; Lieberman, Campbell, & Yashkina, 2015, 2016) as leaders of current and future improvements in and for Ontario's education system. The appropriate balance of responsibilities and working relationships between government, formal leaders in districts and schools, and teachers has come into particular focus during the most recent round of labor negotiations with calls for a renewed approach to teachers' professionalism. In practice, Ontario has drawn on a combination of approaches to improvement with shifting balances between government direction and professional autonomy evolving over time and continuing to be debated, contested, and experienced.

In this case study report, we provide evidence, documentation, and voices from teachers, school administrators, teacher unions, provincial organizations, and government officials to detail the policies and practices implemented in Ontario to support the development of teachers and teaching quality. To situate the study, an overview of Ontario and of the Ontario education system is provided. The report focuses mainly on education developments from 2003 onwards, when a new government was elected with a priority commitment to improving the publicly funded education system.

Ontario's Theory of Action for Educational Improvement

Underpinning the specific details of teaching practices and policies, it is important to understand that Ontario has developed and operates with a theory of action. Senior government officials and political advisors spoke of the Ontario theory of action involving five key elements:

1. Focus: identification of key priorities for improvement
   Three goals have informed the focus of Ontario's educational improvements over the past decade: increasing student achievement; reducing gaps in performance; and increasing public confidence in publicly funded education. In 2014, these goals were revised and renewed with the introduction of a fourth priority focus on enhancing well-being.

2. Tri-Level Reform: system-wide coherence and alignment
   A vast array of policies, strategies, initiatives, and actions has been undertaken over the past decade. However, all actions are intended to be aligned with the core goals outlined above and have involved coordinated attention at provincial, school district, school, and classroom levels. To support systemic action and coherence, a central feature has been an emphasis on developing professional partnerships, trust, and respect between the provincial government, all provincial stakeholders, the teaching profession and wider public.

3. Support and Positive Pressure: capacity building with a focus on results
   A key element of the Ontario strategies is "capacity building with a focus on results" involving the development of educators'

knowledge, skills, and practices with a particular focus on instructional improvements to support students' learning and achievements. Where student achievement is identified as being lower, for example for particular groups of students and/or schools, additional attention, resources, and supports are provided to target and improve educational practices. The Ontario approach emphasizes developing the capacity of all people involved through fostering collective commitment and collaborative action for educational improvement.

4. Shared Leadership: respect for professional knowledge and practice
The Ontario approach to educational change has placed emphasis on valuing and developing professional capacity and leadership throughout the education system. Existing professional knowledge is valued and respected. A combination of professional knowledge, identification, and sharing of successful or promising practices plus the use of data and research locally and from international leading practice are combined to inform the Ontario strategies and actions.

5. Professional Accountability: results without rancor or ranking
Educators are considered to be professionals with responsibility for self- and peer-improvement. The government does not label "failing" schools by requiring firing of staff or takeover models. Rather where underperformance in student achievement is identified, the view of the Ministry of Education is the need to develop the "will and skill" of educators to improve programs and instructional practices, plus supporting conditions, to enable students to learn, achieve, and thrive at school and beyond.

Informed by this theory of action, Ontario has developed a culture and infrastructure for implementation of policies and practices to support teachers' development and teaching quality, including attention to: initial teacher education; attractiveness of teaching as a career; recruitment; induction; continuing professional learning; performance management; retention; and career and leadership development.

Overview: Ontario Education System

The province of Ontario (Link 3-2) spans over one million square kilometers and is Canada's most populous province with a population of over 13.5 million people (38.5% of the total population of Canada) (see Figure 3–1). Ontario generates almost 37% of Canada's GDP. Ontario is a highly diverse province. In the 2011 national census, 70.4% of Ontario's population was Canadian born and 28.5% was born outside of Canada.

Figure 3–1 Province of Ontario

Source: Natural Resources Canada.

Two percent of the Ontario population is identified as First Nations, Métis, or Inuit (FNMI). Ontario's diversity is increasing over time; over 40% of immigrants to Canada settle in Ontario. In Ontario's capital city, Toronto, over 100 languages and dialects are spoken. English is Ontario's official language, and French language rights have been extended to the legal and educational systems (Government of Ontario, 2014a, 2014b).

Relatedly, Ontario's student population is large and diverse. Over two million students attend Ontario's publicly funded school system. Twenty-seven percent of students in Ontario were born outside Canada; with 20% self-identifying as members of a visible minority, and 4.5% of Ontario students are French speaking (Pervin & Campbell, 2011). O'Grady and Houme (2014, p. 119) report:

According to the 2011 census by Statistics Canada, the six languages most commonly spoken at home in Ontario for ages 5–19 are English (1,936,345), French (50,830), Punjabi (19,085), Urdu (17,740), Spanish (16,610) and Arabic (14,610). An estimated 64,000 Aboriginal students between the ages of 5 and 19 attend provincially funded elementary and secondary schools.

Ninety-five percent of school-age children in Ontario attend the publicly funded education system. This system is overseen and funded by the provincial government, through the Ontario Ministry of Education. Children are required to attend school once they turn six years old and to stay in school until they graduate or turn 18. The levels are primary (grades 1–3), junior (grades 4–6), intermediate (grades 7–10), and senior (grades 11 and 12). In 2010, a policy to provide full day kindergarten (FDK) for four and five years was introduced. FDK involves children being cosupported by a teacher and an early childhood educator. By 2014–2015, full roll out of the FDK policy had been achieved extending to 265,000 children across 3,600 schools.

There are almost 5,000 schools in Ontario; in 2012–2013, there were 3,978 elementary and 913 secondary schools. Schools are governed through four publicly funded education systems: English Public, English Catholic, French Public, and French Catholic. These education systems are administered through 72 school districts, encompassing 31 English Public districts, 29 English Catholic districts, 8 French Catholic districts, 4 French Public districts, and 11 smaller school authorities. School districts range widely in size, from a few hundred students in remote rural areas to more than 250,000 students in Ontario's largest board, the Toronto District School Board (TDSB).

Currently (2012–2013), there are approximately: 115,492 full-time equivalent (FTE) teachers (73,031 elementary and 42,460 secondary), 7,326 administrators (principals and vice principals; 5,220 elementary and 2,105 secondary), and 4,390 early childhood educators in Ontario (Ontario Ministry of Education, 2014). In general in Ontario, teachers constitute almost 90% of the education workforce.

Length of School Year, Instructional Time, and Organization of the School Day

The length of the school year is set by the Ministry of Education and currently stands at a minimum of 194 school days. Instructional time in Ontario schools is mandated to be not less than five hours per day, exclusive of recess and lunch breaks. In primary and junior schools, instructional time is usually chunked into blocks of time ranging from a half an hour to an hour and a half, depending on the subject matter. Students take a range of subjects including math, language arts, science, social studies, religion, health, art, music, French, and physical education over the course of the whole school year. Many upper intermediate and secondary schools are semesterized, meaning students take one block of four subjects for the first half of the school year and another block of four in the second half. The instructional day in these schools is typically divided into four equal periods of 75 minutes, with one block per subject each day. Non-semesterized schools often divide the school day into five or six equal periods of an hour or less and students take eight subjects over the course of the full year. In either case, students receive the equivalent of eight courses at 110 hours of instruction per course. Sample student schedules are provided in Figures 3–2 and 3–3.

Governance at the Provincial and Local Level

The governance of the Ontario education system involves a range of provincial and local organizations with distinct roles yet interconnected responsibilities. There is an emphasis on working in partnership to govern and administer the education system across partners and agencies with a

Figure 3–2 Sample Junior Student Schedule—Grade 5/6, Toronto District School Board

Period/ Time	Day 1	Day 2	Day 3	Day 4	Day 5
1 8:45 9:15 2 9:15 9:55	Language	Language	Language	Language	Language
9:55 10:10		R E C E S S			
3 10:10 10:50 4 10:50 11:30	Mathematics	Mathematics LIBRARY (Book Exchange)	Physical Education Mathematics	Mathematics	Mathematics
11:30 12:25		L U N C H			
5 12:30 1:10 6 1:10 1:50	Science or Social Studies	COMPUTERS Science or Social Studies	FRENCH Health	FRENCH Drama/Dance	Health FRENCH
1:50 2:05		R E C E S S			
7 2:05 2:45 8 2:45 3:15	FRENCH Visual Arts	FRENCH Visual Arts DPA (Daily Physical Activity)	Science or Social Studies	MUSIC Drama/Dance DPA (Daily Physical Activity)	Reading Buddies Physical Education
Band: Day 2, 4 (1:50-3:10pm)					

Figure 3–3 Sample Secondary Student Schedule, Grade 11, York Catholic District School Board

Semester 1

Period	Day 1	Day 2	Day 3	Day 4
1	World Religion	World Religion	World Religion	World Religion
2	Chemistry	Chemistry	Chemistry	Chemistry
3	Biology	Biology	Healthy Living	Healthy Living
4	Healthy Living	Healthy Living	Biology	Biology

Semester 2

Period	Day 1	Day 2	Day 3	Day 4
1	Physics	Physics	Physics	Physics
2	Personal Fitness	Personal Fitness	Personal Fitness	Personal Fitness
3	Applied Math	Applied Math	English	English
4	English	English	Applied Math	Applied Math

focus on benefits for students and the education system. Some key organizations related to teachers and teaching quality are outlined below.

The Ontario Ministry of Education

The Ministry of Education administers the system of publicly funded elementary and secondary school education in Ontario, in accordance with and under the authority of the Education Act (Link 3-3). The political leader is the Minister of Education and the civil service lead is the Deputy Minister of Education. The Ministry oversees funding, legislation, regulation, strategy development, and supports for capacity and implementation throughout the education system. Over the past decade, the Ministry has restructured and refocused its activities to put a priority focus on supports for student achievement, instructional leadership, equity, and student well-being. The Ministry has incorporated responsibility for childcare as part of implementing universal full-day kindergarten across the province. With new responsibilities for early learning and with ongoing responsibilities for postschool transitions and adult education—in partnership with the Ministry of Advanced Education and Skills Development—a holistic focus on children's development and lifelong learning is further developing.

Consistent with Ontario's theory of action emphasizing the development of shared leadership and capacity building at all levels of the education system, the Ministry's internal capacity, culture, and infrastructure to support educational improvement has also been developed. A key feature of the Ministry's approach is a blending of policy and educational knowledge which has become embedded in a staff model which combines government officials and experienced educators working together in the Ministry and in partnership with the education sector. For example, discussing the work of the Literacy and Numeracy Secretariat (LNS), which was established in 2004 to lead the new Literacy and Numeracy Strategy (see Glaze, Mattingley, & Andrews, 2013), Mary Jean Gallagher (former Chief Student Achievement Officer and Assistant Deputy Minister of the Student Achievement Division, Ontario Ministry of Education) explained that the combination of government and educational expertise is considered to be particularly important for working appropriately with educators to achieve goals for students, teaching, and learning (Link 3-4):

> I would say the LNS have been designed as a particularly effective infrastructure for implementation. The staffing itself is a combination of school system staff and government staff. OPS [Ontario Public Service] people bring the public policy piece forward; they bring a deep understanding of how policy can affect action and structure, what the strategic levers that might work and how you build these logic models that actually are thorough and careful. On its own, that gives you policies or programs that can be implemented, not necessarily policies that are implemented. Because the reality is in a school, everybody is running down the hallway so busy dealing with day to day issues that, too often, really good documents, research, concepts and programs sit on a shelf and never become implemented in a way that the system owns them. So the other side of LNS staff is a collection of exceptional educators. Whether they have come into our research staff, whether they've come into our field staff or our leadership staff, they are embedded at every level of our organization. It's a combination of both of those kinds of staff, because you have to design the program's policies and documents with implementation and an understanding of how schools and Boards function in mind and then you have to continue to be nimble and modify as you go along.

Similarly in the Ministry of Education's Teaching Policy and Standards Branch, interviewees commented on the importance of blending policy knowledge from government officials with experienced educators working in the Ministry and with the sector to build relationships:

> We now hire people who know how to work with our stakeholders/partners, know who the stakeholders/partners are . . . it's about that relationship. Our HR (Human Resources) practices reflect our vision

in a way. It's not just "yes, know your technical program," that's important, and hopefully you're hearing some of that, but that stems from knowing the people you are working with. It sounds simple, but it's core to the change that has happened and is reflected in the renewed vision.

(Demetra Saldaris, Teaching Policy and Standards Branch,
Ontario Ministry of Education)

You can have any policy you want, but if you don't have the right people in place to implement it, it's either not going to work and everybody will say "oh, it didn't work." Well, the policy may have been just fine, it wasn't implemented properly, or you didn't have the right people to implement it properly. So it's not a matter of "just" policy. That's a really good point. You've got to have the right people driving it. (Paul Anthony, Teaching Policy and Standards Branch, Ontario Ministry of Education).

So that idea that the people who are implementing it have walked in the shoes of the people that they are working with. I think maybe that's one of the strengths of the blended model of educational policy.

(Jim Strachan, Teaching Policy and Standards Branch,
Ontario Ministry of Education)

Importantly, the focus on capacity building to support improved educational outcomes includes attention to the capacity of those working in the Ministry and their relationships with the education sector.

Provincial Curriculum and Assessment

Ontario has a provincially developed and implemented curriculum K–12 and linked provincial testing.

Curriculum Council

The Curriculum Council was first formed in 2007 to provide strategic policy advice on the elementary and secondary curriculum. The Council is comprised of community leaders and education experts and may also work with specifically formed working groups with relevant curriculum expertise, including teachers. Areas of curriculum on which the Council has advised include: environmental education, financial literacy, the elementary curriculum, strengthening equity, inclusive principles, and prevention of bullying across the curriculum. The Ministry of Education is responsible for the development of the Ontario Curriculum, K–12. Curriculum documents are available by grade and by subject for both elementary and secondary. The curriculum documents include provincial standards for the knowledge and skills students are expected to develop in each subject at each grade level. By developing and publishing curriculum documents for use by all Ontario teachers, the Ministry of Education sets standards for the entire province. In addition to curriculum documents, there are a range of supporting resources and materials available for the Ontario curriculum.

Education Quality and Accountability Office (EQAO)

EQAO was established as a Crown agency by Act of Parliament in 1996. The mandate of EQAO is to provide independent scrutiny of the quality and standards of the Ontario education system. Currently, EQAO administers province-wide tests of students in grade 3 for reading, writing, and mathematics, grade 6 for reading, writing, and mathematics, grade 9 Academic Math and Applied Math, and the Ontario Secondary School Literacy Test in grade 10 linked to the Ontario curriculum. EQAO administers and oversees Ontario's participation in national and international testing also.

District School Boards

District school boards operate the province's publicly funded schools. The professional head of each school board is a Director of Education who is assisted by Supervisory Officers and a range of staffers. These various professionals each have provincial organizations to support their work and to represent their interests and voices, such as the Council of Ontario Directors of Education (CODE).

Each school board is governed by a board of trustees, which includes those publicly elected, those appointed by First Nation communities, and student(s) elected by the student body (for more information on the qualifications of trustees see http://cge.ontarioschooltrustees.org/en/read/becoming-a-school-board-trustee). As members of the school board, trustees serve as important connections between local communities and the school board, communicating the issues and concerns of their constituents to board discussions and decision making. Trustees are elected every four years during municipal elections. Trustees receive a salary ranging from $6,000 to $26,000 (CDN) depending on the specific board they are elected to. Only the elected board has the power to make decisions under the law, and their collective roles include working in partnership with school councils (local advisory parent groups), explaining the policies and decisions of the board to community residents, and supporting and encouraging public education. Trustees are supported also by provincial organizations for trustees in the public, Catholic, and/or French-language education systems. Increasing attention is being paid to providing training and supports to enable trustees to fulfill their important role.

The responsibilities of school boards are set out in Ontario's Education Act which states that every school board shall:

- promote student achievement and well-being, a positive school climate that is inclusive and accepting of all pupils, and prevention of bullying;
- ensure effective stewardship of the board's resources;
- deliver effective and appropriate education programs to its pupils;
- develop and maintain policies and organizational structures that,
    i. promote the boards goals and,
    ii. encourage pupils to pursue their educational goals;
- monitor and evaluate the effectiveness of policies developed by the board in achieving the board's goals and the efficiency of the implementation of those policies;
- develop a multi-year plan aimed at achieving the boards' goals;
- annually review the multi-year plan with the board's Director of Education or the supervisory officer acting as the board's Director of Education; and
- monitor and evaluate the performance of the board's Director of Education, or the supervisory officer acting as the board's Director of Education, in meeting,
    - his or her duties under this Act or any policy, guideline or regulation made under this Act, (including duties under the multi-year plan), and
    - any other duties assigned by the board.

Beyond these broad areas of accountability, the Education Act also spells out duties for school boards that include such obligations as effective operation of schools, setting the board's budget, implementing the Ministry's curriculum policies, and ensuring that appropriate staff are hired as required by schools. Boards will also make determinations about such matters as pupil transportation, school libraries, continuing education, and childcare facilities on school sites.

School Councils

School councils are local advisory boards comprised of parents, students, community members, school staff (both teaching and nonteaching), and a school administrator. Every school in the public system is required to elect a new school council at the beginning of each school year. The term of office is one year, however, there are no limits on the number of times a member can seek reelection. Being a council member is a volunteer position, and there is no remuneration outside of reimbursement for expenses incurred as part of required council business. The council advises the school administration, and sometimes the school board, on issues related to the program and operations of the school including student codes of conduct, curricular priorities, strategies to improve student achievement, communication to parents and broader school community, community use of the school, fundraising, special events and field trips, and the selection of principals. Principals are required to take the recommendations of the council into consideration when making decisions and must report to the council why particular recommendations were or were not implemented.

Teachers' Federations

Established in 1944, all public teachers in Ontario are required to be members of the Ontario Teacher's Federation (OTF). Teacher candidates participating in provincial initial teacher education become associate members of OTF. Through the Teaching Profession Act (Link 3-5) the core objectives of the OTF are:

(a) to promote and advance the cause of education;

(b) to raise the status of the teaching profession;

(c) to promote and advance the interests of teachers and to secure conditions that will make possible the best professional service;

(d) to arouse and increase public interest in educational affairs;

(e) to cooperate with other teachers' organizations throughout the world having the same or like objects; and

(f) to represent all members of the pension plan established under the Teachers' Pension Act in the administration of the plan and the management of the pension fund.

Members of OTF also become a member of one of four affiliate teacher organizations depending on the education system in which they are working or affiliated: L'Association des enseignates et des enseignants franco-ontariens (AEFO), The Elementary Teachers' Federation of Ontario (ETFO), The Ontario English Catholic Teachers' Assocation (OECTA), and The Ontario Secondary School Teachers' Federation (OSSTF), who represent teachers' voice in educational policy and negotiate working conditions and terms of employment between teachers, the province's 72 school boards and government. As Rhonda Kimberley-Young, Secretary-Treasurer of the OTF, explains:

> We see ourselves as the professional organization or association for Ontario's teachers. Because we are unlike other jurisdictions where there would just be one Federation that does everything that we and the Federations do together, we're different. We see ourselves as that place where the four Federations come together to promote and to protect public education and to safeguard and support the profession.

OTF and each of the affiliates are involved in a variety of advocacy initiatives related to broad issues around teaching and learning in the province including equity and social justice, Aboriginal education, the status of women, and teacher working conditions. The teachers' organizations are also engaged in areas of curriculum development and provide professional development, additional qualification courses, and leadership training to their members. More broadly, the teachers unions are concerned with supporting public education:

> So while we're an organization committed to our members, we are very much involved in trying to support public education as it impacts students, as well.

(Suzette Clark, OSSTF)

The Ontario College of Teachers

In 1997, the Ontario College of Teachers (OCT) was established to regulate the teaching profession in the public interest. All teachers in Ontario's publicly funded school system are licensed by OCT. As Michael Salvatori, Chief Executive Officer and Registrar of OCT, explained:

> Our primary role is to protect and serve the public interest. It's very much aligned with one of the Ministry of Education's vision statements about maintaining and enhancing public confidence in the system. . . I see the role of the College in assisting in promoting the professionalism of the profession.

OCT advances this role through responsibilities and actions to:

o Ensure Ontario students are taught by skilled teachers who adhere to clear standards of practice and conduct;

o Establish standards of practice and conduct;

o Issue teaching certificates and may suspend or revoke them;

o Accredit teacher-education programs and courses.

Principals' Associations

In Ontario, principals and vice principals are not part of the teacher unions. Rather, there are additional professional organizations for administrators who can voluntarily become members of one of three principals' associations—depending on the system they are working in—l'Association des directions et directions adjointes des écoles franco-ontariennes (ADFO), The Catholic Principals' Association of Ontario (CPCO), and the Ontario Principals' Council (OPC). The principals' associations aim to promote and develop exemplary leadership for student success in Ontario's schools. Their main roles include to represent, support, protect, and promote their members' professional interests, provide opportunities for the professional growth of principals and vice principals, and to advocate for public education. Notably, the principals and vice principals associations are not unions and do not participate in negotiating salary, benefits, or working conditions.

Table 3–1 summarizes roles and responsibilities of educational stakeholders. For a series of videos on who does what in Ontario's public education system, visit http://www.otffeo.on.ca/en/about-otf/public-education-ontario/.

Partnership Working among Provincial and Local Organizations

The Ontario theory of action emphasizes coherence and partnership working at provincial, district, and school levels through the development of shared leadership and collaboration.

Rather than individual autonomy as isolated professionals, Ontario is striving to develop "collective collaborative autonomy" where members of the profession develop and work together. Fundamentally, there is an emphasis on an education system that values and fosters teachers' professionalism in partnership with school, district, and provincial leaders. However, the nature and exercise of professionalism and partnership working have both developed and been contested over the period of Ontario's reforms.

Following a period of distrust and labor unrest between teacher unions and the previous government, in 2003 the newly elected government set about building partnerships for "peace and progress" in the education system. An important element of the Ontario's approach has been a concern to "remove distractions" from the core focus on educational improvement, including fractious relations that could undermine a

Table 3–1 Summary of Roles and Responsibilities of Educational Stakeholders in Ontario (Link 3-6)

Group	Roles and Responsibilities
Ministry of Education	Oversees all aspects of Ontario's public education system including: Developing education policies and administration of provincial statues and regulations Setting policies and guidelines for school boards, including the length of the school year Allocating funding to school boards using the Funding Formula (which includes provisions for teacher salaries) Establishing the provincial curriculum (what students will learn in each grade) Setting requirements for graduation (diplomas and certificates) Creating lists of approved text books and other learning resources

School Boards	Ensure that school board governance responsibilities in the *Education Act* are fulfilled and provide local governance for the development and implementation of Ministry policies, including:
	
	Deciding how to spend the funds they receive from the province, for example for hiring teachers and other staff, building and maintaining schools and purchasing school supplies
	Deciding where new schools should be built and when and if schools should close
	Promoting student achievement and well-being, a positive school climate that is inclusive and accepting of all pupils, and prevention of bullying;
	Delivering effective and appropriate education programs to its students, such as special education, programs for newcomers and French Immersion;
	Developing and maintaining policies and organizational structures that,
	  • promote the board's goals and,
	  • encourage pupils to pursue their educational goals;
	Monitoring and evaluating the effectiveness of policies developed by the board in achieving the board's goals and the efficiency of the implementation of those policies;
	Developing a multiyear plan aimed at achieving the boards' goals;
	Ensuring schools follow the rules set out in the Education Act;
	Establishing a school council at each school and a Parent Involvement Committee for the board.

(Continued)

Table 3–1 Summary of Roles and Responsibilities of Educational Stakeholders in Ontario (*Continued*)

Group	Roles and Responsibilities
School Councils	Provide recommendations on school programs and operations including: Sharing information with parents and the community and seeking their input on matters the council is discussing; Providing advice to the principal and school board on issues such as school year calendars, strategies to improve school performance, codes of conduct and dress, selection criteria for principals, and board policies that will affect the school.
Ontario College of Teachers	Regulates the teaching profession in the public interest by: Establishing the requirements for a teaching certificate and setting standards for teacher training programs; Maintaining a provincial register of qualified teachers Investigating complaints against teachers.
Teachers' Federations	Represent the interest of teachers in their employment relations with school boards and the Ministry by: Negotiating the terms of collective agreements which outline provisions for teacher working conditions, benefits, and salaries; Ensuring that due process is carried out in disciplinary matters between members and the Ontario College of Teachers; Collaborating with the Ministry on curriculum development and teacher professional development programs; Collecting dues from members to fund member services and programs.
Principals' Associations	Support principals and vice principals to develop exemplary leadership by: Representing their membership; Promoting the professional interests of members; Supporting and protecting members; Advocating on behalf of public education; Providing professional growth opportunities for principals and vice principals.

Sources: Ontario Teachers' Federation, Public Education in Ontario: Who does What? and People for Education, Who Does What in Education.

focus on student achievement and equity goals. One of the early actions of the Liberal government was to form the Education Partnership Table, bringing together groups and associations representing students, parents, trustees, directors of education, supervisory officers, teachers, early childhood educators, support workers, principals, and relevant provincial organizations to meet with the Minister of Education and senior government officials. According to the Ontario Ministry of Education website, the intended purpose is to provide:

> A practical forum designed to get broad and diverse insights from the education sector on provincial education policy early in the government's policy development process. . . Collaboration is needed to bring real, positive change to the education system and to achieve better results for students. Participants have the opportunity to contribute to the common public interest in publicly funded education. In return, they agree to work toward consensus and, wherever possible, to raise issues first at the Table for all to examine and help address collectively.

The principles of collaboration and consensus seeking, while recognizing diverse interests and perspectives, have become fundamental to Ontario's way of developing educational improvement. Emerging from the Education Partnership Table approach and also from a broader commitment to creating forums and opportunities for collaboration, a host of working tables and stakeholder forums bringing together Ministry, provincial partners, and professionals currently exist, including for example:

- Student Achievement Division Working Table
- Early Years Advisory Group and Francophone Early Years Advisory Group
- Ontario Education Research Panel (OERP)
- Institute for Education Leadership
- Permanent Task Force on French-Language Continued Learning
- French as a Second Language Provincial Working Group and Principal Focus Group
- Minister's Advisory Council on Special Education (MACSE)
- Minister's Advisory Council on First Nations, Métis, and Inuit Education
- Accepting Schools Expert Panel
- Healthy Schools Working Table
- Minister's Principal Reference Group

o Capital Advisory Committee

o Minister's Student Advisory Council (MSAC)

o Provincial Municipal Early Years Reference Group

While there are times of contention and differences of opinion, the practice of principles of partnership working are valued. For example, as Susan Perry from OECTA commented:

> The fact that we are at the table with the Ministry regularly and with all the stakeholders, I think really says that we are valued for the work that we do. We may not always agree, but we can usually come up with some form of consensus or an agreement around how things might roll out. So I think that we are regarded as professionals . . . that makes a big difference. We are trusted with our professional development of our teachers. . . We are trusted to make those professional judgments. . . Our voices even on things like curriculum changes, when new curriculum is being developed and rolled out, we are usually at the table and are allowed to voice our opinions and sometimes we are standing up pounding our chests and other times we are saying this is great. So to be able to have that freedom and ability to be trusted . . . makes a huge difference in teacher autonomy and self-worth.

Educational Funding

Historically, educational funding in Ontario was a combination of provincially provided grants and district level funding, which was generated through local taxation. In 1995, however, educational funding was centralized at the provincial level in an effort to reduce discrepancies in funding levels between districts with different taxation capacities. Currently, the Ontario Ministry of Education provides funding (Link 3-7) to school boards through a series of annual grants called Grants for Student Needs (GSN). As outlined in Figure 3-4, in 2013–2014 these grants consisted of a Pupil Foundation Grant (teacher salaries, educational assistants, textbooks, learning supplies, and library and guidance services), a School Foundation Grant (principals, vice principals, secretaries, office supplies), 12 Special Purpose Grants (special education, First Nations, learning opportunities, safe schools, facilities, student transportation, etc.), and Debt Service (interest expense), which totaled a projected $20.80B (Ontario Ministry of Education, 2014a). These grants are distributed equitably to ensure that all districts are able to provide comparable student programming, with additional funding available to high need schools. Most categories are broad in scope and school boards have some discretion in determining the direction and focus of the allocations

Figure 3–4 Projected Educational Funding 2013–2014

2013–14 Grant Allocations (Projections)

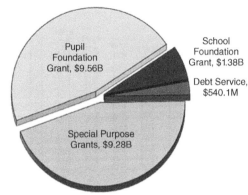

Total: $20.80B*

Pupil Foundation Grant, $9.56B

School Foundation Grant, $1.38B

Debt Service, $540.1M

Special Purpose Grants, $9.28B

Special Purpose Grants

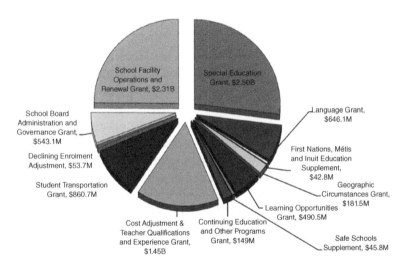

School Facility Operations and Renewal Grant, $2.31B

Special Education Grant, $2.50B

School Board Administration and Governance Grant, $543.1M

Declining Enrolment Adjustment, $53.7M

Student Transportation Grant, $860.7M

Cost Adjustment & Teacher Qualifications and Experience Grant, $1.45B

Continuing Education and Other Programs Grant, $149M

Language Grant, $646.1M

First Nations, Métis and Inuit Education Supplement, $42.8M

Geographic Circumstances Grant, $181.5M

Learning Opportunities Grant, $490.5M

Safe Schools Supplement, $45.8M

Source: Ontario Ministry of Education, Educational Funding Technical Paper 2013–2014, Spring 2013.

in each area. At the school level, funding is allocated by the boards and managed by the principal. As is the case at the board level, some allocations at the school level are targeted and others are more open-ended and can be used in ways that best suit the needs of the school.

The GSN in 2014–2015 was projected to be $22.53B (see Figure 3–5), an increase of about 3.1% over 2013–2014; when compared to

Figure 3–5   GSN Funding per Pupil 2002–2003 to
2014–2015

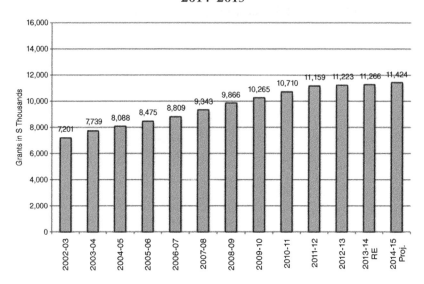

Source: Ontario Ministry of Education, 2014–2015 Grants for
Student Needs Technical Briefing, Spring 2014.

the 2002–2003 school year this represents an increase of over $8 billion (56%) in operating funding. Per pupil funding in 2014–2015 is projected to be $11,424—equivalent to 1.4% more funding per pupil than in 2013–2014 ($11,226).

In addition to GSN funding, which covers the operation of the education system (including salaries and capital), education programs other (EPO) funding is provided annually and targeted to priority initiatives and identified needs. This funding can be a lever for targeted implementation of provincial policies and priorities and also be adapted by school boards to local contexts. In 2014–2015, $178.9 million was identified for EPO funding (Ontario Ministry of Education, 2014b).

These increases in overall funding over the past decade have supported major strategies and actions to support professional capacity, student achievement, equity, and well-being.

Improving the Ontario Education System: Provincial Goals and Results

If your focus is the student and you are trying to improve learning, you have to be able to improve teaching. . . it's not about building a specific program or initiative, it's about building approaches that are cognizant of the fact that you have to be able to implement things in the school system.

(Mary Jean Gallagher, Student Achievement Division,
Ontario Ministry of Education)

In 2003, a new provincial government was elected with a commitment to making improvements in public education the top priority. The previous government, elected in 1995, had enacted substantial cuts in public services and spending, including reductions in school boards' budgets resulting in teacher layoffs and cuts in programs and services. In addition, their education policies—building on the former government—enacted the introduction of a standards-based core curriculum and the creation of the EQAO for provincial testing (Anderson & Jaffar, 2006). Controversially, the Harris government of 1995–2003 also introduced the "Ontario Teacher Testing Program" to test teachers for certification, recertification, and performance evaluation. This combination of cuts and policies were unpopular with the education profession and resulted in strikes and significant professional and public disquiet about the changes to the education system.

Elected in Fall 2003, the new Liberal government committed to making significant improvement in education with an emphasis on building partnership, trust, and respect with the education profession. For example, by the end of 2004, the "Ontario Teacher Testing Program" was canceled and a process of establishing "peace and progress" in 2005 resulted in a four-year collective agreement with the teacher unions. As Mary Jean Gallagher commented:

> The newly elected Liberals were more about raising the outcomes of the system, predicated on a deep respect for the members of the teaching profession and leadership of schools and Boards to be able to accomplish that kind of improved result if they were supported in the right ways. So starting in 2003 you saw a number of things happen after that election and change of government.

(Mary Jean Gallagher, Student Achievement Division,
Ontario Ministry of Education)

Focus on Priority Goals

Three priority goals were identified and became the focus for the work of the Ministry of Education, the education system, and partners in a tri-level system-wide reform for:

1. Increased student achievement
2. Reduced gaps in student achievement
3. Increased public confidence in publicly funded education

Related to these goals, targets were established to have 75% of students achieve at the provincial standard (70%, or a B grade) in reading, writing, and mathematics in the sixth grade (age 12) and a secondary school graduation rate of 85% of students. Targets to reduce primary class sizes (grades 1–3) to an average of 20 students, with flexibility of up to 23 students if required for practical reasons, were also established.

To deliver both improved relationships with the education sector and improved results, the government committed substantial new policies, strategies, infrastructure, and resources for educational improvement. Central to the Ontario strategies is a focus on improving student outcomes:

> There's this moral imperative of reaching every student. The understanding that every student can learn and every student can be successful is at the core of our work.

> (Mary Jean Gallagher, Student Achievement Division,
> Ontario Ministry of Education)

Moreover, there is a belief that achieving improvements for students requires attention to supporting the capacity of educators:

> If you look at the strategic priorities, it's all about the students, but in every branch [of the Ministry], there's recognition that teachers are number one in terms of being able to positively affect student achievement and well-being and leaders are number two. . . although the focus is student learning, all branches recognize the power of teachers and leaders.

> (Demetra Saldaris, Teaching and Policy Standards Branch,
> Ontario Ministry of Education)

Consistent with the theory of action developed since 2003—focus, tri-level reform, support and positive pressure, shared leadership, and professional accountability—the development of a culture, capacity, and implementation infrastructure to achieve the priority goals have been put in place. Two of the major student achievement strategies have been the development of a Literacy and Numeracy Strategy with a focus on improving instruction and learning in elementary schools and a Student Success/Learning to 18 Strategy with changes in programs and pathways to support high school students through transitions in schooling and to succeed in graduating from high school.

 A range of supporting strategies have also been developed and implemented. For example the Ontario Equity and Inclusive Education Strategy (Link 3-8) was introduced to provide a framework to assist the education community in addressing discriminatory biases and systemic barriers to student achievement. Targeted policies and initiatives have been implemented to support the goal of closing gaps in performance, for example for students identified as having special education needs and for Aboriginal learners and communities (Link 3-9). New policies to support French-language students and the francophone education system have also been implemented. A common focus has been on improving strategies, programs, pathways, and instructional practice for all learners with targeted supports for struggling students and schools to fulfill goals for achievement *and* equity. Increasing attention has also been placed on the use of evidence through an Ontario Ministry of Education Research and Evaluation Strategy (Link 3-10).

As discussed further in later sections, attention to developing teacher and administrator capacity is common throughout all of the strategies, as well as new policies and initiatives dedicated to teacher and leader development.

Focus on Results

Considerable progress on the government's education goals and related targets has been achieved.

Increased Student Achievement   From a starting point of 54% of elementary students achieving or exceeding the provincial standard in reading, writing, and mathematics, 72% of students met or exceeded the provincial standard in 2013–2014 (see Figure 3–6). Nevertheless, while

Figure 3–6 Combined Reading, Writing, and Mathematics Results for Elementary Schools

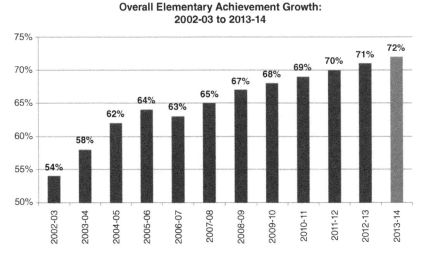

Source: Ontario Ministry of Education, Student Achievement Division.

Figure 3–7   High School Graduation Rates

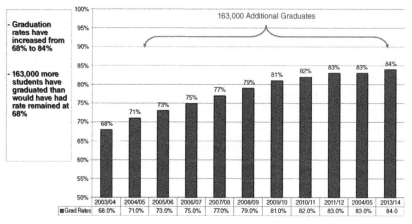

Five Year Cohort Graduation Rate
Provincial
2003/04 to 2013/14 *

	2003/04	2004/05	2005/06	2006/07	2007/08	2008/09	2009/10	2010/11	2011/12	2004/05	2013/14
■ Grad Rates	68.0%	71.0%	73.0%	75.0%	77.0%	79.0%	81.0%	82.0%	83.0%	83.0%	84.0

- Graduation rates have increased from 68% to 84%

- 163,000 more students have graduated than would have had rate remained at 68%

163,000 Additional Graduates

* 2013/2014 data is based on a full data set and excluded students who deceased or moved out of province

Source: Ontario Ministry of Education, Student Achievement Division.

the target is for literacy and numeracy combined, provincial results indicate considerably stronger performance in literacy (reading and writing) than in mathematics. Hence, there is a current emphasis on improving mathematics understanding and achievement.

The high school graduation rate has also improved considerably, as outlined in Figure 3–7. Based on analyses of students who graduate from Ontario publicly funded schools within five years, Ontario's graduation rate has increased from 68% of students in 2003–2004 to 84% of students in 2013–2014.

Reduced Gaps in Performance   Alongside an overall increase in student achievement, the Ontario government and education system are committed to reducing gaps in performance. At the school level, this has involved a focus on supporting all schools to improve with additional supports for schools identified as lower achieving or struggling to improve. Consistent with the theory of action of "support and positive pressure," the Ontario Ministry's approach is to identify schools that are struggling to improve and provide targeted resources and professional development support to build the capacity of teachers and school administrators to improve teaching, learning, and educational outcomes. Initially, the Ministry of Education established a targeted initiative for schools where less than 33% of grade 3 students were at the provincial standard (equivalent

Figure 3–8 Distribution of elementary schools
by EQAO achievement category (2005–2006 to
2012–2013)

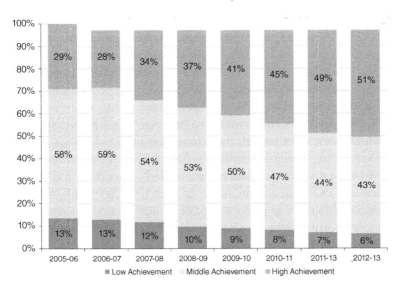

Low achieving: Fewer than 50% of their students meet/exceed provincial
standard on more than half of the assessments in the school
High achieving: 75% or more of the students meet or exceed provincial
standard on at least half of the assessments
Middle achieving: All other schools

Source: Ontario Ministry of Education, Literacy and Numeracy Secretariat.

to a B grade) in Reading. At the outset, this accounted for almost 20%
of elementary schools in Ontario. However, with focused action and
improvement, the number of very low performing schools reduced and
the Ministry redefined the criteria of "low performance" to be less than
50% of students achieving the provincial standard in more than half of
the provincial assessments for that school. As indicated in Figure 3–8,
over the period from 2005–2006 to 2012–2013, the proportion of elementary schools identified as low performing has more than halved from
13% in 2005–2006 to around 6% currently. At the same time, there
has been an increase in the proportion of "high performing" schools—
identified as schools where 75% of students are achieving the provincial
standard on at least half of the provincial assessments administered in
the school. Indeed, the majority of elementary schools in Ontario are
now in the "high achieving" category—an indication of both "raising
the bar" for high performance and also reducing lower performance.

Examples of schools that have improved, particularly in challenging circumstances, are available here: http://www.eqao.com/ProvincialReport/Files/14/PDF/provincial-report-elementary-school-stories-2014.pdf.

At the student level, the most substantial improvements in reducing gaps have been for English language learners (ELL). For example, Figure 3–9 indicates the gap in performance as measured by comparing the difference in provincial test results for all students overall compared with the results for ELL students in each of the provincial assessments in elementary schools. As indicated, in 2002–2003, the performance gap for ELL students ranged from 32 to 17 percentage points; whereas in 2013–2014, the gap has been narrowed to between 9 to 3 percentage points. Although not as substantial, there have also been reductions in performance gaps for students identified as having Special Educational Needs. Attention to equity is considered particularly important for Ontario's diverse and changing communities. As with Canada overall, there is no significant difference in performance of immigrant students compared to Canadian born students in Ontario. There is, however, continued need for considerable attention to support Aboriginal students and also Youth and Children in Care.

For a video on how Ontario is working to close the achievement gap visit http://www.edutopia.org/education-everywhere-international-canada-video.

Figure 3–9 Percentage point difference in achievement between ELL students and all students overall on EQAO assessments

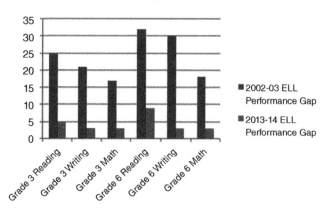

Source: Campbell (2014). Student achievement division literacy and numeracy strategy: evidence of improvement study.

Public Confidence Ninety-five percent of school-age children in Ontario attend a publicly funded school. Nevertheless, the majority of the tax-paying public do not have a school-age child (although they may have had previously or have someone in their extended family). In this context, the Ontario government places an importance on demonstrating the successes and improvements in schools and for students to continue to ensure public commitment to education and funding for the public systems. A key element has been to emphasize positive communication about education, students and teachers in public.

Encouragingly, public opinion survey data indicate increasing satisfaction levels with the Ontario education system For example, according to Hart (2012):

o In 2012, 65% of the public were satisfied with schools, compared to 44% of the public in 1998.

o In 2012, 70% of the public were satisfied with the job teachers are doing, compared to 62% in 1998.

Satisfaction rates are higher for parents than for the general public. In 2012, 77% of parents were satisfied with schools and 76% of parents were satisfied with the jobs that teachers are doing.

The goal of reducing class sizes has been popular with the general public and parents (Hart, 2012). The targets for class sizes have been met:

o In 2003–2004, 25% of primary classes had 25 or more students.

o In 2013–2014, all primary classes have 23 students or fewer and 90% of classes have 20 students or fewer.

Looking to the Future: A Renewed Vision for Achieving Excellence

After a decade of educational change and improvement, Ontario is looking to the future with a renewed educational vision. While there have been improvements in overall achievement results and reductions in performance gaps, Ontario recognizes that there is more to be done. Within the literacy and numeracy goals, achievements in reading and writing are stronger than in math. There have been concerns about ensuring a broader focus on improvements across the curriculum and for supporting all aspects of a student's learning and well-being. There are concerns also about students who continue to struggle and whose needs may not be being as well-served by the Ontario education system currently, including priority foci on Aboriginal Learners and Children and Youth in Care.

Hence, the Ontario government—under the leadership of a new Premier, Kathleen Wynne, and Minister of Education, Liz Sandals—and Ministry of Education embarked on an extensive consultation process in 2013–2014 resulting in a renewed vision for Ontario education. This renewed vision, Achieving Excellence (Link 3-11), has also been informed by the Minister's Student Advisory Council's aspirations for the future of Ontario's education system and for their future as Ontario students (see Figure 3–10):

http://www.videodelivery.gov.on.ca/player/download.php?file=http:// www.media.gov.on.ca/a0efff64e63ac895/en/pages/text.html

The mission statement for a renewed vision seeks to build on Ontario's successes while also continuing to improve for students' and society's future needs:

> Ontario is committed to the success and well-being of every student and child. Learners in the province's education system will develop the knowledge, skills and characteristics that will lead them to become personally successful, economically productive and actively engaged citizens.
>
> Ontario will cultivate and continuously develop a high-quality teaching profession and strong leadership at all levels of the system. Our education system will be characterized by high expectations and success for all. It will be responsive, high quality, accessible and integrated from early learning and child care to adult education.
>
> Together, we will build on past achievements and move forward with ambitious goals.
>
> (Ontario Ministry of Education, 2014c)

Importantly, the renewed vision reaffirms a commitment to partnership working and collaborative, collective capacity building.

Achieving Excellence builds on Ontario's previous three goals and adds a new goal for well-being. Specifically, the renewed goals for education are:

> *Achieving Excellence:* Children and students of all ages will achieve high levels of academic performance, acquire valuable skills and demonstrate good citizenship. Educators will be supported in learning continuously and will be recognized as among the best in the world.
>
> *Ensuring Equity:* All children and students will be inspired to reach their full potential, with access to rich learning experiences that begin at birth and continue into adulthood.
>
> *Promoting Well-Being:* All children and students will develop enhanced mental and physical health, a positive sense of self and belonging, and the skills to make positive choices.

Figure 3–10 The Future of Ontario's Education System

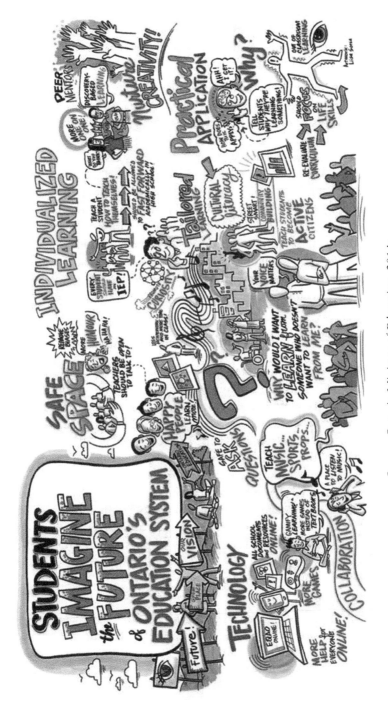

Source: Ontario Ministry of Education, 2014c.

Enhancing Public Confidence: Ontarians will continue to have confidence in a publicly funded education system that helps develop new generations of confident, capable and caring citizens (Ontario Ministry of Education, 2014c).

Following the June 2014 provincial election, when Premier Wynne was elected with a majority government, the Premier's mandate letter to the Minister of Education detailed realizing the vision of Achieving Excellence as top priority (Ontario Ministry of Education, 2014c). As well as continuing vital partnerships within, among, and across provincial, school board, school, and community partners, the Premier and Ministry of Education have appointed four Education Advisors—Carol Campbell, Jean Clinton, Michael Fullan, and Andy Hargreaves—to provide expert advice on how to proceed with realizing the renewed vision in collaboration with the professionals, stakeholders, students, and communities involved. In 2016, a new Minister of Education, Mitzie Hunter, was appointed to further realize the renewed vision for excellence, equity, well-being and confidence in Ontario's education system.

Supporting Teachers and Teaching Quality

Ontario's education strategy includes a strong emphasis on developing professional learning and instructional leadership to support student learning and equity. In 2004, the government released a discussion paper *Teacher Excellence—Unlocking Student Potential through Continuing* *Professional Development.* This was followed, in 2005, by the establishment of the Working Table on Teacher Development (Link 3-12) to bring together education partners to provide recommendations on teachers' professional development. The membership of the Working Table included a wide range of provincial stakeholder organizations, including vitally the OTF and all four teacher union affiliates.

Going forward, based on a review of relevant research, five characteristics were recommended for the design and provision of professional learning for Ontario's teachers:

1. Coherent
   Teacher professional learning is ultimately about best practices for student learning and development and occurs in the context of the Ministry/board/school and parent/community/classroom continuum. Coherence is also built on the "three R's" of respect, responsibility and results, recognizing teacher professionalism and the complexity of teacher learning. . .

2. Attentive to Adult Learning Styles

Teachers come to each professional learning experience with a wide variety of skills, knowledge, education, teaching, and training background. As a result, when planning professional learning, adult learning principles should be addressed by:

- Considering the role of choice. Research supports the importance of choice and self-direction in personalizing the learning.

- Providing programming that is viewed as meaningful, relevant and substantive.

- Providing differentiation in the content and delivery models.

- Considering "best fit" within a culture of collaborative learning. The "one size fits all" approach may prove problematic in many circumstances. Effective learning must recognize and include the participants' understanding and perspective in order to bring about a culture of reflection and transformation.

- Providing appropriate recognition for the successful completion of professional learning.

3. Goal-oriented

Professional learning is enhanced when it is goal oriented and is clearly:

- Connected to improved student learning and achievement.

- Connected to daily practice (job embedded), both directly and indirectly.

- Situated within and respectful of varied contexts (i.e. relevant to Ministry, board, school/community, classroom).

4. Sustainable

Professional learning that will have impact in the classroom must:

- Be planned and progress over time (i.e. it is a process).

- Be supported by appropriate resources focused on its success.

- Involve the learners and allow time for practice (job embedded).

- Include time for self-assessment through reflection (construct/de-construct/reconstruct thinking about practice) within its processes.

- Include, wherever possible, congruency in professional learning for other staff who support student learning. . .

5. Evidence-informed

Professional learning should be considered and be built upon current research as well as both formal and informal data.

(Ontario Ministry of Education, 2007, pp. 4–5)

The Working Table concluded that there should be no one-size fits all approach to professional learning in recognition of the variety of needs, experiences, interests, contexts, and career stages of teachers and the variety of their students, classrooms, and practices. Stemming from the conclusions of the Working Table on Teacher Development, Figure 3–11 provides an overview of the key provincial policies and practices supporting the development of teachers and teaching in Ontario over the past 10 years.

As important as the new policies was the development of a new way of collaboratively making and implementing policy through partnership working:

> It's worth mentioning that it wasn't just a change in policy, but it was also change in how we do policy. This suite of programs was developed over a ten-year period and each program grew out of the work that we did collaboratively with our stakeholders. This work was done through a working table, which included the Teacher Federations, the Ontario College of Teachers, parent groups, student groups, and school boards all around the table working out these programs.
>
> (Camille Chenier, Teaching Policy and Standards Branch,
> Ontario Ministry of Education)

Figure 3–11 Teacher Development in Ontario

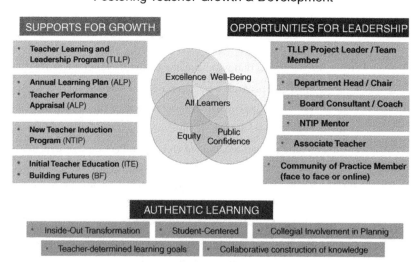

Fostering Teacher Growth & Development

SUPPORTS FOR GROWTH	OPPORTUNITIES FOR LEADERSHIP
• Teacher Learning and Leadership Program (TLLP)	• TLLP Project Leader / Team Member
• Annual Learning Plan (ALP) • Teacher Performance Appraisal (ALP)	• Department Head / Chair
	• Board Consultant / Coach
• New Teacher Induction Program (NTIP)	• NTIP Mentor
	• Associate Teacher
• Initial Teacher Education (ITE) • Building Futures (BF)	• Community of Practice Member (face to face or online)

Excellence Well-Being
All Learners
Equity Public Confidence

AUTHENTIC LEARNING

• Inside-Out Transformation   • Student-Centered   • Collegial Involvement in Plannig
• Teacher-determined learning goals   • Collaborative construction of knowledge

Source: Ontario Ministry of Education, Teaching Policy and Standards Branch.

We examine key provincial policies and practices for teacher quality in detail below.

Initial Teacher Education

We're trying to develop teachers who are going to continue to learn throughout their careers.

(Kathy Broad, Teaching Policy and Standards Branch,
Ontario Ministry of Education)

Teacher certification is highly regulated in Ontario. To be certified, teachers must:

ɔ Have completed a minimum three-year postsecondary degree from an acceptable postsecondary institution.

ɔ Have successfully completed an acceptable teacher education program.

ɔ Apply to the Ontario College of Teachers for certification and pay the annual membership and registration fees.

ɔ Complete application processes include providing proof of identity and a Canadian Criminal Record Check Report.

For additional information on teacher certification requirements visit https://www.oct.ca/%7E/link.aspx?_id=25CD74DDD6A14F3BA96849 0666FB1733&_z=z.

For teacher candidates who meet the certification requirements, the OCT issues a Certificate of Qualification and Registration, which outlines the applicant's teaching qualifications including: university degree, program of teacher education, the school divisions for which the candidate is qualified (primary: K to 3; junior: 4 to 6; intermediate: 7 to 10; and senior: 10 to 12), and additional qualifications for in-service professional learning. Teachers must hold a Certificate of Qualification and Registration to teach in Ontario's publicly funded education system.

All initial teacher education in Ontario is provided by university Faculties of Education, accredited by the OCT, to fulfill the above requirements. For teachers trained outside of Ontario, including internationally, teachers must also register with the OCT and fulfill equivalent standards, including language requirements, to become licensed to teach in Ontario. There are some variations to requirements to enable First Nations, Métis, or Inuit applicants who do not fulfill the university degree requirements to teach in elementary schools.

Programs typically prepare teachers to teach content in two divisions (primary/junior, junior/intermediate, intermediate/senior). At the intermediate and senior levels, preservice teachers are subject specialists that have completed a concentration in one or more content areas prior to beginning the teacher preparation portion of their studies. Intermediate/Senior programs generally require students to complete two subject-specific methodology courses for each area of specialization. Content areas can include a range of subjects such as business, computer science, English, family studies, math, science, French, geography, history, music, religion, technology, health, and art.

At the primary and junior levels, preservice teachers may complete a subject specialization prior to beginning their teacher education but it is not required. Rather than subject-specialists, teachers in these levels are considered generalists who typically teach all subject areas. Typically students complete content courses in a wide range of subjects (either in their previous studies when enrolled in a consecutive program or during their B.Ed. in a concurrent program) as well as methodology courses in a host of subject areas including language arts, math, social studies, science, health and physical education, music, and visual arts. Junior/intermediate programs may require students to take both a broad-based methodology course and a subject-specific course in their area of choice. For a sample of course syllabus and program structure please see Western University's Course Description document (Link 3-13).

Up to 2014–2015, teacher candidates typically completed three or four years of undergraduate study and a one-year teacher preparation program at a faculty of education in one of two routes: concurrent (where teacher candidates simultaneously complete a bachelor of arts or science and a bachelor of education) or consecutive (candidates apply to a Faculty of Education having already completed a bachelor's degree). Candidates who are preparing to be teachers of technological studies may enter a consecutive program and complete a Diploma in Education using prior work experience or an undergraduate degree as the prerequisites for program entry. While most programs are offered on a full time basis, a small number of Ontario Faculties of Education offer a part-time option. Programs are expected to: reflect current research in teacher education; integrate theory and practice; reference the Ontario curriculum; include theory, methods, and foundation courses; and require teacher candidates to complete a minimum of forty days of practice teaching, although most Ontario programs offer at least 50 or 60 days. In addition to the specific theory and practices involved in teacher preparation, the goals of teacher education include the development of teachers' as reflective continuing learners. As will be discussed further in this chapter, the requirements for teacher education changed with effect from September 2015 onwards.

Perceptions of Teacher Education Quality

In 2008, four Faculties of Education in Ontario, in collaboration with the Ministry of Education, researched the views of their graduates, other teachers, and employers regarding teacher education in 21 school districts in Ontario (Herbert et al., 2010). Just over half of the teachers in the survey rated their teacher-education preparation as "good" or "very good." The practicum experience was rated highly (83% responded "good" or "very good") more often than the course work (53%). Consistent with these findings, data from the OCT's 2011 Transitions to Teaching Survey (Link 3-14) indicate that almost nine in ten of teacher education graduates (87%) rate their practicum teaching experience as good or excellent in terms of career preparation, with the majority also rating their course work positively. Of the six top priorities, graduates identified four as being tied with practical experience: more practicum time; more teaching opportunities for candidates during the practicum as well as observation time by experienced teachers; and more coaching and feedback throughout the practicum. The other two priority items for graduates were related to hands-on teaching experience: classroom management and assessment; and testing and evaluation. Similarly, research by Gambhir et al. (2008) indicate that Ontario principals were reasonably satisfied with teachers' preparation (91% rated it "adequate," "good," or "very good"), but felt that improvements could be made in terms of having more current teachers instruct teacher-education program; longer practicum periods, with more frequent interaction; and more emphasis on current issues, such as data-driven instruction, balanced literacy, and special needs.

Teachers interviewed for this case study were generally pleased with their teacher preparation programs. One teacher who had completed a concurrent program spoke very highly of her program:

> My initial teacher preparation was excellent and prepared me well for my career ahead. Because it was a three-year concurrent program, there were various opportunities to observe, implement and reflect upon various teaching methods and classroom dynamics in three different schools. Beyond the usual theory and lesson training, we learned to work together as colleagues, share information, advise each other and listen to and solve problems. We prepared lessons for each other and experimented with different ways to make learning come alive. There was a community of learners, which included

alumni, to answer questions at any given time. The learning never stopped. We still keep in touch after fifteen years.

(Cathy)

Most teachers interviewed enjoyed the practical application of their methodology courses and rated their practicum as being the greatest component in their preparation:

> By far the strongest part was my practicum, because I was in the classroom with a teacher. I was lucky to have two strong professionals who gave me very constructive feedback. . . I don't want to be told "you're great." I want a lot of constructive feedback and so that was, by far, the most effective part of my preservice training.

(Heather)

> The absolute best part of my teacher training was the practicum. I got to learn from many different teachers, engage in PD (professional development), help plan lessons and eventually teach the class myself. . . . Those wanting to be a teacher need to be in the classroom. The real life experience is so much more valuable than anything they will learn from a book.

(Darcy)

However, interviewees also indicated areas for improvement in teacher education, particularly the need for a stronger focus on equity and technology, coupled with more practical and contextual experiences observing and teaching in classrooms. One teacher, for instance, commented that a one-year program was not long enough to prepare them for the "real life" of a classroom teacher. This perceived need for additional time has been incorporated into changes to initial teacher education programs in Ontario from 2015 to 2016 onwards.

Changes to Teacher Education Programs from 2015 Onwards

In 2008, a study on teacher education in Canada (Gambhir et al., 2008) noted that, at 40 days, Ontario had the shortest required practicum of any Canadian teacher education program (although it should be noted that many universities required more than the minimum). In particular, the study noted that:

> Depending on the university, candidates can spend anywhere from eight months to two years earning their B.Ed degree. One of the greatest challenges of the consecutive model is the intensity of delivering comprehensive courses and practical placements in the shorter

programs (e.g., Ontario's eight-month degrees). Critics feel that more time is needed for development of teaching skills and knowledge than can be achieved in a short program. Another concern is the limited depth and breadth of topics that can be covered.

(Gambhir et al., 2008, p. 10)

In 2013, the provincial government announced significant changes to teacher education, with the introduction of a four-semester (two-year) program with an increased practicum of 80 days, to begin in September 2015. Additional changes going forward include an enhanced focus on diversity, meeting the needs of students with special needs, children's mental health, and the integration of technology (Ontario Ministry of Education, 2013b). In an effort to curb the oversupply of teachers in the province (discussed in further detail in later sections), the government also reduced enrolments from 9,000 to 4,500 places per year. Although the total number of applicants to initial teacher education has declined in recent years (hitting a peak of about 16,500 in 2007), data from the Ontario Universities' Application Centre (2014) shows that there were approximately 9,400 applicants to teacher education programs in Ontario in 2014, suggesting that a reduction in available placements will also likely increase the competitiveness of entry into the profession.

The provincial government provides funding to universities to offset the cost of operating initial teacher education programs. In 2009–2010, the government provided universities with approximately $8,517 for each full-time teacher candidate to complete one year of preservice education. Under the new two year program in 2015–2016, Faculties of Education receive $5,684 per candidate in each of two years for B.Ed. programs (equating to a total of $11,386 CDN per FTE for the full program). The Ontario Institute of Studies in Education (OISE) at the University of Toronto has decided with the new two-year program to move to masters' level teacher education only. As a graduate program, OISE receives approximately $13,200 per FTE in annual operating grant for masters' provision. While the government funding to universities supports partial subsidizing of the costs of teacher education, students still pay tuition and fees within a government regulated system—currently these fees range by institution and type of provision. B.Ed. fees in 2015–2016 ranged from $6,000 to $10,000 CDN. As the number of funded places has halved, the total funding to universities per year has declined resulting in some financial challenges for providers. For example at OISE, the shifts from 1,167 B.Ed. places per academic year to 502 masters' places equates to around a 32% (or $3 million) reduction. For smaller universities, an early impact has been reductions in B.Ed. provision and in some cases closure of programs or regional satellite offerings.

More positively, a goal of the two-year program is to provided more extensive practical experiences for teacher candidates during their training, focus more in-depth on priority areas for learning and experience, and also rebalance supply and demand over time. Some interviewees are hopeful that these goals can be reconciled and achieved:

> I do not understand it (reform of teacher education) purely as a response to oversupply. I'm seeing it as well as a response to and a thinking about what teachers should bring to the table as 21st century learners and 21st century educators meeting the needs of a 21st century society, and so looking at issues such as the environment, recognizing the needs of students who learn differently, special education must be foregrounded, this kind of knowledge must be embedding in the curriculum. It is supporting teacher candidates to develop a mindset and culture of learning and as learners who respond to the needs of all students. Whether you are teaching in a homogeneous setting or a diverse setting, these are important issues and topics for all educators wherever you may be. As Ladson-Billings said, "it is just good teaching," and so for me, that is an ongoing, important, crucial debate and I think it must be front and centre. I think the Ministry is responding to that in the new two-year program highlighting the importance of culturally relevant and responsive pedagogies and ensuring that we infuse Aboriginal knowledges in the curriculum and do a better job of educating students from our Aboriginal communities. I see these as important issues in the new teacher education curriculum.

(Ann Lopez, OISE, University of Toronto)

Teachers and administrators interviewed for this case study thought that the move to a two-year format could improve the quality of Ontario's teacher education program, particularly with respect to the extended practicum (Link 3-15):

> To be honest [the practicum] wasn't enough time to really understand the profession. We saw the superficial aspect of it, teaching a lesson, maybe some classroom management techniques but the everyday life of a teacher is not something that I left understanding. How to navigate colleagues that don't have the same mindset that you have, there wasn't enough time spent on that. I didn't learn how to have those courageous conversations with my teacher colleagues or with my administrators or with parents and my students in terms of how

to move the learning forward. So the two years could be great in terms of getting that extra time in the classroom.

(Paul)

The extension of the program is intended to strengthen learning and experience rather than to emphasize longer academic study time:

> I think you've heard how important a learning stance has been. Not just for the teacher, but for the system. It is not a learning stance in terms of academia; it is learning about what the students need, being open to learning at all levels of the system. The learning stance we mean is based on how is society changing, therefore, what do students need to know and to be able to do to be part of that society and what do educators need to learn to address these needs? That's the learning stance we're talking about. . . and it's a stance we all have to take whether at the Ministry, board, school or classroom level. It's not a "study longer" stance.

(Demetra Saldaris, Teaching Policy and Standards Branch, Ontario Ministry of Education)

Interestingly, the outcomes of consultations on the future of initial teacher education emphasized the importance of teacher training provided by universities and rejected alternative teacher preparation routes:

> Whether it was in Ministry consultations or at the College when it did its consultations around initial teacher education, there was some discussion about these alternative models for teacher preparation, the kind where it's employment based, so the focus is almost an apprenticeship model. It's learning on the job. There was also discussion around whether we could introduce teacher education programs that are done almost entirely by distance education, and the answer generally was "we're not comfortable with that," not in terms of where we're at with distance education. Not yet, because there's this value on building the relationship, whether it's between the instructors and then the teacher candidates or the teacher candidates amongst themselves, learning amongst themselves, and doing that in face-to-face classrooms.

(Camille Chenier, Teaching Policy and Standards Branch)

There are, however, some concerns that moving to a two-year program of university studies may be a disincentive for some individuals to enter into teacher education, for example whether for academic and/ or financial reasons. Other areas of concern include greater difficulty

Figure 3–12 Cumulative Ontario Teacher
Education Application Statistics as of September
for the Past 10 years

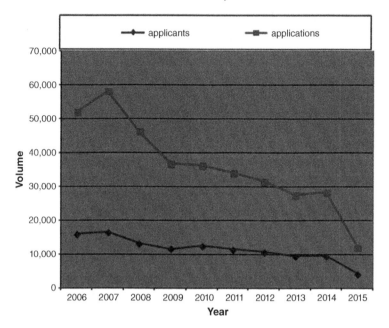

Source: OUAC, 2015.

in attracting candidates to technological education programs as well as
sufficient numbers of French First Language and First Nations, Métis
and Inuit teacher candidates. As the two-year program rolls out over
time, it will be important to monitor whether the potential benefits of
an extended program are realized and whether anticipated issues can be
mitigated.

Admission to Teacher Education   Like all university students in Ontario,
students apply to teacher education programs though the Ontario Universities Application Centre (OUAC) where they complete one application that can be submitted to up to four programs, which they rank
in order of preference (see Figure 3–12). Competition for places is very
strong. For example, prior to 2015, Ontario's largest Faculty of Education, OISE at the University of Toronto, routinely received around
4,000 applications for just over 1,000 places. Overall application statistics for the past 10 years and applications by institution for the past
two years are presented below. Note that numbers in Figure 3–13 for

Figure 3–13 Applications and program choices for Ontario teacher education programs from 2014 and 2015

* Denotes no valid information as OISE at U of T no longer offers a B.Ed. program and has switched to a Master's only program structure.

O.U.A.C. SYSTEM TOTALS

Note: An '*' in any percent change column denotes no valid 2-year comparative data.

	SEPTEMBER 04, 2014 PROGRAM CHOICES					SEPTEMBER 02, 2015 PROGRAM CHOICES					PERCENT CHANGE				
	1ST	2ND	3RD	>3	TOTAL	1ST	2ND	3RD	>3	TOTAL	1ST	2ND	3RD	>3	TOTAL
Brock University	647	463	526	718	2354	435	315	253	299	1302	-32.8	-32.0	-51.9	-58.4	-44.7
Lakehead University	563	447	402	708	2120	156	135	131	177	599	-72.3	-69.8	-67.4	-75.0	-71.7
Laurentian University	213	191	124	96	624	87	76	46	32	241	-59.2	-60.2	-62.9	-66.7	-61.4
Nipissing University	389	381	324	708	1802	187	160	155	275	777	-51.9	-58.0	-52.2	-61.2	-56.9
University of Ottawa	2260	1353	922	608	5143	1039	683	423	228	2373	-54.0	-49.5	-54.1	-62.5	-53.9
Queen's University	408	386	292	417	1503	285	229	136	143	793	-30.1	-40.7	-53.4	-65.7	-47.2
University of Toronto	1753	839	328	218	3138	0	0	0	0	0	*	*	*	*	*
Trent University	208	196	276	569	1249	127	160	166	239	692	-38.9	-18.4	-39.9	-58.0	-44.6
U O I T	227	303	382	327	1239	187	312	129	135	763	-17.6	3.0	-66.2	-58.7	-38.4
Western University	908	689	584	758	2939	386	290	243	247	1166	-57.5	-57.9	-58.4	-67.4	-60.3
Wilfrid Laurier University	276	325	380	585	1566	173	266	245	272	956	-37.3	-18.2	-35.5	-53.5	-39.0
University of Windsor	422	323	274	531	1550	200	171	148	227	746	-52.6	-47.1	-46.0	-57.3	-51.9
York University	1186	1175	394	322	3077	1062	314	194	148	1718	-10.5	-73.3	-50.8	-54.0	-44.2
TOTALS	9460	7071	5208	6565	28504	4324	3111	2269	2422	12126	-54.3	-56.0	-56.4	-63.1	-57.2

Source: OUAC, 2015.

2015 are reflective of the changes to the teacher education program outline above.

Each Faculty of Education has its own set of established criteria for acceptance, typically including academic standards and evidence of competency (e.g., entry interview; teaching statement; experience with children; and teaching).

At OISE, in addition to academic grades, applicants are also asked to complete a teaching profile that outlines their philosophy of teaching and learning:

> So the question over the years for OISE has always been, how do we make that selection and how do we engage in that admissions decision process? So a number of things; there is, of course, the registrarial piece, that each applicant must have a B- average to be in the program, so that's one component. That's the grade component. At OISE we've used also another component, which are the profiles. The profile is a system where we ask teacher candidates to respond to three questions, and in those questions they speak about their experiences engaging in teaching, not necessarily in classrooms, but it can be in a space where they engage with a number of learners. The second question that we ask is really to find out if they're learners and to tell us about their mindset for learning and to articulate why they want to be teachers, and a third question is really foregrounding one of OISE's key principles, which is equity, diversity and social justice, and to get a sense of how our teacher candidates think about those issues and their mindset for wanting to be effective learners and to translate that into the act of teaching.
>
> (Ann Lopez, OISE, University of Toronto)

There is a concern in Ontario to attend to attracting diverse candidates from underrepresented populations and minority groups to increase diversity in the teacher population and recognize increasing diversity in the student population:

> I think that it's important to point that out and that it stems from this real interest in Ontario and in the Ministry to attract and recruit teachers from different backgrounds. We recognized, at one point in Ontario, that we didn't really have enough teachers, for example, from a French language background or teachers who were from a Native ancestry background and so there was a lot of attention paid to that and thinking around how do we make it more accessible for teachers of a diversity of backgrounds to want to and be able to join the profession and then be able to connect with their students,

because we have students from such a diversity of backgrounds in our four systems.

(Camille Chenier, Teaching Policy and Standards Branch,
Ontario Ministry of Education)

Faculties of Education are also concerned to increase teacher diversity. At OISE, this has been a targeted goal with specific actions:

OISE has been cognizant of the need to increase the diversity in the program. The challenge around that has been that diversity does not exist in the pool of applicants who apply. When I say diversity, I mean racial, religious, cultural, ethnic, sexual orientation and so on just wasn't in the pool of potential teacher candidates applying. This year, I think we've made quite a stride. This year we were able, and last year, to ask a question with the profile encouraging prospective teacher candidates to tell us about their particular area of diversity or their particular social identity and how they would use those experiences to teach in classrooms to students who are usually underserved. This was voluntary and each applicant must have a B- average to be admitted. Through the profile system, we were able to read applicants' responses that would give us a sense of their social locations, we were able to factor that information into our admissions process and I think we were very successful in admitting a more diversified group of teacher candidates last year, and this year, even better.

(Ann Lopez, OISE, University of Toronto)

Attending to recruiting and supporting a diversity of teacher education candidates continues to be an area of focus, including attracting Aboriginal teacher candidates who can bring knowledge of Aboriginal issues and connections with Aboriginal communities and students into their teaching practices.

Example of Teacher Education Programs (2014–2015)

We present two examples of institutions offering Initial Teacher Education programs. The first case, OISE is the largest provider of teacher preparation in the province and is known as one of the top teacher education schools in the world. Located in the city of Toronto, the province's capital, OISE has a strong focus on urban education and social justice. Lakehead University was chosen as a contrast to OISE. Located in the northern city of Thunder Bay, Lakehead is a much smaller faculty of education that offers students a range of experiences in specialized Aboriginal teacher education programs. Additional details of the programs offered at each institution are provided below.

Ontario Institute for Studies in Education, University of Toronto   In light of the government's changes to teacher education, OISE has moved to masters' level teacher education provision only, beginning in the Fall of 2015. The masters' provision is based on a revised and expanded offering through the Master of Teaching and Master of Arts in Child Study in Education. The concurrent B.Ed. program is being phased out to enable existing candidates to complete their studies and will end in 2018. The consecutive B.Ed. program ceased to be offered in 2015.

Master of Teaching: The Master of Teaching (MT) is a full-time two-year graduate level teacher education program. Students choose one of three program specializations (divisions): primary/junior, junior/intermediate, or intermediate/senior to become certified as either an elementary of secondary teacher. Students participate in required courses that weave theory and practice, including courses on: Curriculum and Teaching (specific to grade and subject for certification); Educational Professionalism, Ethics and the Law; Practice Teaching; Reflective Teaching and Inquiry into Research in Education; Fundamentals of Teaching; Child and Adolescent Development; Authentic Assessment; Special Education and Adaptive Instruction; Issues in Elementary or Secondary Education; From Student to Professional; and Integrating Technology. In addition, all candidates conduct a Master of Teaching research project.

Master of Arts in Child Study and Education: The Master of Arts in Child Study and Education (MACSE) is a full-time graduate level program involving the equivalent of 16 half-courses in areas such as play and education, psychological foundations of early development, early learning in mathematics, child and family relationships, and theory and curriculum and approximately 600 hours of in-class practical experience. Candidates are qualified to teach in JK–grade 6 in Ontario.

The University of Toronto Concurrent Teacher Education Program: OISE's concurrent program enables students to simultaneously complete the requirements for an undergraduate degree, a Bachelor of Education degree, and professional teacher qualifications over a five-year period. Students build on their subject knowledge from their undergraduate degree combined with specific B.Ed. courses for the concurrent program including: Principles of Teaching; Inclusive Education; Psychological Foundations of Learning; Social Foundations of Teaching and Schooling; Curriculum, Instruction and Assessment; Mentored Inquiry in Teaching; and Practicum. Students enrolled in the concurrent program prior to 2015 will complete their studies; following the current cohort, the program will be phased out as OISE moves to masters' level teacher education only.

As well as specific courses for each pathway, OISE teacher education candidates are expected to demonstrate capacities set out in The Learner document including capacities relating to:

Knowledge of the Learner: for example: "Understand that teaching is more than a methodology. It includes an understanding of teaching redefined as a responsibility for student learning";

Teacher Identity: for example, "Develop a personal philosophy of education that embodies principles of equity, diversity, inclusion, social justice and environmental justice";

Transformative Purposes of Education: for example, "Understand the roles teachers, learners, families, communities, schools and systems play in this transformative process [of education]";

Subject Matter and Pedagogical Content Knowledge: for example, "Make informed pedagogical decisions with the goal of success for all students based on knowledge of the learner, context, curriculum, and assessment"; and

Learning and Teaching in Social Contexts: for example, "Understand how systematic/institutional practices dis/advantage social groups/learners and ways that they can work with others to counter inequalities."

Importantly, OISE aspires for teacher candidates to become excellent teachers who are also critical, thoughtful, action-oriented learners:

> We engage in pedagogies, assignments, assessments, evaluation all coming together to facilitate synthesizing that at the end of the day, they [teacher candidates] should be able to bring together all of the components of the program, developing for themselves an understanding of what it means to be an effective teacher. Being able to articulate that, reflect on what else they need to learn, what they need to unlearn, and if we've done that, we feel very good that our teacher candidates are able to make a difference, and I think that's one of the strengths of our program is truly helping our teacher candidates to understand that they are lifelong learners, but not in a very rhetorical way, but in a meaningful way and how do they do that?
>
> (Ann Lopez, OISE, University of Toronto)

Lakehead University: Teacher Education Preparation for Aboriginal Education   With its main campus residing in the Northern Ontario city of Thunder Bay, Lakehead University is home to Canada's only department of Aboriginal Education. Part of the Faculty of Education, the department offers two unique undergraduate degree programs which focus on aboriginal cultures and traditions. Education programs at Lakehead also changed in 2015 when the two-year requirement for teacher education came into effect. Four-year concurrent programs are being phased out over the next three years and new students, from September 2015, are enrolled in five-year programs. Also beginning in September, 2015, the professional year in all other education programs has become two years in length going forward.

Honours Bachelor of Education (Aboriginal) P/J: This program is specifically designed to prepare people of Aboriginal ancestry to become teachers and leaders in Aboriginal communities. The four-year degree program consists of two years of required courses in Native languages (Cree and Ojibwe) Indigenous learning, English, general sciences, and visual arts, followed by a two-year component on educational theories, practices, and abilities, which includes courses exploring the literacy of Aboriginal children, the context of teaching in Aboriginal settings, and Aboriginal ways of child rearing.

Students must undertake two teaching practicums to be completed either in a Band school or a provincial school with a significant Aboriginal population. In addition, during the final year of the program, students must complete an honors project that demonstrates meaningful learning through one of a variety of mediums including learning portfolios, apprenticeships with elders or other cultural leaders, research projects, or the design of culturally relevant teaching resources. Upon completion of the degree, students are eligible to receive OCT certification to teach grades K–6 in Ontario schools.

Native Teacher Education Program (NTEP): Admission to degrees within this program is open to both people of Aboriginal ancestry as well as non-Aboriginals with a desire to teach in Aboriginal contexts. The program houses four joint degree programs:

○ Bachelor of Arts (General)–Bachelor of Education (Native Education) P/J, J/I, and I/S

○ Bachelor of Science (General)–Bachelor of Education (Native Education) P/J, J/I, and I/S

These four-year concurrent programs consist of three years of course work and one professional year of teaching. Required course work in the first three years includes Ojibwe or Cree, Native Arts and Crafts, First Nations Literature, Native Legends and Myths, and other Indigenous learning courses as well as a minimum of eight full-time equivalents from the Faculty of Social Science and Humanities or the Faculty of Science and Environmental Studies. The professional year includes selected methodology courses as well as courses in sociology of education, Aboriginal education, and teaching exceptional learners. During the professional year students also complete two teaching practicums, which can be completed either in a Band school or in a provincially run school.

⊃ Bachelor of Arts (Indigenous Learning)–Bachelor of Education P/J, J/I, and I/S

In this four-year concurrent program students complete a BA with a major in Indigenous Learning as well as a Bachelor of Education in Native Studies. Required course work during the first three years includes developing an understanding of traditional methods of Indigenous Learning and Ways of Life, Native Perspectives on World Views, First Nations Literature, Native Arts and Crafts, Native Myths and Legends, and Ojibwe or Cree. Elective courses include two additional full time equivalent courses in Indigenous learning (which include offerings in areas such as community well-being, the rights of Aboriginal Peoples, Indigenous women, and gender relations in Aboriginal communities) as well as two 0.25 equivalent courses from areas including Literacy and the Aboriginal Child, Teaching English as a Second Dialect to Aboriginal Learners, and Contemporary Issues in Native Education. The professional year in this program operates in the same manner as in the Bachelor of Arts or Science (General)—Bachelor of Education described above.

⊃ Honours Bachelor of Arts (Indigenous Learning)–Bachelor of Education P/J, J/I, and I/S

The first two years of this five-year program is identical to the Bachelor of Arts (Indigenous Learning)–Bachelor of Education program described above. However, during years three and four, students in the honors program must complete four full-time equivalent electives in Indigenous Learning (as compared with two in the regular BA) and must also complete an honors research project relevant to some aspect of Indigenous learning. The core professional year of education courses comprises year five of the degree.

In addition to these programs, NTEP also offers a specialization as a Teacher of Aboriginal Learners to students enrolled in any of Lakehead's consecutive or concurrent initial teacher education program. To earn this certificate, students must complete the following courses within the context of their home program:

⊃ Native Arts and Crafts

⊃ Literature of Canada's First Nations

○ Ojibwe or Cree

○ Introduction to Indigenous Learning

○ One half-course elective in Indigenous Education

Vignette: Lakehead's Professional Program On-Site Delivery (PPOD)

Students in Lakehead's concurrent program have the opportunity to complete a portion of their education degree as part of Lakehead's professional program on-site delivery (PPOD), a school-based model where students and professors collaborate with local schools and teachers one-day per week. Students who participate in PPOD are embedded in schools for the duration of the education portion of their degree. This makes for seamless learning as theory introduced in course work is reinforced through in-classroom observation. Courses delivered on-site include language arts, classroom management, planning and evaluation, and literacy. Students also engage in literacy coaching at their PPOD school and neighboring schools, learning valuable teaching skills while assisting students' literacy development. This 40-hour literacy internship serves as additional practical training, beyond the regular practicum requirements. The program runs seven cohorts per year: five in primary, and one in each of the intermediate and secondary programs.

Building Futures

Since 2004, the Ministry of Education has provided Building Futures to support teacher candidates in learning key government education priorities as they transition from university to the school classroom. During this one-day session, experienced educators provide teacher candidates with information and resources about education priorities and effective teaching strategies through a series of workshops. The workshops are delivered to preservice teachers at all 13 Faculties of Education and are designed to provide teacher candidates with information about provincial policies, initiatives, and resources that they are expected to be aware of and engage as they enter a teaching career in Ontario. Workshops topics include assessment, Aboriginal education, 21st-century learning, English language learners, literacy, healthy living, e-learning, inclusive schools, mathematics, and a host of others. As the coordinator of Building Futures explains:

The Teaching Policy and Standards Branch works with many other Branches in the Ministry of Education to develop these workshops, which are aligned to the current Ministry priorities and presented by experienced and dynamic educators. The educators that present the workshops, all have experience in the classroom. Probably one of the best things about the program is that it's one of the first initial introductions from the Ministry to the teacher candidates!

(Christina Terzic, Teaching Policy and Standards Branch, Ontario Ministry of Education)

Recruitment

The role of a teacher impacts every single student, every single child in Ontario. Even those who don't attend regularly are still impacted by teachers, and the majority of them are impacted very positively. So I think that when you are a child growing up and you look at the people who influence you, I think the realities of education in Ontario are we have a good solid curriculum, we have schools that are viewed as community hubs and I think that the students growing up in them realize the importance of those roles in society, and if they want to contribute to society as adults, teaching is a career that they would choose.

(Suzette Clark, OSSTF)

School boards are responsible for hiring and appointing teachers to Ontario schools in the public systems. Typically, teachers apply to schools of their choice within a school board and are assigned by principals to positions based on their qualifications and the specific program needs of the school, such as teaching English language learners or French immersion programs (Ontario Ministry of Education, 2011). Generally, evaluations of candidates are based on qualifications and seniority, with the assessment framework outlined by the OCT's Standards of Practice competencies (Link 3-16).

In September 2012, the government of Ontario implemented Regulation 274/12, Hiring Practices (Link 3-17) which requires a school board to interview the five most senior applicants who meet the requirements of the job, when holding interviews for a vacant position. They must also organize their occasional teacher and long-term occasional (LTO) teacher lists according to seniority.

Over the past ten years, retirement numbers in Ontario have declined, and as a result, there has been a decline in the number of opportunities available to unemployed teachers. Meanwhile, the number of graduates from initial teacher education programs has continued to increase, resulting in a surplus of teachers and a highly competitive market. This is a marked shift from the early 2000s, when retirement rates were high and most new education graduates could easily gain employment. Thus, Ontario's employment market is now characterized by an oversupply of trained teachers in most subject areas, particularly in elementary schools. This has created an opportunity for school boards to be highly selective in recruiting teachers. Consequently, the job market for teachers in Ontario is very competitive, with the average new teacher facing longer waiting periods to secure a permanent full-time contract. In 2011, the OCT's Transition to Teaching survey reported the following:

> Almost one in three of the teacher education graduates of 2010 who sought teaching jobs during the 2010–11 school year were unemployed, with no success in finding even daily supply teaching during the first school year of their teaching careers. Only one in eight of them secured regular teaching jobs. And just one in three of those who were on the job market secured as much teaching work as they wanted. . . One in five first year teachers now look outside the province for their first teaching job. . . And more first year teachers are now working in non-teaching occupations (22%) as an alternative when faced with a failed teaching job search or as a supplement to part-time teaching income.
>
> (Ontario College of Teachers, 2011, p. 3)

Data from the Ontario Ministry of Education (Table 3–2) indicates that in 2012–2013, there was a total of 8,328 new teachers hired in Ontario of which 4,836 were permanent hires and 3,487 were long term occasional staffing. Of concern, it is estimated that there are currently approximately 40,000 qualified teachers in Ontario who are unemployed or working in other fields.

Table 3–2 New Teachers in Ontario, 2009–2012

	2009/2010	2010/2011	2011/2012	2012/2013
First Year Permanent Hires	4600	4788	4269	4836
First Year Long-term Occasionals	3306	3950	3895	3487
Total New Hires	7906	8738	8164	8323

Source: Ontario Ministry of Education.

One teacher in our case study commented:

> I worked so hard to volunteer and start to establish a network but that's just seen as "paying your dues" now. . . A lot of teachers struggle with supply teaching and being bumped from school to school and if you get a job right away, it can create a lot of animosity between new teachers. . . So there's a lot of tensions, there's a lot of competition that happens between young teachers.
>
> (Tina)

Likewise, when asked about desirable places to work, another teacher in our study stated, "positions are limited and beginning teachers need to be willing to move to the areas where openings are available" (Cathy).

For internationally trained teachers, even after going through a process to become an Ontario certified teachers, the job market can be particularly challenging. This is an area of concern and attention:

> We know from our surveys [of registered teachers in Ontario] that 90% of those who indicate that they were internationally educated are underemployed or unemployed in their first year of teaching and even into their second, third and fourth years of teaching. So that's where I see a gap. The education community does have an interest in looking at hiring teachers who represent the whole gamut of diversity and yet our internationally educated teachers are not being hired.
>
> (Michael Salvatori, OCT)

The changes to the enrollment in teacher education programs for 2015–2016 include reducing the number of teacher education placed by half (from 9,000 currently to 4,500 per year) with the goal of rebalancing supply and demand.

Attractiveness of Teaching as a Career

> Kids coming out of high school now, heading into university, if they think, "I think I want to go into teaching," I think it's because they have had that good experience themselves. And they think, "That would be a nice place to work." Of course, it's the "I want to make an impact on young people's lives." I think that's what draws you to the profession at a base level, but just that comfort level with "this is a respected profession. I have a good feeling about public education."
>
> (Rhonda Kimberley-Young, OTF)

A virtuous process appears to exist where the public support the education system, individuals' own positive experience in schools may encourage them to become teachers, and hence students then become adults who want to be teachers to further support, contribute to and impact a strong public education system with positive benefits for future students:

> I think the other piece of it is that for the most part, although we have issues that we all work on and we try to improve in our school system, most people have a pretty good experience, and they [aspiring teacher candidates] see the value of education. They understand that education is a great balancing factor, if you want to have a life that is fulfilling for yourself and that you can move forward and you can achieve things, that you need education and I think people get caught up in that passion and they want to share that passion and they want to ensure that others have the same opportunities that they did through education, and in Canada, we are so very lucky that it is a universal education system. And that's part of the tenets that we believe in, universality, comprehensiveness, proficiency and accountability. Those are all things that we believe in and I think people understand that you build the future on education and they want to be a part of that.
>
> (Lori Foote, OSSTF)

As indicated by a public opinion survey conducted at OISE every three years, Ontarians have continued to have a high regard for the teaching profession and support the publicly funded education system (Hart, 2012). Satisfaction rates for teacher quality are at almost 80% among parents, a figure that has steadily increased over the past number of years (Hart, 2012).

Even in the context of unemployment and underemployment, entering into teaching remains a highly desirable career, particularly since salaries and working conditions are relatively good compared to other professions with equivalent training:

> Nobody is ashamed to say, "I am a teacher." People are proud to say, "I am a teacher." People feel that pride.
>
> (Lindy Amato, OTF)

> Teachers are still among the most trusted of professions and I think that helps. You want to be part of a profession where you know the public has a good opinion of the professionals.
>
> (Michael Salvatori, OCT)

Teacher attrition in Ontario is extremely low at less than 5% each year (see Table 3–3). The Ministry of Education's Educator Attrition Indicator measures the number of educators that were actively assigned within the public education system in a particular year, but were not assigned or on leave in the public education system in the following year.

Table 3–3 Education Attrition Rates: Ontario Educator FTE Position Counts

	2008–09	2009–10	2010–11	2011–12	4-year change
Active	122,253	121,804	121,853	122,435	182
Attrition	4,860	4,688	4,578	5,604	744
Educator Attrition Rate	3.98%	3.85%	3.76%	4.58%	0.60%

Note: Provincial totals and breakdowns by age and gender include educators in School Authorities, which excluded in breakdowns by board type.

Source: Ontario Ministry of Education.

This is turned into a percentage by dividing FTE educators leaving by the number of active FTE educators for the base year, multiplied by 100.

Similarly, a survey by the Ontario College of Teachers (2011) revealed that, in spite of the challenges they have been experiencing in the employment market, new teachers are highly committed to their careers. Approximately nine in ten (88–92%) of surveyed graduates from 2006–2010 indicated that they will definitely or probably be in the teaching profession in five years. The commitment levels are even high among the first and second year teachers reporting that they are completely unemployed. Among this group, 87% and 75% of first and second year unemployed teachers respectively report that they will definitely or probably be teachers five years into the future. Only 5–8% indicated that they would likely not be teaching by then. Furthermore, a survey of 2011 graduates (Ontario College of Teachers, 2012) who obtained some teaching employment in the 2011–2012 school year shows that about three in four rated their overall teaching experience as excellent (31%) or good (42%). Eighteen percent evaluated the experience as adequate while 9% rated the experience as unsatisfactory or very unsatisfactory.

Compensation and Working Conditions

Labor Bargaining   Elected on the heels of a Conservative government who had been in conflict with teachers and the public sector, the newly elected Liberal government of 2003 went about repairing the damaged relationships with the teachers' unions through a variety of partnership projects and policy changes around teacher development. Building on a renewed trust, in 2005 and 2009, the government and the teacher unions successfully facilitated a process to implement a provincial bargaining framework to establish four-year collective agreements across Ontario and to avoid labor disruption (Pervin & Campbell, 2011).

However, in negotiations for the next round of contracts in 2012, the policy landscape shifted and the relationship between the government and the teacher unions became more contentious. Unable to come to labor agreement with all four of the teacher organizations in Ontario, in September of 2012 the Government passed Bill 115, the Putting Students First Act (Link 3-18), allowing the Ontario government to impose a collective agreement and establish rules to be adhered to by local school boards when they negotiated with local unions. The bill also established limitations on the legality of teachers' unions and support staff with respect to strike action.

With the passage of the bill, there was discontent among teachers and their unions, including strike activities by two teacher unions. The government has subsequently repealed the Bill (Government of Ontario, 2014c), and, under leadership from a new Premier, Kathleen Wynne, announced a new agenda to work with teacher unions and school boards to formalize a new process for collective bargaining in the province. Talks designed to facilitate a new process for future collective bargaining in the education sector continued into the fall of 2013, and in April of 2014, Bill 122 was passed, establishing a formalized, two-tiered bargaining system where major financial issues are centrally bargained between the school boards, the provincial government, and the teacher unions, while local matters continue to be negotiated between individual boards and the unions that hold bargaining rights in that particular jurisdiction (Government of Ontario, 2014d).

Moving forward, both government and the teacher unions were hopeful that the new bargaining process would facilitate a smoother negotiation for new contracts during the 2014–2015 school year. Unfortunately, the new process proved to be unclear and challenging as local unions and boards questioned what were local and central issues and how local issues could be determined separately from a provincial agreement on major financial matters. Protracted bargaining and impasses occurred during Spring and Summer 2015. Public secondary teachers in three local districts took strike action in the spring of 2015 and there was concern that the school year would be incomplete. The strikes ended after a labor board ruling deemed them to be unlawful since the strikes were local in nature but primarily over central bargaining issues. Following the ruling, the government passed back-to-work legislation in May. Public elementary teachers, however, instituted a province-wide work-to-rule job action in May of 2015, including their members not participating in Ministry/government initiatives, including provincial testing, and school board directed initiatives. Little progress was made over the summer months. However, by early in the 2015–2016 school year, provincial deals were reached and approved by the majority of members of three out of four teacher unions (OSSTF, OECTA, and AEFO). ETFO, however, expanded their Work to Rule in response to their serious concerns about the process and content of current bargaining. By November 2015, the Premier intervened to indicate a deadline on the timeline for reaching a negotiated agreement. Subsequently, a negotiated central agreement was also reached with ETFO and approved by a majority of their members. Across the four unions' agreements, elements include enhancements to salaries, maintenance of specific working conditions (class sizes, preparation time), a commitment to revisit understandings of professionalism and teachers' professional autonomy, and a hiatus on new Ministry initiatives for the current (2015–2016) school year. In practice, the new two-tier system of bargaining has encountered a range of problems in being implemented and understood.

Central to concerns raised by the teachers' unions and areas of contention with management have been the concept of teachers' professional autonomy, for example of their preparation time, and teachers' working conditions, for example concerns about class sizes and students' needs. While all parties continue to want to reach negotiated solutions and to work together in future, the hallmarks of partnership working and professional trust central to the past decade of Ontario's educational improvements have been brought under scrutiny. Moving forward, a renewed understanding and practice of teachers' collective and individual professionalism and of partnership working with district and school leaders and with the government required vital attention and action. By working together in partnership with all professional associations, a new commitment to Collaborative Professionalism has been enshrined in Policy and Program Memorandum No. 159 to value and include the voices and judgment of all education professionals.

Competitiveness of Salaries   Teachers are placed on a salary grid based on educational qualifications and years of teaching experience. The evaluation of educational qualifications is currently the responsibility of the Qualifications Evaluation Council of Ontario (QECO) and the Certification Department of the Ontario Secondary School Teachers' Federation. A teacher is given a salary rating category (with 1 being the lowest and 4 being the highest), which is used by the school board to place the teacher on the salary grid. Teachers can improve their rating category by completing approved university and/or additional qualification (AQ) courses (e.g., specialist qualification) in a combination acceptable to the evaluating body. The salary grid typically provides for ten years of experience and four qualification categories, although there can be local variations. Usually after ten years, salaries will only move if teachers have not already achieved the highest qualification level or through negotiated increases. In addition to their salary, teachers can also receive allowances for additional responsibilities, or for holding other credentials—for example, as subject department heads, or for holding a master's degree. These allowances are locally negotiated, vary from board to board, and are outside of the funded grid.

In 2012, salaries for Ontario teachers with five years of university education ranged between approximately $45,000 (Year 1 at AI—with a degree and a teaching certificate) and $95,000 (Year 10 at A4—with additional qualification courses). Examples of salary grids for elementary and secondary teachers from the Toronto District School Board effective September 2011 (in Canadian dollars) are in Tables 3–4 and 3–5.

According to a report produced by the Laurier Centre for Economic Research and Policy Analysis (Johnson, 2013), teachers in Ontario

Table 3–4   Elementary Teaching Salaries, based on QECO ratings

Step—number of years of teacher experience	A1	A2	A3	A4
0	44,826	46,910	50,739	54,333
10	74,552	77,878	87,882	92,878

Source: Collective Agreement between the Toronto District School Board and the Elementary Teachers Federation of Ontario, http://www.ett.ca/collective-agreement-2008–2012/.

Table 3–5 Secondary Teaching Salaries, based on OSSTF ratings

Step—number of years of teacher experience	Group 1	Group II	Group III	Group IV
0	45,709	47,834	51,738	55,404
10	76,021	79,414	89,614	94,707

Source: Collective Agreement between The Toronto District School Board and The Ontario Secondary School Teachers' Federation, http://osstftoronto.ca/wp-content/uploads/2014/01/2008–2012-SecondaryCA-Nov11–091.pdf.

earn relatively high salaries, in comparison to the average population of individuals with a university degree working full-time at one job. For instance, based on data from 2011, the salary of $66,893 after five years of teaching is above the 75th percentile of average salaries for comparable individuals with a university degree and working one full time job. After 10 years of teaching, teachers are close to the 90th percentile of salaries within the university-educated group. However, after 10 years, teachers reach the top of the current salary grid, so further increases are dependent on additional qualifications, responsibilities, and/or recognition.

Most interviewees felt that teacher salaries in Ontario were fair:

> I think lots of teachers work very hard for their money. So I don't think we're overpaid, but I think that we are very well compensated for what we do for the number of years of school that we do, for the number of hours that we work, for the job that we are doing, I think we are well paid.
>
> (Heather)

> I think the salaries of teachers in general are fine. . . . At the highest category, we max out at about $89,000/$91,000. I think that's a nice number for a teacher to be making at approximately ten years.
>
> (Wahid)

However, some interviewees noted that beginning teacher compensation is not as high as the starting salaries of some other public service professions and that the salary grid maxes at ten years despite many teachers' long careers.

Standards of Practice   As mentioned previously, the OCT sets out Professional Standards of Practice to guide teacher training and certification as well as in-service practice. These standards, listed below, are intended to describe and embody what it means to be a member of the teaching profession in Ontario:

> *Commitment to Students and Student Learning:* Members are dedicated in their care and commitment to students. They treat students equitably and with respect and are sensitive to factors that influence individual student learning. Members facilitate the development of students as contributing citizens of Canadian society.
>
> *Professional Knowledge:* Members strive to be current in their professional knowledge and recognize its relationship to practice. They understand and reflect on student development, learning theory,

pedagogy, curriculum, ethics, educational research, and related policies and legislation to inform professional judgment in practice.

Professional Practice: Members apply professional knowledge and experience to promote student learning. They use appropriate pedagogy, assessment and evaluation, resources, and technology in planning for and responding to the needs of individual students and learning communities. Members refine their professional practice through ongoing inquiry, dialogue, and reflection.

Leadership in Learning Communities: Members promote and participate in the creation of collaborative, safe, and supportive learning communities. They recognize their shared responsibilities and their leadership roles in order to facilitate student success. Members maintain and uphold the principles of the ethical standards in these learning communities.

Alongside the *Standards of Practice* are a set of Ethical Standards that guide the actions and decisions within the teaching profession. These standards are:

Care: The ethical standard of *Care* includes compassion, acceptance, interest, and insight for developing students' potential. Members express their commitment to students' well-being and learning through positive influence, professional judgment, and empathy in practice.

Respect: Intrinsic to the ethical standard of *Respect* are trust and fair-mindedness. Members honor human dignity, emotional wellness, and cognitive development. In their professional practice, they model respect for spiritual and cultural values, social justice, confidentiality, freedom, democracy, and the environment.

Trust: The ethical standard of *Trust* embodies fairness, openness, and honesty. Members' professional relationships with students, colleagues, parents, guardians, and the public are based on trust.

Integrity: Honesty, reliability, and moral action are embodied in the ethical standard of *Integrity*. Continual reflection assists members in exercising integrity in their professional commitments and responsibilities.

Michael Salvatori explains that such standards are aspirational to inform practice and professionalism:

I think it's more of an aspirational philosophy that these are the standards to which we all aspire and they are meant to inspire our practice and guide our practice, and they are there for reflective practice. . . when I look at them, I think I can't possibly embed all of these standards in my practice every day, and they're not meant to be a checklist to assess our performance, but they are really there to guide us, to inspire us, to encourage the professional dialogue, so I think our approach has been that they are aspirational statements.

Teaching Assignments   Classroom teachers at the primary and junior levels are typically assigned to one group of students and tend to teach the majority of subject areas including math, science, language arts, and social studies. Teaching assignments may change from year to year or they may remain stable, depending on the needs of the school and the expertise of new staff members. There is no formalized looping of teachers and students however and it is not typical for a teacher to stay with a particular group of students as they move grade levels.

Teachers with specializations often teach subjects such as music, art, French, or physical education and are assigned to a number of groups of students. Classroom teachers use this time to plan and prepare lessons, assess student work, or complete other essential tasks related to their teaching. This is illustrated by the student and teacher schedules in Figures 3–14 and 3–15. In this instance the classroom teacher teaches

Figure 3–14 Student Schedule, Grade 4, York Region District School Board

Period	MONDAY	TUESDAY	WEDNESDAY	THURSDAY	FRIDAY
Period 1 8:15 – 8:55 (40 min)	Music	Science/Social Studies	ART	Gym	Science/Social Studies
Period 2 8:55 – 9:35 (40 min)	French	⟶			
Period 3 9:35 – 9:55 (20 min)	Health	Science/Social Studies	Science/Social Studies	Science/Social Studies	Library
RECESS 9:55 – 10:15					
Period 4 10:15–10:55 (40 min)	Science/Social Studies	Science/Social Studies	Science/Social Studies	ART	Gym
Period 5 10:55–11:35 (40 min)	MATH	⟶			
Period 6 11:35–11:55 (20 min)	MATH	⟶			
LUNCH 11:55 – 12:55					
Period 7 12:55 – 1:35 (40 min)	Language	⟶			
Period 8 1:35 – 2:15 (40 min)	Language	⟶			
Period 9 2:15 – 2:35 (20 min)	Language	⟶			
Dismissal / Remedial					

Figure 3–15 Teacher Schedule, Grade 4, York
Region District School Board

Period	MONDAY	TUESDAY	WEDNESDAY	THURSDAY	FRIDAY
Period 1 8:15 – 8:55 (40 min)	PREP	Science/Social Studies	4K Gym	Gym	Science/Social Studies
Period 2 8:55 – 9:35 (40 min)	PREP	PREP	PREP	PREP	PREP
Period 3 9:35 – 9:55 (20 min)	Health	Science/Social Studies	Science/Social Studies	Science/Social Studies	Library
RECESS 9:55 – 10:15					
Period 4 10:15–10:55 (40 min)	Science/Social Studies	Science/Social Studies	Science/Social Studies	4K Gym	Gym
Period 5 10:55–11:35 (40 min)	MATH				
Period 6 11:35–11:55 (20 min)	MATH				
LUNCH 11:55 – 12:55					
Period 7 12:55 – 1:35 (40 min)	Language				
Period 8 1:35 – 2:15 (40 min)	Language				
Period 9 2:15 – 2:35 (20 min)	Language				
Dismissal / Remedial					

health, social studies, science, math, and language arts and preparation periods occur while students are in French and music class. This teacher has a specialization in physical education, however, and also teaches gym class to their own class as well as another class of grade 4 students. When the teacher is teaching gym to the other class, their own class is in art.

In intermediate and senior high, teachers are typically assigned to teach courses based on their specific subject-matter expertise. The extent to which this happens, however, often depends on the size of the school. For instance, in a large school, a teacher with a biology concentration may teach four sections of biology. In a smaller school that same teacher may teach only one section of biology and might be assigned to teach other science classes such as physics or chemistry. While administrators do their best to assign teachers to areas that align with their content areas, sometimes teachers may have to teach outside of their subject area in order to offer students the required curriculum. This is more evident in small, northern schools with low student and staff populations. In these instances an effort is made to provide teachers with resources, mentoring, and professional development to ensure quality teaching and learning takes place under these conditions.

Vignette: A Grade 4/5 Teacher's Day

My school day runs from 8:15–2:35. When I arrive around 8 a.m. I usually go straight into my 15-minute parking lot duty, making sure children cross onto the sidewalk and into the school yard safely. Once the bell rings, I hop into my class, greet the students and start to take care of administrative matters. These are things like permission forms, field trip money, reminders, updates, etc. After that we begin work through an engaging and thought-provoking inquiry-based mathematics activity.

It's 9:55 and we all get a 20-minute recess break that includes a snack. During this time I usually step outside the classroom for a stretch and to chat with my fellow colleagues and friends at the school. Other times, I take care of some online preparation for upcoming classes.

When the students make their way back at 10:15, we move into other subjects like science, social studies, or art—whatever the day of the week may be calling for in the schedule. From 10:35–11:15 is my preparation time. During this time every day my grade partner and I sit down and set up our week for mathematics and other subjects. Because mathematics is so demanding and rich in thinking, we often talk about the learning students are doing and how we can further build on it. The way preparation time is used for collaborative planning is key in the success and workflow for the upcoming days and weeks ahead.

The lunch bell hits at 11:55, and it's a rush to grab your lunch and eat it. During my lunch break, I head down to the staff room and eat at our large communal staff table. It's nice to sit with most staff members and catch up.

The 12:55 bell signals the last leg of the day as the students come back in from their outdoor lunch recess. During this uninterrupted block of time until 2:35, we have literacy time every day. We work through reading and writing conventions and use critical-thinking skills as we collaborate regularly online with our thoughts and ideas to push our thinking. By 2:20 we start to wind down and publish our homework online, pack up, stack chairs and then the bell goes and students file out. After 2:35, I try to tie up loose ends on my side by looking at student work, providing feedback, and checking who has and has not handed items in online. All in a good day's work.

Working Conditions and Teacher Workload   The specific allocation of teachers' time is part of collective bargaining. While there are slight variations as a result of agreements between individual boards and local representatives of the teacher unions, the structure of teacher's daily schedule is similar, regardless of where they are employed. In secondary schools, for example, most teachers teach in three out of four daily time slots, with the fourth allotted for preparation. In primary and elementary schools, most teachers have 240 minutes of preparation each week. However, as Lori Foote explains, these preparation periods may be used in a number of ways outside of preparing for instruction, and teachers also have assigned duties outside of the instructional day:

> That prep period can also be used to fill in for absent colleagues, to do hall duty, library duty, to go out and do bus duty. There are a variety of duties. . . Also, before school and after school and at lunch time, teachers attend a variety of meetings. Department meetings, committee meetings, school success meetings, meetings about a student in particular where the group of teachers who has that particular student may want to come together and discuss ways to assist the student. So a teacher's time may be regulated by a collective agreement, that's on paper, and the reality, when you go into a class every day, you're prepped and you're teaching and things like that, but outside of that class, there's still all kinds of responsibilities and all kinds of tasks and duties that you do before and after school or on your lunch time, or on a weekend, whenever it is. So what you see in black and white is not the actual experience.
>
> (Lori Foote, OSSTF)

As outlined in Figure 3–16, a study conducted by the OECTA (OECTA, 2006) on teachers' workload in 2006 reported that full time elementary teachers in the English-Catholic elementary system spend 25.2 hours teaching in the classroom each working week.

In addition to teaching time, teachers spent 7.4 hours per week on teaching preparation and 7.4 hours per week evaluating tests and assignments. Seventy-two percent of the total work hours for full-time elementary teachers was dedicated to teaching, preparing to teach and grading. The remaining 28% of the workweek was comprised of other work-related activities: 2.8 hours per week for working with students outside of class time; 2.5 hours for volunteering for extracurricular activities; 2.3 hours per week for attending staff meetings, meeting with colleagues, and administrative work; and 2.2 hours per week for professional development pursuits. These teachers also spent time supervising students on

Figure 3–16 Secondary Teachers' Average Work Week

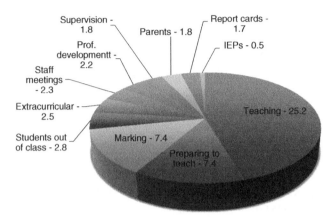

Average work week - in hours
(average work week = 55.7 hours)

Supervision - 1.8
Parents - 1.8
Report cards - 1.7
Prof. developmentt - 2.2
IEPs - 0.5
Staff meetings - 2.3
Extracurricular - 2.5
Teaching - 25.2
Students out of class - 2.8
Marking - 7.4
Preparing to teach - 7.4

Source: OECTA 2006, p. 6.

school property, bus duty, communicating with parents, student evaluation reports (called report cards), and other forms of student assessment
such as individual education plans (IEPs).

While there has been attention to workload and working conditions
in recent years and additional financial and human resources in the education system, workload and working conditions continues to be an
area of concern. As part of a memorandum of understanding signed by
ETFO and the Ontario government in 2013, a large-scale study of elementary teacher workload and its impact on professionalism (Link 3-19)
was conducted in 2014 (Directions Evidence and Policy Research
Group, 2014). Drawing on survey data from almost 3,000 elementary
teachers, the study found that the average elementary teacher dedicates
almost 25 hours to noninstructional tasks per week in addition to their
25 hours of classroom teaching. A breakdown of this noninstructional
time is provided in Table 3–6.

The study also identified, however, a number of factors that helped to
lessen the impact that increased workloads had on teachers' satisfaction
with their working conditions. These included shared decision making,
collaborative working environments, and a school-wide student orientation that focuses on academics. The extent to which respondents agreed

Table 3–6 Average Use of Noninstructional Time per Week

As a teacher of this school, during your most recent complete calendar week, how many 60-minute hours did you spend on the following tasks?

	Mean hours: minutes	n
Individual planning or preparation of lessons either at school or out of school	7:42	1743
Team work and dialogue with colleagues within this school	2:18	1888
Assessing. correcting, evaluating, or marking student work	3:54	1793
Counseling students (providing social or emotional support to students outside of the time devoted to teaching)	1:06	2164
Student supervision outside of class (lunch room, hall, or playground supervision, for example)	1:24	2032
General administrative work (including communication, paperwork, photocopying, and other clerical duties you undertake in your job as teacher)	2:36	1850
Communication and cooperation with parents or guardians	1:18	2170
Engaging in extracurricular activities (e.g., sports, clubs, and cultural activities after school)	1:06	2154
Completing reports required by principal, school board, or ministry of education	2:12	2057
Supervising a student teacher as the primary supervisor	0:30	2198
Providing extra help to students outside of class time	0:54	2165

Source: Directions Evidence and Policy Research Group, 2014, p. 43.

that their school promoted specific aspects of these ideals, however, was variable. As outlined in Table 3.7, the most frequently prevalent forms of collaborative activities were: sharing my teaching materials with others; engaging in discussions about the learning development of specific students; exchanging teaching materials with colleagues; and meeting with colleagues to instructional improvement. This emphasis on professional collaboration focused on instruction is consistent with Ontario's theory of action to develop and embed collaborative, collective professional capacity.

Table 3–7 Frequency of Collaborative Activities

	Domain	% Never	% Once a year or less	% 2–4 times a year	% 5–10 times a year	% 1–3 times a month	% Once a week or more	% Total	n
Teach jointly as a team in the same class	C	45.2%	13.1%	11.1%	7.5%	6.7%	16.4%	100%	2543
Observe other teachers' classes and provide feedback	C	62.2%	19.9%	8.8%	3.5%	3.4%	2.2%	100%	2543
Engage in joint activities or projects that involve different classes or age groups	C	16.1%	15.1%	25.0%	14.8%	14.9%	14.0	100%	2542
Engage in discussions about the learning development of specific students	C	1.9%	4.8%	11.6%	11.4%	21.0%	49.2%	100%	2536
Work with other teachers in my school to ensure common standards in evaluations for assessing student progress	C	15.0	13.3%	24.9%	15.7%	17.3%	13.9%	100%	2541
Attend team conferences	C	30.5%	14.3%	19.8%	15.3%	14.2%	5.9%	100%	2537
Take part in collaborative professional learning	C	5.6%	11.0%	31.6%	24.5%	17.9%	9.4%	100%	2536
Review data from diagnostic assessments to improve instruction	C	8.8%	12.0%	29.2%	16.7%	23.0%	10.4%	100%	2534
Review data from EQAO assessments to improve instruction	C	15.0%	33.6%	37.9%	8.4%	3.6%	1.4%	100%	2538
Meet with colleagues to discuss instructional improvement	C	9.2%	9.2%	20.8%	17.0%	21.1%	22.8%	100%	2537
Exchange teaching materials with colleagues	S	2.5%	4.1%	9.2%	12.0%	24.9%	47.3%	100%	2540
Share my teaching material with others	S	1.5%	1.8%	7.4%	12.6%	23.5%	53.2%	100%	2540

Source: Directions Evidence and Policy Research Group, 2014, p. 53.

The study of teachers' professionalism and workload (Directions Evidence and Policy Research Group, 2014) recommended continuing attention to professional learning for teachers to help manage workloads. However, the report also noted that, where possible, the Ministry should pay attention to the quantity and timelines of existing and new initiatives to avoid exacerbating workloads and initiative fatigue.

Vignette: A Grade 7 Teacher's Day

My teaching day begins between 7:30–7:45 a.m., depending on my arrival to school. I begin my day by reviewing my "To-Dos" for the day, which includes items related to my teaching assignments—English as a Second Language (ESL) resource teacher (AM) and grade 7 Health and Physical Education teacher (PM). I also have duties related to being the grade 7 chairperson, which is a Position of Responsibility within schools.

Preparing for my AM teaching assignment as an ESL Resource teacher consists of reviewing the lessons that I will be implementing for the English Language Learners (ELLs) that I will be providing support to on this day. As a grade 7 Health and Physical Education teacher, my preparation time is focused on organizing the various equipment that will be used in the day's lessons.

Around 8:30 a.m., my principal and I meet to touch base to update each other regarding various school-related items, such as school safety matters that may require attention. Our informal meeting usually concludes in 10–15 minutes, as it is predominately an opportunity for my principal and I to brief each other on items that we should keep in mind for further discussion at a later time.

Being that the majority of our staff arrive to school by this time, I use the next 15 minutes to touch base with any staff members that are involved in my list of "To-Dos" for the day or the near future. For example, meeting with the teacher responsible for the upcoming Future Aces assembly to select a date and time for the assembly.

At 8:51–9:51 a.m., I have my daily supervision duty at our main entrance in which I am able to greet all 280 of our students.

My instructional day begins at 9:01, in which I engage in my ESL Resource teacher duties for the first four periods of the day. In three out of five days of the week, I have one prep period, which is approximately 35 minutes long. I usually use my AM prep period to reflect on the morning's lessons and to plan follow-up lessons. If time permits,

I use the remaining time to prepare for my PM Physical Education duties.

Depending on the day of the week, I use my lunch period (40 minutes) to either oversee our house league or supervise our Future Aces student committees. If it happens to be a day in which I am not involved in one of our school's cocurricular activities, I use my lunch period to set up equipment that would be used in the afternoon's Physical Education lessons.

I have an afternoon prep period (30 minutes) four out of five days of the week, which is used to address the remaining items on my "To-Dos" list. The items I address at this time are usually related to my role as the grade 7 chairperson, such as planning curriculum meetings.

After school (3:01–4:00 p.m.), I coach one of our school teams and/ or address the remaining items on my "To-Dos" list. If I do not have a Leadership Team meeting or a committee meeting to attend, I usually depart school between 4:00–4:30 p.m.

Induction: The New Teacher Induction Program (NTIP)

> NTIP is informed by four goals to enhance teachers' efficacy, practice, confidence, and commitment to continuous learning. . . So there's the goal of increasing their confidence, that as a new teacher you have the supports around you to be successful. The feeling of the new teacher's sense of self efficacy, that what they are doing is making a difference for their students, to improve their instructional practices. . . at a quicker rate. And then the goal. . . is to enhance the ongoing commitment to professional learning, and so if we do a really great job of mentoring our new teacher, they'll become outstanding mentors not just to their students but also to the next generation of new teachers.
>
> (Jim Strachan, Teaching Policy and Standards Branch, Ontario Ministry of Education)

All first-year new teachers hired to a permanent contract in Ontario are expected to participate in the New Teacher Induction Program (NTIP). Established in 2006 and funded by the Ministry, NTIP is intended to provide comprehensive support in terms of early professional development to new teachers placed in regular teaching positions or long-term occasional positions in Ontario school boards. Long-term occasional teachers (LTOs) hold assignments that are a minimum of four months in length. For the purposes of the NTIP, a first-year LTO teacher is a certified occasional teacher in the first long-term assignment, with that assignment being 97 or more consecutive school days as a substitute for the same teacher.

Because of the current labor market conditions for teachers in Ontario, many "new" teachers have in fact completed their initial teacher education and certification several years previously. Becoming a "new" teacher with a full-time teaching position is an important milestone (Link 3-20):

> My own experience working with new teachers, I would say because of the oversupply, people who are entering the profession are highly committed, they have not just graduated and got a job in September, they've done years and years of daily occasional teaching, long term occasional teaching. They've seen the process through over the course of, in some cases, a decade. And now become a "new teacher," so the folks that are entering the profession have a high level of commitment.
>
> (Jim Strachan, Teaching and Policy Standards Branch, Ontario Ministry of Education)

> There's lots of evidence that the more experienced teachers can deliver a better educational experience for their student, but the core notion of the NTIP was, "how do we accelerate that experience." Everything from helping the teacher get comfortable in the physical setting and where the resources are faster to supporting them in terms of all the different issues they will run into with the kids and their parents and the school, etc. and how to handle those faster. So the whole notion behind it was how do we accelerate that experience so that ultimately the students are getting that improved experiential education experience that you get from a more experienced teacher. That was sort of the core, the genesis of it.
>
> (Paul Anthony, Teaching Policy and Standards Branch, Ontario Ministry of Education)

NTIP includes three components: (1) an orientation to the school and school board; (2) ongoing mentoring by more experienced teachers throughout the first year; (3) professional development and training appropriate to the needs of new teachers. Principals conduct two performance appraisals throughout the first 12 months, and if not satisfactory, teachers are given up to 24 months to improve. Once the program is completed, the OCT is notified within 60 days and a notation is made on the teacher's record of certification. Boards of education may decide to extend NTIP supports to the second year for either permanent hires or

LTO teachers. The extension to a second year developed in recognition that after one year of NTIP, new teachers were saying:

> "I'm only just now at the end of my first year, realizing what I don't know. I only know now what I don't know," and they came to us and said, "what about second year?" because second year wasn't initially part of it. That's another one of those things that have evolved directly from the field and people being comfortable saying "I just realized what I don't know and I need more time.
>
> (Paul Anthony, Teaching Policy and Standards Branch,
> Ontario Ministry of Education)

According to data collected by the OCT in 2012, participation in NTIP is high, with 92% of first-year teachers in regular teaching positions, as well as 25% of those in first-time long-term occasional positions, reporting being involved. Similarly, 81% of regular appointees in second year and 37% of long-term occasional teachers reported that they are in the NTIP. Mentors and other experienced teachers involved in the NTIP received positive evaluations from participating new teachers. The majority (90%) of new teachers rated the support they received for practical day-to-day teaching responsibilities as "very helpful" or "helpful" (Ontario College of Teachers, 2012, p. 36).

Mentor Selection

Typically, mentors are colleagues at the same school as beginning teachers. Mentorship is voluntary, although school administrators may invite individuals to take on the role to support a beginning teacher. The following criteria are listed in the NTIP Induction Elements Manual (2010) (Link 3-21) suggesting that a mentor must:

○ Be in good standing with the Ontario College of Teachers;
○ Be an experienced teaching professional, skilled in working with both adults and students;
○ Be knowledgeable and skilled in current curriculum and teaching/ learning strategies;
○ Have demonstrated skills in problem solving;
○ Be an excellent role model of a teaching professional;
○ Be open to the views and feedback of others and be a continual lifelong learner;
○ Be an effective listener and communicator;
○ Have effective interpersonal skills.

Mentees have the option of choosing a mentor or having one assigned to them. Most of the teachers in our study chose their own mentors or were approached by grade-level partners in their school who offered to be their mentors. Increasingly, rather than having only one mentor, new teachers are working with several mentors to support different aspects of their teaching practice and career:

> We think of building a mentoring web. It can be one to one, but it could also be online, it could be a group, it could be a community of practice, it could be informal. Mentorship can be customized based on a person's individual needs. To me it's the ultimate personalization of learning. When the mentor and the new teacher meet, the agenda for the learning are the needs of the new teacher. And that's really powerful.
>
> (Jim Strachan, Teaching Policy and Standards Branch)

Mentor Training

Also listed in the *NTIP Induction Elements Manual* (2010) are components of the mentor training program which is intended to be well structured and based on a curriculum that includes training in consulting, collaborating, and coaching; for example:

- ○ How to develop a mentoring plan;
- ○ Listening and building rapport;
- ○ Sharing information and sources;
- ○ Using appropriate language;
- ○ Conferencing skills and providing meaningful feedback;
- ○ Integration of mentoring activities and ongoing personal and professional development;
- ○ Building capacity for high achievement;
- ○ Assurance that confidentiality between mentors and new teachers is respected;
- ○ A clear and safe exit procedure for both mentor and new teacher in case of noncompatibility;
- ○ Dealing with a teacher in crisis.

Mentoring

Schools may choose from different mentoring models such as one-to-one mentoring and large- or small-group mentoring. Rather than evaluative, the mentorship relationship is intended to be supportive. Mentors provide guidance that is suited to the individual needs of the teacher to help new teachers develop their capacity for learning and growth. Specific supports provided by the mentors of teachers in this study included assisting with goal setting, introducing mentees to professional networks, informing mentees of professional development opportunities, modeling professional relationships, offering tips and advice around classroom management, being a sounding board for teaching strategies, providing insight into the school climate and related politics, and offering emotional support during the first few days of schools:

> In the chaos of getting all your planners and stuff in the half an hour before the kids come in. . . I remember him sitting beside me and saying, "I know you are terrified, but it actually doesn't get any easier, whether that makes it better or worse." And it did make it better for me. I felt that I wasn't out on my own.
>
> (Heather)

> My mentor provided a lot of goal setting support. So sitting together and figuring out what were my goals for the year. They were all centred on my personal visions, but it was in the context of a school. . . . Getting more familiar with how I can increase engagement, which went back to classroom management and then how I could create a broader network. . . So we sat down and we looked at professional development opportunities for classroom management and she walked with me into the Principal's Office to have a conversation and modelled how you could just create that personal relationship that you would need to broaden your network.
>
> (Tina)

Shared release time for mentors and new teachers to collaborate is provided by the NTIP, and can be used for co-planning, classroom observation, and collaborative assessment of student work, among other areas. Participants in our study identified these days as being very valuable to their initial development as a practicing teacher:

> I was given six [release time days] and it was my option to share three of those with my mentor so that we could do professional development together. . . I didn't have to, but I thought it was kind of courteous to do so. . . We talked about teaching and planning and some off-the-record types of advice like what the best ways of doing things were inside the classroom. She was very willing to share, very giving and she provided a lot for me so that made everything worthwhile.
>
> (Wahid)

Some of the teachers in our study had also volunteered to be NTIP mentors, and spoke very highly of their experiences:

> As a mentor, I frequently check in with my mentee to make sure all is well and listen to any questions or issues that may arise. We have frequent discussions, which usually lead to more questions. The goal is to coach and not teach so that the mentee becomes more proficient and confident in their role as teacher.
>
> (Cathy)

Indeed consistent with Ontario's emphasis on developing shared leadership, a positive benefit of NTIP is growing both future teachers to support students and as mentors and teacher leaders to support other teachers:

> The most powerful piece. . . is the mentors themselves, the relationships that are successful, it's reciprocal, and so they are rejuvenated in their own passion for teaching. They feel more connected to their colleagues. They're feeling more positively, not just about interacting with that new teacher, but more involved in their staff or engaged in their work. . . these are all examples of small "l" teacher leadership. So you are leading without title. You are doing it out of a really strong desire to support others, but you are being supported and engaged in doing the work and it is very, very satisfying work for most mentors.
>
> (Jim Strachan, Teaching Policy and Standards Branch, Ontario Ministry of Education)

Continuing Professional Learning

> I feel that I have a lot of opportunity for self-directed learning. I think that people, who want self-directed learning, also have to be self-directed learners.
>
> (Heather)

A key element of Ontario's theory of action and implementation strategies is a focus on capacity building to support continuing professional learning for new and experienced teachers. There is a vast array of professional learning opportunities and supports, including formal additional qualifications (AQs), provincial professional learning initiatives and resources, professional learning led by educators' organizations including teacher unions, school board and school level professional learning, and individual opportunities for teachers to advance their knowledge, skills, and practices. For example, a survey by the Ontario College of Teachers (2012) indicated that the majority of new teachers

Table 3–8 New Teacher Engagement in Professional Development

Nature of professional development	2010 graduates (in first year of teaching)	2009 graduates (in second year of teaching)
Participating in formal courses	50%*	56%
Collaborative learning in my school	46%	57%
Collaborative learning beyond my school	40%	46%
Engaging with subject or specialist associations	35%	40%
Participating in school self-evaluation	31%	37%
Undertaking action research	24%	30%

Source: Ontario College of Teachers, 2012.

were participating in professional development with the most common forms of development outlined in Table 3–8.

More recently, a 2014 study of teachers' workload and professionalism (Directions Evidence and Policy Research Group, 2014) also indicated a high level of participation in various professional development opportunities among practicing teachers. As indicated in Figure 3–17,

Figure 3–17 Number of Professional Learning Activities During Working Hours Over the Past 12 Months

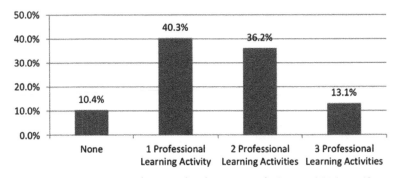

Source: Directions Evidence and Policy Research Group, 2014, p. 68.

90% of respondents reported participating in professional learning activities during the school day, with almost 50% of teacher respondents reporting participation in two of more activities over the past 12 months. As outlined in Figure 3–18, the professional learning activities engaged in outside of the regular work day include a balance between individual research or participation in additional qualifications or study and also collaborative professional learning activities, including participation in learning networks with other teachers, collaborative professional research, and/or mentoring or coaching activities.

Below we outline some of the available professional learning opportunities for teachers.

Additional Qualifications

More than 40,000 teachers voluntarily take AQ programs every year to upgrade their qualifications and enhance their practice. AQ programs are offered by Ontario Faculties of Education, teachers' federations, and other organizations and are accredited by OCT. Completing AQ courses also repositions teachers on the salary scale and is one of the only ways for teachers to advance their salary once they have reached the end of the 10-year scale (see earlier section on salaries). That being said, teachers undertake AQs for a range of professional reasons:

Figure 3–18 Learning Activities Over the Past 12 Months Outside of Regular Work Day

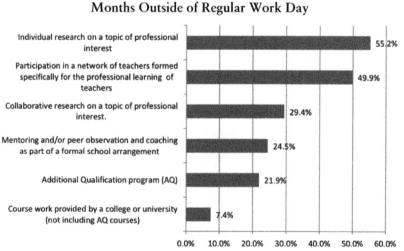

Source: Directions Evidence and Policy Research Group, 2014, p. 69.

In some cases, they are to gain greater depth in an area of study or specialization. In other cases, they're to increase the breadth that teachers have and so allow them to teach to learn about teaching in a different division. If they were certified as a teacher of primary/junior and have an interest of eventually teaching at the intermediate level then they would take one of these courses to increase their breadth. In some cases, it's to make them more marketable, to have access to employment. In some cases, it does allow them to move up on the salary scale in the first few years of the profession, and in most cases, I think it is self-identified areas of interest.

(Michael Salvatori, OCT)

The programs are voluntary, taken on a teacher's own personal time (e.g., during the summer), and the cost of participation is covered by the teacher (up to $1,000 per program). Popular AQs include special education, English as a second language, and French as a second language. New AQs are also developed to keep current with latest developments in education and needs in Ontario. Latest offerings have focused on current provincial priority areas, including: the use of technology integrated with pedagogy; the inclusive classroom; understanding and supporting First Nations, Métis, and Inuit education; and mathematics.

Alongside developing new priority content for AQs, a recent development has been the modularization of some AQ courses so teachers have flexibility to study individual modules at a pace that suits them rather than committing to the full AQ. As Susan Perry from OECTA explained:

The other thing that we have just started at OECTA with the permission of the College of Teachers [OCT] is to allow module learning. We are looking at special education and classroom management, some of those key areas that teachers may not want to take a full AQ, but they may say "this year I have three kids with autism and so I really want to learning more about autism," and they can take a module in any order. They can choose the module as professional learning [in its own right] or they can choose to put it towards an AQ course. It allows teachers flexibility and also in terms of cost. I look at our new teachers who really need and want some additional information around some of those classroom management or special education areas, but they don't have $600 to pay for an AQ course, but they do have $100 to pay for a module and get enough information to get started. That's an exciting initiative and we are seeing that teachers are very interested in professional learning in a modular format.

Provincial Initiatives

The Ontario strategies place a priority emphasis on professional capacity building. Ministry strategies and initiatives generally include resources to invest in, and support, professional learning and improvements in practices. In summary form, key elements of provincial initiatives have included:

o Whole system supports for all schools combined with intervention partnerships with schools at different performance levels.

o Targeted supports and interventions for students and schools that are struggling to improve.

o Support for professional collaboration, teams, and collective capacity within schools and districts with focus on evidence about student learning.

o Range of professional learning, development, and resources for specific education priority areas, plus teacher quality and leadership.

o Facilitation of networks to share and support improved practices across schools and districts.

o Development of culture, value, and practice of using research, evaluation, and data to inform, monitor, and adapt strategies and practices.

o Substantial resources and infrastructure for system capacity.

o Creating an enabling policy environment and partnerships with the profession, stakeholders, and public.

Two main strategies have focused on building professional capacity to support student achievement: the Literacy and Numeracy Strategy has emphasized improving instructional capacity and practices to support student learning and achievement in elementary schools; and the Student Success Strategy has focused on transforming high school programs, pathways, and support for students to graduate from high school and transition to postsecondary apprenticeships, college, university, or work destinations. Initially, the two strategies—for elementary schools and for secondary schools—were separate; however increasingly, there is a focus on aligning and developing capacity across K–12 with an emphasis on instructional leadership and teaching practices:

> We (LNS and Student Success) started out as two separate strategies, from two very different points of view. Student Success (grades 7 to 12) was about creating programs that would build new, relevant,

engaging programming and learning experiences for kids, targeted to build success for all students, but particularly to be successful with those students who would have walked away. Specialist High Skills Majors, Dual Credits focused primarily on students who were the most likely to walk away from school by funding new learning experiences. Student Success teachers were put in place in every secondary school to build an infrastructure with a focus on these kids who were in greatest need of support to be more successful. At the elementary level, with the Literacy and Numeracy Strategy work, right from the very beginning, it was about working with teachers and principals, building the capacity of teachers and leaders. Some of that, I think, is a product of the fact that in elementary we are dealing with 4,000 schools as units of change and in secondary, there are 900 schools. But I think those two different perspectives, one being about program and structural change and the other about instructional change reflect strategic entry points for improvement. The two strategy approaches have become one division in the Ministry and that I think was really important, because it has brought our work together. It is much more now one student achievement strategy. It's becoming increasingly both at elementary and secondary about instructional change and instructional improvement, building capacity of staff on the ground to make the changes in response to student needs.

(Mary Jean Gallagher, Student Achievement Division,
Ontario Ministry of Education)

A K–12 focus on improving instruction is embedded into school board and school planning and implementation processes. For example, the K–12 System Implementation and Monitoring (SIM) initiative provides funding to support school districts to identify a System Implementation Monitoring Team to work with School Improvement Teams within and across networks of schools to improve pedagogy and instructional leadership. According to the Literacy and Numeracy Secretariat, through professional dialogue and study, teams will further develop their capacity to:

○ observe, describe, and analyze student work
○ set specific goals and targets for student learning
○ plan and implement specific teaching and learning strategies
○ monitor student achievement results and adjust strategies as needed
○ support the professional learning required to raise achievement
○ align resources to meet achievement goals
○ engage students and parents in school improvement

A K–12 School Effectiveness Framework (Link 3-22, see Figure 3–19) is intended to inform and provide a focus for identification of goals, priorities, and actions at the school district level through the Board Improvement Plan for Student Achievement (BIPSA) and for schools through School Improvement Plans.

School boards receive funding and support from the Ministry to support professional learning and capacity building linked to priority strategies and needs each year, for example in 2014–2015, examples of capacity building funding provided to school boards included attention to: special education K–12, professional learning communities to support the development of French language, support for Aboriginal students, mathematics support, differentiated instruction, literacy, innovative practices integrating assessment and feedback, teacher inquiry, and supporting transitions for students between grades and schools (for additional information on this funding please visit http://faab.edu.gov. on.ca/Memos/B2014/B05E.pdf).

There is a complex theory and practice of professional capacity building for educational improvement embodied in, and evolving from, the

Figure 3–19 K–12 School Effectiveness Framework

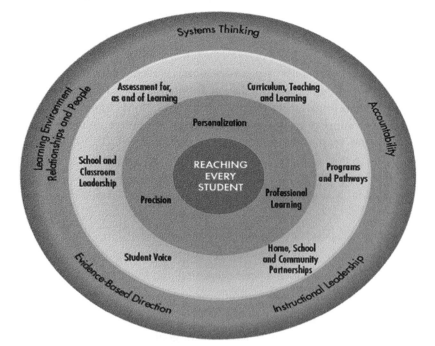

Source: Ontario Ministry of Education, 2013c.

educational reforms in Ontario. Consistent with Ontario's theory of action for tri-level reform, there is commitment to continuous improvement with accompanying processes at classroom, school, board, and provincial levels in combination with differentiation of professional learning and resources to meet the variety of student and professional needs across the province. However, the emphasis is not simply on each level of the education sector, it is about developing a coherent approach to system-wide reform. For example, as Mary Jean Gallagher comments about board and school improvement planning processes:

> Things like BIPSA [Board Improvement Plans for Student Achievement], the School Effectiveness Framework, school improvement planning structures and Board improvement planning structures fit into what I would refer to as the systemization of reform. It's how you take it from happening in some isolated schools or one Board and try to build it as a comprehensive activity for everyone. It can't simply be done by saying, "Oh, we're going to have a policy that says Boards have to have an improvement plan or schools have to have an improvement plan." What we were building was an infrastructure to engage reflective thinking, and also to deliver reform, but the reform we were delivering was not just the reform of the government's making or the Ministry's making, it was the reform of the schools' making and the School Boards' making and building that partnership. So it became about a structured way of systematizing the de-privatization of teaching and leading.
>
> (Mary Jean Gallagher, Student Achievement Division,
> Ontario Ministry of Education)

While "systematizing" approaches to improvement, the emphasis is not intended to be a standardization of top-down directives. Rather the goal is to identify, value, and develop professional capacity linked to professional accountability:

> When we're working with Boards or schools or teachers, it's a treasure hunt not a witch hunt, and all of our processes are founded on a deep respect and regard for the work of teaching and learning and a deep respect and regard for our educators. We would never go in and deliver to them "look, here is 'the' strategy for how you teach math, or 'the' strategy for how you teach literacy and if you would just do it this way results will improve," because that is not how kids learn. Kids learn when you have a dedicated teacher who understands deeply where kids are and has a whole backpack full of teaching strategies. The professional capacity, the professional judgement

comes in deciding how you are going to do that. So the question for us is how do we work with teachers all across the province and leaders in ways that share that professional judgement and competency and enhance it and build it. How we work in partnership with them?

(Mary Jean Gallagher, Student Achievement Division,
Ontario Ministry of Education)

The intent is fostering a "collaborative professionalism" throughout the education system:

I don't believe that professionals are independent of each other, and certainly in teaching, they can't be independent. They need to be interdependent. And so I talk less about autonomy and more about a collaborative professionalism that is, in my view, the responsibility of a professional educator to engage in that collaborative discourse that augments personal reflection and research with a robust dialogue about improved practice and practicing to improve.

(Mary Jean Gallagher, Student Achievement Division,
Ontario Ministry of Education)

As noted previously, however, the recent labor negotiations had centered on teacher unions' concerns about a perceived potential erosion of teachers' professional autonomy and calls for a reduction in the volume and nature of Ministry initiatives.

Through fostering individual and collective capacity in schools and school boards, while also learning and sharing across the province, the aim is shared leadership and ownership for system and school improvement:

Here is a quintessentially Canadian approach or quote for you. Wayne Gretzky, when he was a professional hockey player, was asked how he was so successful. He talked about the fact that he moves where the puck is going. Part of what we are doing here is working with the system to create a common focus and then using that to telegraph where the puck is going and people move there. It is a collaborative leadership at the same time that it's a horizontal knowledge mobilization exercise.

(Mary Jean Gallagher, Student Achievement Division,
Ontario Ministry of Education)

For teachers' professional learning specifically, the approaches involved in the Ministry of Education's Student Achievement strategies have evolved over time. The earliest phase of the Literacy and Numeracy Strategy involved "building consensus" to engage educators in school boards and schools in a shared purpose of a priority commitment to improving student achievement and equity (Glaze, Mattingley, & Andrews, 2013). A starting point was funding for Local District Initiatives to foster action and innovation linked to local school board needs, plus a parallel process of identifying and sharing existing successful and promising practices in and across school boards and schools (Campbell & Fullan, 2006). The Literacy and Numeracy Strategy quickly placed a central focus on capacity building across the province of Ontario. Early strategies, beginning in 2005, included large-scale provincial training on literacy, numeracy, differentiated instruction, and assessment through summer programs for teachers and provincial events for school and school board leaders. Increasingly, training was provided to teams involving teachers and administrators collaborating together. Feedback from these events was very positive; however, participants also indicated a desire for less province-wide events requiring teachers and administrators to attend centralized training outside of their school or school board, and rather an interest in access to on-demand resources linked to evidence of effective practices and supports for job-embedded collaborative learning opportunities within and across classrooms, schools, and boards (see Campbell and The Literacy and Numeracy Secretariat, 2008; Glaze & Campbell, 2007).

Subsequent phases of the Literacy and Numeracy Strategy included increasing availability and access across the province to professional learning resources to support all teachers and students to succeed. For example, the Ministry provides a range of professional learning resources and materials for educators, students, and parents. Over three million visitors have accessed the Student Achievement Division's Webcasts for Educators, YouTube resources, and online videos. In addition to province-wide resources, the Student Achievement Division's approach to capacity building has become increasingly focused on local professional collaboration and inquiry centered on understanding students' learning, using data, and sharing knowledge and practices across schools, districts, and provincially. For example, initiatives have included an emphasis on developing collaborative inquiry processes involving a culture of professional inquiry and collaboration, building pedagogical content knowledge, engaging in professional discourse to learn, reflect on, and improve practices, and ensuring professional learning is relevant to students' learning in local contexts (Literacy and Numeracy Secretariat, 2010; Campbell, 2014). Funding and resources to support professional collaborative inquiry is being provided from early learning through to high schools. For an example view the following video of the Collaborative

Inquiry for Learning—Mathematics (CIL-M) http://www.edu.gov.on.ca/eng/research/cilm.html.

As one interviewee commented:

> I think that one of the things that the Literacy and Numeracy Secretariat has demonstrated is change. So we started off with a dissemination model of professional learning. . . Then we shifted and revised and evolved our ideas about most effective approaches to change through professional learning. Now we are implementing change through a variety of different initiatives that support collaborative inquiry. . . They provide different entry points for professional learning through collaborative inquiry founded on the idea of forming a question based on individual student needs and working toward finding ways of supporting that.
>
> (Judi Kokis, Literacy and Numeracy Secretariat,
> Ontario Ministry of Education)

Evidence across the LNS initiatives suggests considerable changes and improvements in professionals' knowledge, efficacy, and practices, with benefits for student engagement and learning. However, there are variations in the effectiveness of specific initiatives (Campbell, 2014) with evidence suggesting the importance of quality pedagogical and content knowledge being vital for supporting improved student outcomes.

Alongside system-wide support for school effectiveness, improvement planning, professional collaboration, and teacher learning there are also targeted supports for schools, student groups, and/or areas of practice that are identified as needing additional assistance which have had considerable impact on raising achievement and reducing performance gaps (Campbell, 2014). Consistent with the theory of action for "positive support and pressure," the strategy for lower performing schools involves provision of targeted resources and supports for leadership and teacher development through collaborative capacity building. For example, the Student Success strategy includes a School Support Initiative for schools identified based on low achievement results:

> It is one of the ones that we work most closely with teachers. In school we look at schools that are well below the provincial rate in terms of performance indicators for student achievement and the Principal is a key driver of that, and so we try and leverage the capacity of the Principal. We work with the Ontario Principals' Council and the Catholic Principals' Council of Ontario to provide support to do that. We have provided some coaching for the Principal to support this, but at the

core of the process is a school team. The school team will focus in on two or three courses where the performance gaps are. They generally tend to be applied courses. The team of teachers and the Principal leader come together in the school and the Principal has access to coaching, but they also come together with us [the Ministry's Student Success branches] we work through how their process is going in terms of assessing the student need and looking at the teacher learning need in terms of what they need to help the students to improve, and then we provide them with what we call "high yield strategies." These are a collection of different approaches that they can look at trying. When they select which courses and which students they will focus on, based on the evidence they have, they then look at the specific strategies they will implement. Then they monitor their process and results as that happens. They implement their strategies and they see what the effect is, based on an assessment of students before they start and an assessment of students once they finish. It's a collaborative inquiry, and when we bring those teams of schools together from across Ontario there's an opportunity to network, and the teachers are learning from each other. It's a really good teacher engagement tool. I think there's a lot of power in that and I think that's why it works—because the teachers are deeply engaged in the process at all levels and stages.

(Rob Andrews, Student Success/Learning to 18 Implementation, Innovation and Support Branch, Ontario Ministry of Education)

Through providing funding for release time and professional learning, professional resources, and supports as well as a range of system-wide, differentiated, and targeted initiatives, the Ministry of Education is engaged in significant work to develop teachers' capacity in partnership with schools, boards, and provincial organizations.

Teacher Organization Led Initiatives

The teachers' federations play a significant role in the provision of professional learning in Ontario, with thousands of teachers participating annually in activities, developed "by teachers, for teachers." Opportunities throughout the school year include short-term experiences such as one- to three-day workshops on a variety of topics including leadership skills, curriculum delivery, and equity mindedness as well as longer-term experiences like ETFO's yearlong teacher action research program, Reflections on Practice (ROP). Teacher organizations also support development of curriculum resources and materials:

We've produced all kinds of curriculum initiatives. We have what is called our "Common Threads" project, which produced curriculum documents that our teachers can use. There are lessons, there's videos, there are reproducible materials and resources, and we provide the funding for that. We have teams of educators who come in and, for example, we've done one on the sweatshops in Guatemala. We did one on HIV/AIDS in South Africa, and so we send our curriculum team that applies for this and they go there to these countries and they research and they talk to the people there and they live there for a week or two depending on the length of the project, and they come back and they create these ready-made curriculum projects. We also had one on our First Nations, and we had a very successful curriculum resources produced on that that are very much used by our members and other members, other teacher members across the province. So we are very committed to that educational piece, very committed to that curriculum development, very committed to supporting members who go forward for professional development opportunity.

(Lori Foote, OSSTF)

Teacher organizations also partner with subject association, the Ministry of Education, and other appropriate organizations to deliver a range of professional learning resources and activities during the school year and over the summer months. ETFO's Summer Academy and OEC-TA's Summer Institutes, for example, offer a wide variety of workshops and collaborative sessions, many of which are designed and delivered by teachers themselves. In the summer of 2014, over 3,000 teachers voluntarily participated in summer programs provided in partnership with the OTF on provincial priority topics including mathematics, technology, and mental health. Other union-sponsored professional learning includes a variety of conferences, collaborative professional learning opportunities, AQ courses, and union schools which prepare teachers to take on various leadership roles within the union itself.

Professional learning through Ontario's teacher organizations is very teacher-driven and designed to meet member learning needs as assessed through member surveys and other forms of member feedback. The importance of teachers' choice of professional learning to meet their needs is considered vital:

We are very proud of our role in providing our members with good quality professional development. I think the most critical thing that we believe about professional development for teachers and everyone in education is that it should be self-driven. There are some good initiatives that the Ministry brings on that requires some training and some PD opportunities to enhance the quality of their role as a teacher in a school, but for the most part, we believe very strongly that professional development should be something that people self-select.

(Suzette Clark, OSSTF)

Participation is voluntary and release time, travel, and accommodations are typically funded by the teacher organizations, which usually earmark a portion of their revenue from member dues to support such initiatives. In addition, the Ministry of Education has provided substantial funding to teacher federations to support professional learning activities, including support for release time. As Susan Perry of OECTA commented:

> That is a stand that we have taken for many, many years, that if teachers are doing professional learning, if there's an expectation that they do it, then they are provided with release time in order to do that.

Teacher unions are a trusted source of high quality professional learning for their members (Link 3-23):

> We [teachers] know that if it's coming from the Federation (a) it's good, (b) it comes from our perspective, and (c) the main objective is to do something for me as a teacher.

(Lindy Amato, OTF)

Particularly important is that those providing the professional learning are mainly teachers:

> I think a particular style of professional learning that teachers find particularly valuable, is the "by teachers, for teachers," kind of approach. The TLLP is one example, but all the summer workshops, the conferences, the on-line learning, the various networked learning opportunities that exist, whether it's within one of the affiliates or through OTF initiatives, the growth has been dramatic and response from teachers has been excellent.

(Rhonda Kimberley-Young, OTF)

Teachers who participate in federation supported professional learning opportunities tend to speak very highly of the activities and their benefits for teachers' knowledge and practices.

Ministry and OTF Partnership Projects: The Teacher Learning and Leadership Program

Rather than professional learning being government-driven only or based on individual teachers working independently, Ontario is striving to provide a range of professional learning activities and opportunities. Coming out of the Working Table on Teacher Education, the Teacher Learning and Leadership Program (TLLP) (Link 3-24) was launched in 2007. A key feature of the TLLP is that it is developed and delivered in partnership between the Ministry of Education and the Ontario Teachers' Federation (OTF). This partnership has been critical to the initiation, implementation, and ongoing success of the TLLP:

> So the Teaching Policy and Standards Branch of the Ministry was smart to engage us in the base level thinking around what we would do around the TLLP and around teacher performance appraisal and around the new teacher induction program, and to share ownership with us on that, because if you don't have that input or presence of the Federation at the beginning, you're not going to get it after the fact, because you lose the ownership piece. So when it's shared ownership, I think, you have a much greater sense of success. But I think the Federations really do go a long way to changing practice and again, if a government is smart, they will see that.

> (Lindy Amato, Ontario Teachers' Federation)

The shared goals for the TLLP are to:

○ support experienced teachers who undertake self-directed advanced professional development;

○ develop teachers' leadership skills for sharing their professional learning and exemplary practices; and

○ facilitate knowledge exchange for spread and sustainability of practices.

Each year, experienced teachers—individually or more commonly in teams—can apply to conduct a TLLP project. School board committees review applications and submit their priority choices to a provincial committee comprised of teacher union and government representatives, who select projects for funding. Approximately 100 projects per year are funded.

Successful applicants receive training, support, and funding for their TLLP projects. Prior to embarking on their TLLP projects, teacher leaders attend a Leadership Skills for Classroom Teachers training to support their preparation to take on the professional learning, project management, and leadership expectations of a TLLP. Throughout their TLLP project—and beyond—participants become part of Mentoring Moments, an online community to share resources, learning, and discussion and, at the end of their TLLP project, TLLP teams attend the Sharing the

Learning Summit to showcase completed projects and to strengthen the spread and sustainability of practices. Participants in the TLLP are highly enthusiastic about the benefits of these projects. In 2014–2015, 97% of participants in the *Leadership Skills for Classroom Teachers* training rated being very satisfied or satisfied with the experience. At the end of their TLLP project, 98% of participants reported being very satisfied or satisfied with the *Sharing the Learning Experience*. These are excellent results (Campbell et al., 2015).

In our research on the TLLP (Campbell et al., 2013a, 2013b; 2014a, 2014b; 2015; Lieberman, Campbell, & Yashkina, 2017), a range of project themes were identified with the most prevalent including differentiated instruction; technology; math; literacy; and professional learning communities. Based on a sample of projects, the majority of professional learning activities included teacher collaborative learning (85% of projects), reviewing research (55% of projects), and/or engaging in research (52% of projects), in addition to other forms of professional learning and networking. Related to the goal of teachers' professional learning, the TLLP has had considerable benefits. The "TLLP approach" is grounded in a commitment to "authentic learner led learning . . . by teachers, for teachers." The teacher-led, self-directed nature of TLLP was considered to be unique and vital, particularly for experienced teachers looking for new ways of developing their professional learning.

As part of our longitudinal research, in 2014–2015, we surveyed current and previous TLLP project leaders over all cohorts (Campbell et al., 2015). All (100%) survey respondents indicated TLLP-related professional learning benefits. Specifically:

o 78% of respondents reported new knowledge and/or improved understanding
o 75% of respondents reported improved instructional practice
o 73% of respondents reported improved communication/collaboration between teachers
o 58% of respondents reported improved energy/inspiration
o 54% of respondents reported improved self-efficacy
o 50% of respondents reported improved technological skills
o 48% of respondents reported improved assessment skills

Related to the goal of developing teacher leadership, TLLP teacher leaders valued the opportunity to learn leadership "by doing" and by being supported to develop their leadership by the OTF and Ministry. As one TLLP interviewee commented: "This is grassroots leadership at its finest. . . . This has been some of the best and most rewarding work in my career." With regard to teacher leadership, 97% of survey respondents indicated that the TLLP had supported development of their leadership skills (Campbell et al., 2015). Specific leadership skills that improved were:

o Facilitation/presentation skills for 74% of respondents

o Project management skills for 70% of respondents

o Communication/listening skills for 54% of respondents

o Interpersonal skills/relationship building for 53% of respondents

o Trouble shooting/problem solving skills for 47% of respondents

Vignettes written by TLLP teacher leaders include consideration of their developing leadership. All the TLLP vignette writers who worked with someone else wrote that part of their learning was gaining the ability to work with others and keep everyone involved, learning, and contributing. Learning *how* to do this was an important part of the work:

> The opportunity that this project gave me to utilize strategies dealing with collaboration, empowering others in the group, and motivating colleagues that were less confident than others at the outset of this project, was incredibly valuable. Leading this project was the most useful leadership based professional learning that I have been involved with in my teaching career.

In writing down what they learned about leadership, various themes emerged including collaboration; building relationships; creating a vision and sharing leadership; planning a project; implementing a project; going public with their teaching; and learning technology. In particular, moving from working alone in isolation to working with others in the development of a project was a huge part of participants' learning as it was new and complicated for them. Participating teachers strongly valued the development of their leadership through the TLLP:

> With respect to what our project was to me, it was more than just helping students. It was an opportunity for me as team leader to become a better leader. Our TLLP project was a way to heighten our professionalism and do something that really mattered. The project is proof that teachers can learn and lead when they are provided the support/conditions they require to do good work.

The third goal of TLLP to support knowledge exchange has supported teachers to deprivatize their practice and share their learning and practices across classrooms, schools, districts, provincially, and, in some cases, internationally. In our analysis of recent TLLP projects, the majority of projects were sharing their learning through developing and providing professional learning sessions and also through the use of online media, including Twitter, blogs, and websites. Other forms of sharing included: staff meetings, professional learning communities, conferences, modeling, mentoring, communications/publications, and events. TLLP teachers were also developing professional resources and materials including lesson plans, resource lists, assessment tools, and instructional materials. The strategies of developing professional collaboration, communication (in-person, online and in print) and co-development of practical resources for teacher use appear to be the most impactful and prevalent approaches for sharing knowledge and practices among and between teachers through the TLLP.

Very encouragingly, 98% of our TLLP survey respondents reported that their TLLP activities had been sustained in some way (Campbell et al., 2015). Reported aspects of sustainability included:

⊙ Further implementation of TLLP learning/strategies/tools (82% responses);

⊙ Further development of professional learning (80% responses);

⊙ Continued or further collaboration with colleagues to develop and/or improve teaching practice (70% responses);

⊙ Further sharing of professional learning/strategies/tools (66% responses).

These findings concerning sustainability or spread and/or implementation of TLLP-related activities after the initial funding are highly important.

To further spread sharing of practices, completed TLLP projects can be identified by a school board to apply for additional funding through the Provincial Knowledge Exchange (PKE) to provide resources and release time to enable sharing of practices from the TLLP with other schools in their board and/or school boards across Ontario. Most recently, Ontario's public broadcaster, TVO, has collaborated with the advice of TLLP teachers to develop an online platform, TeachOntario, where teachers can share their practice, explore research, collaborate on new projects, and access resources to support knowledge mobilization with, for, and by teachers across Ontario.

While TLLP teacher leaders faced—and mostly overcame—challenges of time, resources, logistics, and change management, the overall experience is rewarding and enriching for experienced teachers to further develop their professional contribution:

> Professionally, I don't have a leadership position within my school community. I'm not a chairperson, I'm not a vice principal; I'm a teacher. I felt that it was a way for me to become a specialist in a particular area in a short period of time. There is kind of a dichotomy in terms of the challenge within the practice, I guess, where there is this extra amount of work on top of your regular job. But on the other hand, the connection, the collaboration, the brainstorming, and the creative sort of outlet was rejuvenating for us. It was rewarding, enriching, inspiring, invigorating, captivating, so that the three of us on the core team would just sort of feed off one another and just dream big thoughts that normally we would never have the time to do, nor offered the opportunity.

> (TLLP teacher leader)

Vignette of Practice: Balanced Math Provincial Knowledge Exchange, Simcoe County District School Board

The Balanced Math program began as part of a TLLP project in 2012 led by Kirsten Muscatt-Fennell when she was a primary-junior teacher at Fieldcrest Elementary School in the Simcoe County District School Board (SCDSB). Kristen's passion for math encouraged her to bring the Balanced Math program to her classroom and the school. Starting as a TLLP in one school, the Balanced Math program became a Provincial Knowledge Exchange (PKE) involving 15 schools across SCDSB in 2013–2014. The PKE team, led by Kristen Muscatt-Fennell, includes also her colleagues Darrell Bax, a special education resource teacher, and Stephanie Skelton, a grade 8 teacher at Fieldcrest Elementary School. Each team member brings complementary skills to the program combining leadership, project management, technological, and pedagogical knowledge and skills. Importantly, the project has experienced strong support from current and past school principals as well as the board's Superintendent of Education, Anita Simpson.

Balanced Math provides opportunities for modeled, guided, shared, and independent math experiences in an engaging, interactive learning community. The three-part lesson model follows the following format:

1. Whole group instruction (60–70 min.)
   - New concepts taught in a 3-part lesson (using open questions and parallel tasks)
   - Consolidation task assigned and/or completed
2. Balanced math rotation (20–30 min.)
   - Students are directed to their next Balanced Math rotation and proceed independently
3. Optional follow-up work time (15–20 min.)
   - Students begin work independently on lesson consolidation task if not completed during 3-part lesson

Teachers have the option of incorporating Balanced Math rotations in their weekly lesson plans. These rotations include the following six components as part of a differentiated instruction program, plus a "Share the Wealth" activity for whole group consolidation:

- Guided Math/Problem Solving
- Shared Problem Solving
- Independent Problem Solving
- Math Journal
- Math Games
- Math Facts

The key learning goals of this PKE included: growth in numeracy instruction and assessment using technology; strategies to enhance student achievement in the mathematical processes; and enhanced differentiation of instruction. The PKE operated on the basis of collaborative learning where the PKE team told teachers about the Balanced Math program and modeled use of resources and activities, they provided practical resources for use by the participating teachers, teacher participants observed the resources in use (through demonstration classrooms and modeled by the PKE team), there were opportunities for teachers to co-plan and co-learn for their own use of the Balanced Math strategies, and teachers were supported to apply Balanced Math in their own classrooms and to share their learning within and across the schools.

Through release time for professional development, the PKE team shared and developed the Balanced Math approach in a three-part series involving a total of 2.5 days. The first session introduced teachers, coaches, and administrators to the TLLP project and learning goals that may culminate into a plan for implementation. The second session included opportunities for sharing successes and challenges, a focus on the use of technology to support Balanced Math, visits to demonstration classrooms and sharing of student work, and professional collaboration on additional strategies. The final session involved a culmination of the project including moderation of student work, a survey to measure the project's success, and plans for further sharing. As part of the final session, teachers were asked to bring a sample lesson plan for the collective Balanced Math resource binder. The sessions were based on the premise that teacher learning comes through collaboration. As such, each session built in time for the exchange of ideas, and the co-planning of lessons. The project team shared their learning using a Wiki space designed to highlight a variety of instructional strategies and resources linked to the Board's Essential Practices. Teachers also collaborated on the Wiki Space by uploading and exchanging resources, including lessons, assessment resources, tip sheets, and samples of student work. In addition, all teachers participating in the PKE received a resource binder, books, and materials for their own use in their classrooms and schools. Teachers were encouraged to share knowledge and resources from the PKE with other staff at their school. For further sharing of practices provincially, the PKE team has developed math tutorials as short video clips to be made available online.

Teacher participants indicated substantial appreciation for the practical nature of the Balanced Math professional development sessions and its potential benefits for their teaching practices and for students' learning. Teachers pointed to the immediate applicability and usefulness of resources provided and to the expert support provided by the PKE project team.

A video profiling the TLLP is available here http://www.youtube.com/watch?v=3DCiHTSaZu8&feature=youtu.be

School District and School Professional Learning

The Ontario school calendar currently (2015–2016) includes six professional activity (PA) days for schools—two for provincial priorities and four to be locally determined. The provision of an additional PA day is part of the discussions for the current round of labor negotiations. In addition, school boards and schools are involved in initiating and leading a range of professional learning connected to local needs. The provision of additional PA days is currently being negotiated as part of new collective agreements with the teachers' unions.

The teachers interviewed for this case study participated in a variety of professional learning experiences. At the board level, such experiences included opportunities to visit the classrooms of other practicing teachers to observe the implementation of particular teaching and learning strategies (for example, termed "Learning Forward," "Demonstration Classrooms," or "Exploration Classes" in different boards), collaborative inquiry groups, and a variety of curricular and methodology workshops:

> I have attended a number of Professional Development workshops on the topic of reading and writing led by board personnel and authors who specialize in the field over the past year. This year my focus has been on Mathematics and the three-part lesson (Activation, Implementation, Consolidation). This has been a series of six workshops with neighbouring schools in grades 2–3 who have the same student-identified focus this year. Under the guidance of the school board math resource person, we explore, implement and discuss new strategies for effective teaching.
>
> (Cathy)

> Our Board implemented TLCPs, Teaching Learning Critical Pathways, maybe five years ago now, where every elementary teacher in the Board had to do one. So a group of teachers get together and look at a need that they see with the kids. They work together to develop a formal diagnostic. So if we say the kids need help with writing a paragraph, we'll give them a diagnostic. You'll do that in your class. I'll do it in my class. We come back together, we moderate, and we mark the diagnostic to see where the kids are. It's good because then teachers are also talking about how they mark, and we think about well, if this is where they are, what do they need?
>
> (Heather)

School-based programs included book study groups, "lunch and learn" mini workshops, and a variety of school based communities of practice and professional learning groups where teachers work on specific problems of practice or school improvement initiatives (termed "Professional Learning Team," "School Improvement Team," and "Learning Circles"):

Through the School Improvement Team, I am able to examine school data with my colleagues on the team and determine a focus for the year(s) ahead. For example, last year the focus for the primary division was reading comprehension. We used the Daily 5 format (Boushey and Moser) and Text Structures writing program (Diane Dillabough) to enhance our teaching. Our principal guided our learning by providing us with the materials needed. Through biweekly divisional meetings, frequent grade level meetings and various board workshops, we were able to implement and discuss strategies for implementation regularly with our colleagues and offer support and suggestions for improvement.

(Cathy)

These groups allow teachers to engage with their colleagues in collaborative activities including co-planning, co-teaching, and reflection on practice. Time for engaging in such collaborative work is often provided through a combination of designated PA days provided by the Ministry, release time provided by the principal (who receives an allotment of discretionary days to use for teacher PD, extracurricular, and other professional activates that would require the use of an occasional teacher), and time outside of the instructional day. A sample schedule and timeline of a professional learning group in one of the schools in this study is provided in Figure 3–20.

Although many of the experiences described by the teachers in our study aligned with specific board and school goals, most felt that they had opportunities to direct their own learning. However, some noted that not all teachers shared this sentiment:

There are a lot of initiatives that are happening at the Board. So you could be a part of a number of them, or you could just be part of one or none, really. I think I'm in a good spot where I can be part of the ones that I want to be a part of, but I have heard that there are teachers at other schools who are told to participate in certain initiatives by their administration.

(Wahid)

Evaluation and Performance Management

I always take what the principal and VP says [on my Teacher Performance Appraisal] quite seriously. It's always good to get a different perspective on your teaching. Any advice they give can be processed and used to better what you teach and how you teach it. I also think

Figure 3–20 Professional Learning Group Master
Schedule, York Region District School Board

Cycle	Topic of Discussion	Date	Group	Note
1	Long Range Planning/Creating Report 1 comments	Thursday, October 31 2013 Friday, November 1, 2013	1 to 6 7 & 8	4 supply teachers required for each cycle
2	Reviewing Current Practice What are stall learning needs? • Linked to the challenge of practice	November 18th at divisional meetings	1 to 6 7 & 8	
3	**Selecting skills/strategies and rasks** tasks to focus on to address student needs • Share COP to the challenge of practice	Thurs., November 28 2013 Fri., November 29, 2013	1 to 6 7 & 8	- PD component - Something practical
4	Review the strategy and focus for the first 4Cs (continue discussions from the staff meeting)	Thes., January 14 2014 Wed., January 15, 2014	1 to 6 7 & 8	- Look at the subject area and strategy on which group will focus. - discuss subject/curriculum - go over 4Cs process (and roles) - revisit the 7 norms
5	4Cs - Co Planning, Co Teaching/Co Debriefing/Co Reflecting (1)	Weeks of Tues., January 28, 2014 - Fri January 31, 2014 (schedule to follow)	1 to 8	- create the task and how to assess it - discuss how to observe objectively (observations on stickies) • full day PLG • teach and observe the lesson (in roles) • analyze student observations • Reflection should include next steps for the next 4C. • information gathered from the lesson would be the diagnostic
6	Implementing What We Learned (50 min. periods = 4 OTs)	Week of march 31st	All	• incorporate in an existing unit plan the focus strategy from the 4C • create common assessments to monitor student progress
7	4Cs - Co Planning, Co Teaching/Co Debriefing/Co Reflecting (2) (Full day for each group = 12 OTs)	April 22 to April 25, 2014	1 to 6 7 & 8	full day for each group
8	Engage in Reflection	Staff Meeting on May 5th	1 to 6 7 & 8	**Implementing What We Learned**
9	21st Century Classroom Planning • What is a 21st Century Classroom?	May 29th	Lead Team	What is a 21st Century Classroom? How do we support 21st century classrooms?
10	Revise the Challenge of Practice	June 5th	Lead Team	**Work with a Round Facilitator to revise the COP**
11	Planning for Next Year	June 10		

it's a great way for them to see who isn't doing a satisfactory job and get them the help that they need. This not only helps the teacher, but the students as well.

(Darcy)

The Teacher Performance Appraisal (TPA) (Link 3-25) was first introduced as a legislated requirement in Ontario in 2002 and revised in 2007. The system is intended to provide teachers with meaningful appraisals that encourage professional learning and growth. The process is designed to foster teacher development and identify opportunities for additional support where required. The key components of the TPA include a pre-observation meeting, classroom observation, a post-observation meeting, and a summative report. The principal is responsible for the appraisals, and vice principals or supervisory officers may act as designates for the principal. Experienced teachers are normally appraised once every five years, although a teacher can be evaluated at any time if there is a performance concern. In addition to formal evaluations, teachers are also given feedback during the mentoring process early in their careers and often receive informal feedback from school administrators on an ongoing basis. In conjunction with the OCT and the teacher federations, there are provisions for support and due process in cases where unsatisfactory performance results in termination of a teacher's employment.

The appraisals are based on sixteen competencies that reflect the standards of practice set out by the OCT. New teachers are evaluated on eight out of sixteen competency statements based on three domains (commitment to students and student learning, professional knowledge, and professional practice). Experienced teachers are appraised on all sixteen competencies, including the domains of leadership in learning communities and ongoing professional learning.

All of the teachers in our study had been evaluated within the current TPA system at various points in their careers. For most the process was standard and precisely followed the TPA implementation guidelines:

> My Principal essentially arranged the date. He set up a few meetings prior to that where I had to sit with him and he would debrief me as to what was going to happen, what the protocol was and all the steps along the way. And he came in [to the class], took some notes and he wrote up a long report. . . There was another meeting after the lesson, which he observed to reflect and debrief about his observations, and what he saw happening inside the classroom, based on the evaluation. So that was it. It was pretty standard. It was by the book and detailed.
>
> (Wahid)

> I have been evaluated by three different supervisors, at least three, maybe more, and it's kind of the standard TPA process. . . where we set a meeting and then we talk about what we are going to do and then the Principal comes to watch and then we have a third meeting. . . the Principals have all come to a full class, and in my case, every Principal has written up the report themselves, and as far as I can remember, each Principal has given me a copy of the report to ask if there are things that they missed.
>
> (Heather)

Teachers highly valued effective feedback from administrators as part of the TPA:

The feedback that my principal gave was enough for me to think things over a little bit and kind of reevaluate how I might approach a new English language learner, or how you would change things for a special education student with the use of technology, how do you ensure students are responsible for their learning and so on. Things like that that I need to be thinking of every single day.

(Wahid)

On the other hand, teachers lamented when the feedback provided by principals was "nothing very detailed or practical."

In addition to the TPA, each year, experienced teachers must also complete an annual learning plan (ALP) (Link 3-26), which outlines their plan for professional growth. In collaboration with their principals, teachers set growth goals, along with a rationale, a set of strategies, and an action plan for achieving them. In doing this they reflect on their previous performance appraisal, the prior year's professional learning, and input from parents and students. In a year not involving a TPA, teachers are required to submit their ALP's to their principal by the end of October. In a year involving a TPA, teachers meet with their principal to review their ALP as part of the TPA process. The plan is reviewed during the pre- and post-observation meetings and refined where necessary.

The Ministry and the teacher federations both provide teachers with a variety of supports and resources to aid in the creation of ALPs that are intended to be both manageable and self-directed in nature. Areas of professional growth may include expanding curriculum knowledge, implementing new teaching strategies, exploring new assessment strategies, or incorporating new technologies into teaching practice, to name just a few. Strategies to accomplish such goals might include conducting classroom research, enrolling in an AQ course, reading professional publications, attending workshops or seminars, developing new curriculum materials or assessment tools, volunteering on school, district, or federation committees, or being involved in a mentorship. Growth strategies should be relevant to both the professional needs of the teacher and focus on improving teaching practice and student learning.

Teachers' Career Development

Teachers can advance through their career through a combination of experience, expertise, further training such as AQs, and changes in assignments. As outlined previously in Figure 3–11, teachers can aim to move into a range of positions at school, board, and/or provincial levels, such as being an Associate Teacher to support teacher candidates in their practicum schools, becoming a NTIP mentor for newly qualified teachers, developing teacher leadership opportunities, participating in teacher federation or provincial organizations, and/or moving into school or board leadership positions. In addition, there are new teacher opportunities linked to the Ministry's student achievement strategies. For example, the Student Success strategy includes the appointment of a Student Success Teacher and a Student Success Team in each secondary school:

> The student success teacher is an advocate for students who are struggling. The term we typically use is "students with persistent achievement challenges," but the students could be at risk for any reason that the school identifies. So there may be a critical event or more persistent challenges facing the young person, but if they are on the radar for the student success teacher, the idea is that that teacher is working with those students; they're watching the student, they're tracking how the student is doing and they are advocating for those students with other teachers, as well. In the description of a student success teacher, there's also an opportunity for them to work with staff to promote some of the ideas that will support the students. As it is with many things, how that actually plays out is really a question of the context of the school, every school and every student success teacher situation is different.
>
> (Rob Andrews, Student Success/Learning to
> 18 Implementation, Innovation and Support Branch)

There are also dual credit teachers identified as part of the Student Success Strategy. At the elementary level, student work-study teachers collaborate and co-learn with host classroom teachers to understand students' learning and to inform improvements in instruction and assessment practices. The Ministry of Education provided school boards with funding for these positions and, through the Student Achievement Division, support sharing of learning and local practices across the province. Similarly, boards fund a number of positions of additional responsibility, including teacher coaches, board consultants, and department heads.

In addition to funding new positions for the Student Achievement strategy in schools and boards, the Ministry also seconds experienced educators to work—usually on a time limited basis—in the Ministry to inform strategies and to support implementation in the education sector:

> So we go out and we find the people who are really good at what they do. They understand literacy and numeracy and improving instruction really well, in their school and in their Board, and then they come in and they work for three years, ideally, if we can keep them that

long, in a group of different Boards. They get to see how things are done elsewhere, and learn with our internal staff, and we do a lot of development of our own staff. So they are not a group of independent operators out there, they are pretty closely connected on similar wavelengths, because we bring them in for some discussions and modelling of what needs to go on. They grow so much in that three-year period and then they go back and we end up with new people working for us, but those old people are still working for us out there too. So we end up with all of these people who really understand the work deeply and can lead their schools and their classrooms and their Boards in ways that make sense. We are now at a point where, I want to say we're beyond 25% of that have come through student achievement roles, either student success leads out in the Boards or school effectiveness leads out in the Boards or staff that we have seconded and have gone back. It is all part of Ontario's growing focus and attention on the student achievement agenda.

(Mary Jean Gallagher, Student Achievement Division)

However, while there are opportunities for career advancement whether through promotion into senior positions or secondments into specific roles, several of our teacher interviewees commented that it was a concern that taking on a leadership position may mean leaving their classroom responsibilities behind (Link 3-27):

> You can't be a resource teacher and a classroom teacher. You have to be one or the other. It would be nicer to see almost split responsibilities where you have the day to be a resource teacher and support your department and half the day to still be in the classroom.
>
> (Tina)

> I want to feel like I have the opportunity to not just teach in another school or teach another grade, but do something where I would still be in the role of a teacher but do my role in a different way. . . for people like me that want to change it up or see what their strength is and how best they can make use of that strength in the system its either classroom teacher or a system leader and I think a blend would be amazing.
>
> (Paul)

For many teachers in Ontario, they will remain classroom teachers for the majority of their careers:

> The places to be promoted in education are pretty limited. So, I come from the secondary panel where you are a teacher and then you may

potentially become a department head, you may go off to work at the Board level as a coordinator or consultant or, if you want to stay in the schools, you get promoted to Vice Principal and Principal. And that's it. There really are not that many career advancement opportunities for teachers. At the elementary level, of course, they will have division lead, primary lead or intermediate or senior lead perhaps. They are structured a little bit differently, but there is very little room to move from being a teacher, except to either go to Board Office wide positions, like coordinators and consultants. Maybe a literacy lead now or a literacy/numeracy lead at a Board level or if you want to be in the school in admin, it's Vice Principal and Principal, and so I don't know that that is necessarily problematic, but it's not like a lot of industries where there are so many middle levels and upper levels that one can migrate through, many people start their career as a teacher and they end their career as a teacher having never become department head, coordinator, consultant, anything else. It's not necessarily a problem. . . But the majority of people start as teachers and retire as teachers.

(Rhonda Kimberley-Young, Ontario Teachers' Federation)

Initiatives such as the TLLP are intended to provide opportunities for experienced classroom teachers to remain in the classroom while also developing and extending their leadership to support other teachers. For teachers seeking promotion into administrative positions, there are a range of leadership development strategies and supports, as discussed further below.

Leadership Development for Administrators

For teachers who select to move into administrative roles, there is a range of supports and resources through the Ontario Leadership Strategy (OLS) (Link 3-28), a comprehensive plan of action designed to support student achievement and well-being by attracting and developing skilled and passionate school and system leaders. The theory of action driving the OLS is that significant progress toward the province's education priorities can be accomplished by:

o directly improving the quality of school and district leadership;

o supporting and adding value to efforts of others responsible for leadership development; and

o working to improve conditions for teaching and learning in schools and classrooms.

Figure 3–21 The Ontario Leadership Framework

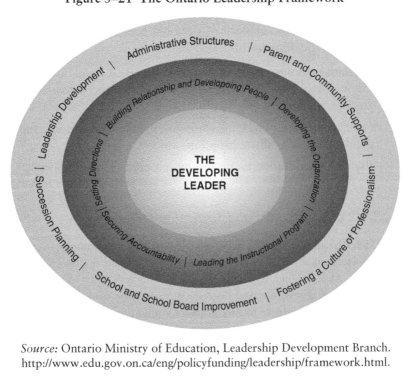

Source: Ontario Ministry of Education, Leadership Development Branch. http://www.edu.gov.on.ca/eng/policyfunding/leadership/framework.html.

The OLS is underpinned and informed by a research-based framework for leadership development (Leithwood, 2012) (see Figure 3–21).

The Ontario Leadership Framework (OLF) is a tool to guide leadership practice. Its purpose is to promote a common language that fosters an understanding of leadership and what it means to be a school and system leader, to make explicit the connections between leaders' influence and the quality of teaching and learning, and to guide the design and implementation of professional learning and development of school and system leaders. The framework contains core leadership practices to inform vice principals and principals in schools and supervisory officers in school districts.

The OLF was updated, refined, and revised in 2013 to ensure the practices within each domain took account of latest research. Changes included:

o Revised leadership practices for school and system leaders

o Introduction of the District Effectiveness Framework

⊃ More explicit connections to the Ministry's K–12 School Effectiveness Framework

In addition, a new category of personal leadership resources were introduced for the domains of:

⊃ Cognitive resources: problem-solving expertise; and knowledge about school and classroom conditions with direct effects on student learning.

⊃ Social resources: perceiving emotions; managing emotions; and acting in emotionally appropriate ways.

⊃ Psychological resources: optimism; self-efficacy; and resilience.

Leadership Recruitment and Succession Planning

> I felt that after so many years of teaching and affecting students lives, hopefully in a positive way, I wanted to go beyond the classroom walls. Also, I found myself, as a teacher, I was very much into helping other teachers too. And I became a department head, and so the opportunity was there to help teachers within the department with resources that I had or other connections where they will be able to find resources. So that gave me satisfaction in helping a wider range of teachers being in a department, and having done all of that I wanted to go beyond the classroom walls and affect more teachers and more students at a larger scale.
>
> (Alex)

School boards decide on the placement of principals in specific schools by looking at the talent pool of candidates, the needs of their schools, and the career preferences of their current leaders where possible, taking into account advice from school councils.

 Through the OLS, each school district in Ontario is provided with funding and support to develop and implement a Board Leadership Development Strategy (BLDS) (Link 3-29) which focuses on school and system leaders and all those within the district who aspire to take on leadership roles, whether on the academic or business side of the organization. The BLDS focuses on four key areas:

Recruiting and selecting leaders through structured and innovative succession planning;

Placing and transferring leaders in ways that sustain school and system improvement;

Developing leaders through mentoring, performance appraisal, and differentiated learning opportunities that meet the needs of leaders in diverse contexts and at various stages of their careers;

Coordinating support for leaders to buffer them from distractions, make information easily accessible, and assist them in building coherence across different initiatives.

Several factors may serve as deterrents for teachers to become vice principals or principals, including a negligible salary increase, the further qualifications required, and the fact that teachers must leave the protection of their federation or union and give up their seniority ranking in order to take on the new role:

> The process sometimes can discourage people. There are the principal qualification courses to go through and that is after you have completed your master's degree. In our Board, we also have to take leadership discernment series before you can put forward your application. The application process itself is tasking, which also includes being interviewed by senior administrators at the end. Those are the kinds of barriers that discourage many teachers from considering administration. People think, "I don't have time for that; I'm just happy where I am."
>
> (Judith)

In particular, the compensation package for school administrators was deemed to be unattractive by almost all of the teachers and administrators interviewed:

> The compensation between a secondary department head and a Vice Principal is a few thousand bucks. So for those headaches, is it worth those few thousand bucks?
>
> (Peter)

> Teachers say, "I don't want your job because you do so much more and there is not much more money you are getting out of it." I have heard that many times. We are having difficulties in getting people to apply for positions of responsibility. They don't want spend so much time to qualify, be responsible for so much more and at the end receive very little compensation.
>
> (Judith)

> I don't think people go into administration because of the money. I think it's such a difficult job that I can't imagine somebody saying that that amount of money is worth it.
>
> (Heather)

Still, most school leaders indicate that they like their jobs, and very few leave prior to the average retirement age. In a recent study of principals' work in Ontario (Pollock with Wang & Hauseman, 2014, p. 28), in response to the survey question "If I had to do it again, I would remain a teacher than a principal," the majority of principals responding disagreed (60%). Principals reported mainly feeling respected with 92% believing that "my job makes a difference in the school community" (Pollock et al., 2014, p. 28). Rather than monetary compensation or climbing the professional ladder, all of the administrators in our study were motivated to move into their positions out of a desire to widen their range of impact and to help larger numbers of students and teachers:

> For me it was the fact that I knew that as a teacher I was able to make a difference for my class, but thinking that as an administrator, I could make a difference for an entire school. So that is what inspired me to move up, to move to a different role.
>
> (Krista)

> I became a department head and I was asked to fill in as a VP on a number of occasions and I saw that it gave me an ability to make a difference on a different level. So when I was in my classroom, I was making the difference in the lives of those kids in my classroom and feeling really positive about that, and I thought here, maybe I could start implementing some of my ideas around programming that I felt was just good for kids' learning. I started off my teaching career as a technological education teacher. It's a very experiential type of learning that I thought kids would benefit from in all classes, and so that was my thought around it, was that maybe I could try some innovative programming, but in order to do that you had to be in a VP or Principal position. So that's what happened.
>
> (Dawn)

Preparation and Professional Development of Administrators

Job Requirements

 Principals and vice principals in Ontario must attain principals' qualifications by completing the Principals' Qualification Program (PQP) (Link 3-30). Participants self-fund their participation in PQP courses. The program is accredited by OCT and consists of two parts, each totaling 125 hours, plus a practicum. The program is provided by Faculties of Education and by principals' associations across the province. Structured around the OLF, the Ontario College of Teachers (2009) has set the following learning expectations for PQP candidates:

o reflect on the Standards of Practice for the Teaching Profession and the Ethical Standards of Practice for the Teaching Profession in relation to the principal's role

o establish a shared vision aligned with school board and provincial policies and initiatives

o expand leadership skills and knowledge required to shape school culture

o expand leadership and managerial skills related to the role of school administrator

o demonstrate curriculum leadership in facilitating the implementation and assessment of instructional programs to improve student achievement

o expand skills in managing human resources for the promotion of efficient and effective schools

o initiate, facilitate and manage change

o expand knowledge of legislation and policy related to education in Ontario

o enhance the knowledge and skills needed to collaborate with parents, the community, and other educational stakeholders to meet the needs of students and advance the goals of education use, current research, performance data and feedback from students, teachers, parents and community to make decisions related to improvement of instruction and student performance

In addition to completing the PQP, principals must have an undergraduate degree, five years of classroom experience, qualifications in three divisions of the school system, and a master's or double-subject specialist degree. In Catholic boards, principals must also complete a specialist in religious studies.

All administrators in our study had completed the PQP program and satisfied all the additional requirements prior to beginning their administrative careers. Most found the PQP to be beneficial in gaining an understanding of the policy and legislation around educational administration in Ontario but commented that the best preparation was the hands on experience gained either in the PQP internship or their boards' job shadowing program.

Principal Preparation and Mentoring

As part of their succession planning, many school boards offer a leadership development program as a first step for aspiring leaders, which in some boards includes those interested in becoming consultants or resource personnel in addition to those wanting to become principals and vice principals. Some boards offer the program to anyone with interest in moving into such positions and in other boards teachers must be recommended to the program by their principal. Typically these programs include a number of professional development seminars around leadership topics such as developing positive relations with parents, the link between leadership and student achievement, and work-life balance. Some programs also include a job shadowing component where prospective administers are placed with a practicing principal or vice principal. This allows those thinking about moving into leadership positions to get firsthand experience of the expectations and demands of such roles. The boards of four of the five principals interviewed for this study offer such programs and participants tended to speak highly of their impact in terms of preparing future administrators for the reality of the job as well as assisting boards in finding the strongest candidates for leadership positions:

> In a Vice Principal's position, really, you learn a lot more when you are in the position. You can know the theory, but it's the day to day practical way of doing things. There is a big lesson there by itself, and for example, right now I have a person who is aspiring to be a leader. The person is coming to my school tomorrow morning and I am going to be with him the whole day tomorrow, just job shadowing. Just going through the kind of things that are happening—the interruptions and the discipline and all the other interruption within. Yes, the programs (PQP) do prepare you to some extent, but there is a little bit more to that than just the theory and the courses we do.
>
> (Judith)

One principal in our sample participated in her board's leadership development program and identified it as being the most influential aspect of her preparation:

> The Leadership Development program was really valuable work in that we were all doing the internship at the same time. So the debriefing of problems and the coming up with ideas of alternative solutions gave us a little support group to reach out to. The job shadowing was invaluable. I thought that that was one of the best things that the board did. I worked with my Principal. He said, "okay, you're just

the fly on the wall. You are going to see whatever I do and follow along and we'll ask questions later," and I had the opportunity to do that once a month for 10 months, and that was really, really helpful.

(Dawn)

As part of the OLF, all principals and vice principals are expected to be offered mentoring for their first two years in each role, funded by the ministry and delivered by school boards according to ministry guidelines. Features of the leadership mentoring program include training for mentors, a learning plan outlining how the mentor and mentee will work together, and a transparent matching and exit process to ensure a good fit between mentor and mentee.

Principal Performance Appraisal

All principals and vice principals are appraised every five years through the Principal Performance Appraisal (PPA) (Link 3-31) process (see Figure 3–22). As part of the appraisal process, principals, in consultation with their supervisors, must set a few challenging yet achievable goals based on ministry, school board, school, community, and personal

Figure 3–22 Principal Performance Appraisal
Process

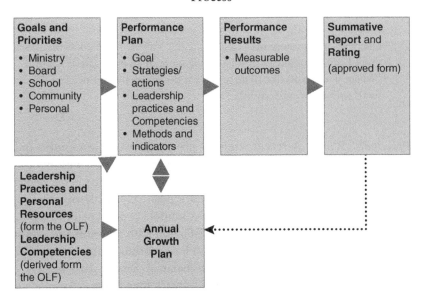

Source: Ontario Ministry of Education, http://www.edu.gov.on.ca/eng/
policyfunding/leadership/PPA_Manual.pdf.

priorities, plus taking account of leadership practices in the OLF, and develop strategies to meet these goals. At the end of the appraisal year, principals are appraised according to the progress they have made in meeting their goals. If this is unsatisfactory, a process is followed that includes an improvement plan, time for improvement, and the offering of supports. If insufficient improvement is made, the board has the authority to demote, transfer, or terminate employment. An annual growth plan—connected to the OLF—outlines the activities that the principal will engage in to support the performance plan.

Of the five administrators interviewed for this case study, four had been evaluated within the PPA program. They considered the process to be more valuable when there was a consistent approach to implementation involving an opportunity to receive feedback, to create awareness of challenges and possible solutions, and to reflect on their progress and their future goals:

> The feedback was good. I was able to recognize the areas that were maybe challenges for me and the areas where I felt efficacious. . . with the challenges I might think about different ways of approaching the issue so if it wasn't really going the way I had hoped or my behavior of the action that I took or decisions on a particular challenge, then I considered approaching it in a different way.

> (Alex)

> I think it is helpful if you take the process seriously, so I do try to be reflective during those times and write out some truthful goals that I think I can accomplish. . . it has to be more of a conversation about "where would you like to go and what do you think you need to do [with senior administration].

> (Dawn)

Principals' Work   A recent study of principals' work in Ontario indicated that the majority of principals (79%) "feel satisfied with my job" compared to 10% who disagreed and 10% who reported being neutral (Pollock et al., 2014, p. 28). Even more positively, 91% of principals surveyed agreed with the statement "my school is a good place to work." However, alongside high levels of satisfaction with their job and school, principals also reported concerns about long working hours, work intensification, and challenges of work-life balance. Seventy-two percent of principals reported feeling "pressured to work long hours." As indicated in Figure 3–23, Ontario principals reported working an average of 59 hours per week. The activities reported as involving the most of the

Figure 3–23 Principals' Hours Spent on Different
Tasks, Duties, and Responsibilities—Per Week

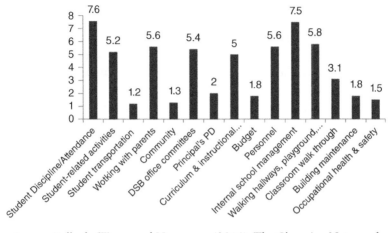

Average Number of Hours Spent per Week

Source: Pollock, Wang, and Hauseman (2014). The Changing Nature of
Principals' Work.

principals' time during a typical week were attending to student discipline/attendance issues and internal school management. Activities relating to curriculum and instructional leadership involved an average of five hours per week. The concept of instructional leadership where principals are involved in facilitating teachers' professional learning and engaging in providing instructional expertise are central to the Ontario Leadership Strategy. A tension between time on managerial tasks contrasted with instructional leadership was identified with 82% of principals indicating that they wished to spend more time on curriculum and instruction (Pollock et al., 2014, p. 16). Relatedly, 74% of principals reported they would prefer to spend more than the current average of two hours per week on professional development activities.

Conclusion

The Ontario approach to developing teachers and supporting teaching quality for over the past decade did not start with a technical approach to mandating "teacher quality," rather a theory of action linked to knowledge of educational change and professional capacity building has informed the mindset, values, principles, strategies, and actions developed and implemented. Specifically, the Ontario theory of action for educational improvement involved five key elements:

1. Focus: identification of key priorities for improvement

   Three goals have informed the focus of Ontario's educational improvements over the past decade: increasing student achievement; reducing gaps in performance; and increasing public confidence in publicly funded education. In 2014, these goals were revised and renewed with the introduction of a fourth priority focus on enhancing well-being.

2. Tri-Level Reform: system-wide coherence and alignment

   A vast array of policies, strategies, initiatives, and actions has been undertaken over the past decade. However, all actions are intended to be aligned with the core goals outlined above and to involve coordinated attention at provincial, school district, school, and classroom levels. To support systemic action and coherence, a central feature has been an emphasis on developing professional partnerships, trust and respect between the provincial government, all provincial stakeholders, the teaching profession, and wider public. Distractors to a focus on student achievement, equity, well-being, and improving the public education system are addressed, for example, by attending to the quality, development, recruitment, retention, and working conditions of teachers.

3. Support and Positive Pressure: capacity building with a focus on results

   A key element of the Ontario strategies is "capacity building with a focus on results" involving the development of educators' knowledge, skills, and practices with a particular focus on instructional improvements to support students' learning and achievements. Where student achievement is identified as being lower, for example for particular groups of students and/or schools, additional attention, resources, and supports are provided to target and improve educational practices. The Ontario approach emphasizes developing the capacity of all people involved through fostering collective commitment and collaborative action for educational improvement.

4. Shared Leadership: respect for professional knowledge and practice

   The Ontario approach to educational change has placed emphasis on developing professional capacity and leadership throughout the education system. A combination of professional knowledge, identification and sharing of successful or promising practices, and the use of data and research locally and from international leading practice are combined to inform the Ontario strategies and actions.

5. Professional Accountability: results without rancor or ranking

   Educators are considered to be professionals with responsibility for self- and peer-improvement. The government does not label "failing" schools requiring firing of staff or takeover models. Rather where underperformance in student achievement is identified, the view of the Ministry of Education is the need to develop the "will and skill" of educators to improve programs and instructional practices, plus supporting conditions, to enable students to learn, achieve, and thrive at school and beyond.

Underpinning this theory of action and linked strategies and practices for implementation is strong support for the transformative power of publicly funded education and support for the continuous learning of professionals working in the education system as well as their contributions to supporting students' learning, equity, and well-being. The keywords for Ontario are learning, collaboration, and capacity building. For example, in teacher education, OISE's Learner Document emphasizes developing teachers' identities linked to the "transformative purposes of education." Likewise, Ontario's Professional Standards for Teachers embody commitments to students' learning, professional learning, and leadership in learning communities, and from New Teacher Induction through to ongoing career development the cultivation of a continuous "learning stance" is supported. Importantly, teachers' professionalism is considered to include collaborative professional learning to develop collective capacity and shared leadership for improvement in educational outcomes.

Ontario's education system has developed a culture of professional learning to improve practices for students' learning. First elected in 2003, a Liberal government has provided a consistent focus on education as a top priority with the urgent imperative of reaching every student. While students are the central priority, the professional capacity of teachers and administrators are considered to be the keys to developing, delivering, and sustaining improved knowledge, processes, and practices for educational improvement. The government has developed and sustained an intentional strategy of improving public confidence and of fostering productive partnerships with the education profession. Partnership has informed both the content of the policies and, as importantly, the processes of how policy is developed and enacted. One of the early actions of the newly elected government back in 2004 was the formation of a

Working Table on Teacher Development, bringing together the teachers' unions, the government, and all main provincial stakeholder organizations in education. This partnership has been critical to informing appropriate teacher development policies, including the New Teacher Induction Program, the Teacher Performance Appraisal System, and the Teacher Learning and Leadership Program. Over the years since the first election of a Liberal government, there have been changes and, at times, challenges and contention about the details of professional respect and partnership in principle and in practice. Moving forward, the nature of teachers' professional autonomy contrasted with the work of administrators in schools and boards and Ministry initiatives will be an area for further attention as teacher unions have called for a (re)envisioning of professionalism and partnership. A joint process involving all education and related professional associations has resulted in a new commitment to develop "collaborative professionalism" in working together.

As well as a culture and practice of partnership, a key feature of Ontario's changes over the past decade has been the development of an infrastructure for the implementation of capacity building and instructional improvement. It is recognized that it takes capacity in order to build capacity. Attention has been paid to developing professional educational knowledge, skills, and practices at all levels of the education system, including restructuring and refocusing the work of the Ministry of Education, school board and school improvement processes, leadership development, and teacher development.

Essential to capacity building is fostering, recruiting, developing, retaining, and valuing a high quality teaching profession. In Ontario, as in Canada more widely, teaching is a respected and attractive profession. A virtuous process appears to exist whereby the public holds education in high regard, schools are generally improving, and students' experiences in schools can positively influence their valuing of teachers and their aspiration to become future teachers making a difference for students and society. There are more applications to teacher education programs than there are places and, for those who complete teacher education, there are more teachers qualified than there currently are positions needing filled. Entry into and recruitment for teaching is highly competitive. This enables teacher education programs to take account not only of strong academic performance, but also consider factors concerning diversity and candidate's demonstrated approach as a learner and future teacher.

Ontario wants its teachers to be excellent educators and continuous learners. Teacher education and certification are regulated to ensure quality. To become a teacher in Ontario, you must have completed at least three years of postsecondary education plus university-provided graduate teacher education. All teacher education in Ontario is provided by accredited Faculties of Education. Once qualified, teachers are expected to aspire to and uphold high standards and ethics of professionalism. However, alongside regulation of the teaching profession, there is trust for teachers and support for teachers' development throughout their careers linked to their professional needs and contexts. This includes induction and mentoring for new teachers, annual learning plans and performance management for all teachers, opportunities for additional qualifications, as well as an array of continuing professional learning and teacher leadership opportunities for experienced teachers. The principles, approaches, and content of teachers' professional development policies and practices are informed by evidence from research combined with professional experience. The majority of teachers in Ontario will have long careers, therefore opportunities for teachers to select and participate in a range of learning and development is critical. Opportunities to develop teacher leadership to enable experienced teachers to support other teachers' learning and to share and spread new knowledge and practices are highly valuable. For teachers who decide to move into administrative positions, a comprehensive leadership framework and support for administrator development, recruitment, and succession planning is important. There is recognition that there is no one size fits all approach to teachers' professional development so a range of opportunities and professional choice are important.

As well as career stage developments, approaches to capacity building in Ontario combine system-wide improvement processes, targeted initiatives for identified provincial priorities, and differentiated professional learning opportunities linked to local needs. Linked to the theory of action emphasizing "capacity building with a focus on results," the Ministry funds, supports, and provides a range of initiatives to support strategy implementation. Leadership development and teachers' professional learning focused on students' learning and needs to inform changes in professional knowledge and instructional practices are vital. There is attention to alignment and coherence through school, board, and provincial planning processes. There has also been attention to the sequence of capacity building approaches from building consensus through valuing and honoring local innovation and practices, to province-wide training and professional resources, to a current emphasis on collaborative professional learning, inquiry, and innovation connected to professional practices for identified students' needs, plus access to on-demand and online professional learning resources and supports. There continues to be a need to attend to the appropriate balance between system-wide initiatives from the Ministry, board, and school-led initiatives, and opportunities for school leaders and teachers to engage in their own professional learning linked to their identified local needs and priorities. There are also concerns about the quantity and intensity of initiatives affecting educators' workloads and conditions. Teachers particularly value self-directed "by teachers, for teachers" and collaborative professional learning opportunities. The Ontario strategies suggest system-wide, targeted, differentiated, *and* teacher-led collaborative professional learning opportunities are all important, particularly in combination at provincial and local levels, rather than one model of professional development. Finally, while Ontario has undertaken a comprehensive system-wide approach to professional development for teachers and administrators for over a decade, partnership development and capacity building require constant attention and continues to adapt, evolve and innovate in pursuit of continuous improvement in professional practices and educational outcomes.

In conclusion, the Ontario case study demonstrates the importance of a theory of action emphasizing consistent focus, systemic actions, supportive but challenging expectations for improvement, shared leadership for improvement, and a collective professionalism. This theory of action has informed, and been influenced by, an evolving culture prioritizing a focus on students' learning, equity, and well-being linked to serious attention to developing an infrastructure to develop professional capacity for implementing improvements in educational practices throughout the public education system, including work in classrooms, schools, school boards, the Ministry of Education, and with provincial and local partners. A collaborative and collective approach to capacity building is central to Ontario's systemic approach to educational improvement. At the heart of these strategies has been a valuing of administrators' and teachers' practices combined with high expectations and standards for continuous learning and further improvement to realize Achieving Excellence for Ontario's current and future students.

Appendix

METHODOLOGY

THE INTERNATIONAL TEACHER POLICY STUDY employed a multi-method, multiple case study design in order to investigate the policies and practices that support teaching quality within education systems. Seven jurisdictions across five countries were selected for the study based upon their highly developed teaching policy systems, as well as indicators of student performance on international assessments such as the Programme for International Student Assessment (PISA). In larger countries, both national and selected state or provincial policies were examined to develop an understanding of the policy system. In these cases, the state or province was treated as a case nested within the larger country case.

The same research design was followed in each jurisdiction, with adaptation to local circumstances. The research was conducted in several phases:

o First, we conducted extensive document analysis, including education policy documents and descriptions of curriculum, instruction, and professional development practices and programs in primary, secondary, and higher education institutions. Reviews of the academic literature within and about each jurisdiction were also completed.

o These were supplemented with analyses of international, national, and, where applicable, state data sources. Quantitative data were used to support document analysis prior to the interview phases, and later, to triangulate findings from interviews. Quantitative data sources consulted included the latest PISA and TALIS reports, OECD country profile documents, surveys conducted by teacher federations and other professional teaching bodies, as well as data around various indicators of student success and educational funding provided by Ministries of Education.

⟳ Two interview phases were conducted in 2014, beginning with interviews with policymakers and education experts in each jurisdiction. This was followed by interviews with school district administrators, principals, teachers, teacher educators, and other education practitioners. In each case interviews were audio- or video-recorded and transcribed for analysis.

⟳ The interviews were supplemented with detailed observations of selected activities in schools and classrooms, along with other key meetings and professional learning events.

Each jurisdictional team consisted of one or more locally based researchers, and one or more U.S.-based colleagues. This approach provided both an "insider" perspective, and an external lens on the data in each. Key lessons and themes from the each jurisdictional case study have also been drawn together in a cross-case publication that serve as a companion to the individual studies.

Across the Alberta and Ontario studies, we interviewed 58 respondents as follows: 16 teachers, 6 school and district administrators, 7 representatives from faculties of education, 6 representatives from teacher federations, 1 representative from the Ontario College of Teachers, individual and groups interviews with senior level officials and staff from the Alberta and Ontario Ministries of Education (21 participants in total).

Observations were conducted in two schools and one school district professional learning center. These schools were selected as one provided an opportunity to observe one of our teacher interviewee's teaching and the second was the site of a professional learning event for teachers including visits to classrooms to observe teaching practices. In contrast, we also observed a professional learning event for teachers across a school district. Interview data were supplemented with qualitative data drawn primarily from observations of key meeting and learning events. Additional data sources included professional learning materials and resources provided by teachers, including examples of teaching materials, teachers' schedules, and vignettes of a day in the life of two teachers.

REFERENCES

2012–2013 Iowa Public School and AEA Teacher Salary. (2013). Iowa Department of Education, Bureau of Information and Analysis, Basic Educational Data Survey. Retrieved September 18, 2014, from http://www.ia-sb.org/HumanResources.aspx?id=10770

Aboriginal Affairs and Northern Development Canada (AANDC). (2015). Federal funding levels for First Nations K–12 Education. Retrieved from https://www.aadnc-aandc.gc.ca/eng/1349140116208/1349140158945

Alberta Education. (2010). Education sector workforce planning framework for action. Edmonton: Alberta Education. Retrieved September 2, 2015, from https://education.alberta.ca/media/1155749/2010--03--03%20education%20sector%20workforce%20planning%20framework%20for%20action.pdf

Alberta Education. (2012). *Spotlight on... professional development: What we have learned from AISI.* Edmonton, Alberta: Author.

Alberta Education. (2013). A transformation in progress: Alberta's K–12 education workforce 2012/2013.

Alberta Canada. (2014). "Economy." Retrieved September 4, 2014, from http://albertacanada.com/opportunity/choosing/economic-economy.aspx

Alberta Education. (2014). A transformation in progress: Alberta's K–12 education workforce 2012/2013. Edmonton, Alberta: Author. http://education.alberta.ca/admin/workforce.aspx

Alberta Education. (2014). About Alberta education. Retrieved September 18, 2014, from http://education.alberta.ca/department/about.aspx

Alberta Education. (2014). Breakdown of student population. Retrieved September 18, 2014, from http://education.alberta.ca/department/stats/students/studentpopulation.aspx

Alberta Education. (2014). Diploma general information bulletin. Retrieved September 18, 2014, from http://education.alberta.ca/admin/testing/diplomaexams.aspx

Alberta Education. (2014). National and international testing. Retrieved September 18, 2014, from http://education.alberta.ca/admin/testing/nationaltesting.aspx

Alberta Education. (2014). Number of Alberta schools and authorities. Retrieved September 18, 2014, from http://education.alberta.ca/department/stats/numberofschools.aspx

Alberta Education. (2014). Putting students first. Retrieved September 18, 2014, from http://education.alberta.ca/department/budget/studentfirst.aspx

Alberta Education. (2014). Questions about. . .teacher salaries. Retrieved September 18, 2014, from http://education.alberta.ca/admin/workforce/faq/teachers/teachersalaries.aspx

Alberta Education. (2014). Student learning assessments. Retrieved September 18, 2014, from http://education.alberta.ca/admin/testing/student-learning-assessments.aspx

Alberta Education. (2014). Teacher certification requirements in Alberta. Retrieved September 18, 2014, from http://www.education.alberta.ca/teachers/certification/requirements.aspx

Alberta Education. (2014). Teacher growth, supervision, and evaluation policy. Retrieved September 18, 2013, from http://education.alberta.ca/department/policy/otherpolicy/teacher.aspx

Alberta Education. Alberta Initiative for School Improvement. (2010). *Improving student learning: Summary report for cycle 3 (2006–2009)*. Edmonton, Alberta: Author.

Alberta Education (May 2014). Taskforce for Teaching Excellence: Full Report. Retrieved on 8/1/15 from http://open.alberta.ca/dataset/0c3c1074-b890-4db0-8424-d5c84676d710/resource/1315eb44-1f92-45fa-98fd-3f645183ac3f/download/GOAE-TaskForceforTeachingExcellence-WEB-updated.pdf

Alberta Education (2014). Curriculum redesign 101. Edmonton: Alberta Education.

Alberta Government. (7 July 2015). Alberta official statistics: Proportion of immigrants, Alberta economic regions. Retrieved 7 July 2015 from http://data.alberta.ca//sites/default/files/datasets/07072015_94_PropOfImmigrantsByEconomicRegion_OnePage.pdf

Alberta Human Services. (2014). Child care subsidy. Retrieved September 4, 2014, from http://humanservices.alberta.ca/financial-support/15104.html

Alberta Learning Information Services. (2013). Alberta wage and salary survey, jobs, skills, labour, and training. Average wages by industry and economic region. Retrieved September 18, 2014, from http://alis.alberta.ca/pdf/wageinfo/2013_AWSS_Wages_By_Industry_and_Region.pdf

Alberta Teachers Association (2003). Mentoring beginning teachers: A program handbook. Edmonton, AL: Alberta Teachers Association.

Alberta Teachers' Association. (2010). *A framework for professional development in Alberta*. Edmonton, Alberta: Author.

Alberta Teachers' Association. (2011). *The early years of practice: Interim report of a five-year study of beginning teachers in Alberta*. Edmonton, Alberta: Author.

Alberta Teachers' Association. (2013). *Teaching in the early years of practice: A five-year longitudinal study.* Edmonton, Alberta: Author.

Ambrose University College. Accessed March 22, 2015, https://ambrose.edu/arts-science-programs/education

Anderson, S., & Ben Jaffar, S. (2006). *Policy trends in Ontario 1990–2006.* Retrieved from: http://icec.oise.utoronto.ca/PDFfiles/FinalPolicyNarrative.pdf.pdf

Becoming a School Board Trustee. (2014). Retrieved from: http://cge.ontarioschooltrustees.org/en/read/becoming-a-school-board-trustee

Brochu, P., Deussing, A., Houme, K., & Chuy, M. (2013). *Measuring up: Canadian results of the OECD PISA study.* Toronto: Council of Ministers of Canada.

Calgary Herald. (17, February, 2015). Big budget cuts trigger outrage among unions and public interest groups. Accessed September 2, 2015, from http://calgaryherald.com/news/politics/big-budget-cuts-trigger-outrage-among-unions-and-public-interest-groups

Cammarata, L., Cavanagh, M., & d'Entremont, Y. (2015). Restructuring the teacher education program at Campus Saint-Jean of the University of Alberta: The importance of the role of academic leaders. In *Leadership for change in teacher education: Voices of Canadian deans of education.* Edited by Susan E. Elliott-Johns. Sense: Boston.

Campbell, C. (2014). *Student achievement division literacy and numeracy strategy: evidence of improvement study.* Ontario Institute for Education, University of Toronto. Retrieved from: http://www.edu.gov.on.ca/eng/research/uoftReport.pdf

Campbell, C. (2015). Leading system-wide educational improvement in Ontario. In A. Harris & M. Jones (Eds.), *Leading Futures: Global Perspectives on Educational Leadership.* London and New York: Sage.

Campbell, C., & Fullan, M. (2006). *Unlocking potential for learning: Effective district-wide strategies to raise student achievement in literacy and numeracy.* Toronto, Ontario: Queen's Printer of Ontario. Retrieved from: http://www.edu.gov.on.ca/eng/literacynumeracy/inspire/research/ProjectReport_full.pdf

Campbell, C., Lieberman, A., & Yashkina, A. (2013a). *The Teacher learning and leadership program: Research project.* Retrieved from: http://www.otffeo.on.ca/en/wp-content/uploads/sites/2/2013/09/tllp_full_report-.pdf

Campbell, C., Lieberman, A., & Yashkina, A. (2013b). *The teacher learning and leadership program: Executive summary.* Retrieved from: http://www.otffeo.on.ca/en/wp-content/uploads/sites/2/2013/09/tllp_summary.pdf

Campbell, C., Lieberman, A., & Yashkina, A., with Carrier, N., Malik, S., & Sohn, J. (2014a). *The teacher learning and leadership program: Research report 2013–14.* Retrieved from: http://www.otffeo.on.ca/en/wp-content/uploads/sites/2/2014/08/TLLP-Final-Report-April-2014.pdf

Campbell, C., Lieberman, A., & Yashkina, A., with Carrier, N., Malik, S., & Sohn, J. (2014a). *The teacher learning and leadership program: Executive summary—research report 2013–14.* Retrieved from: http://www.otffeo .on.ca/en/wp-content/uploads/sites/2/2014/08/TLLP-Executive-Summary-April-2014.pdf

Campbell, C., Lieberman, A., & Yashkina, A., with Hauseman, C., & Rodway Macri, J. (2015). *The teacher learning and leadership program: Research report for 2014–15.* Toronto, Ontario: Ontario Teachers' Federation.

Campbell, C., and The Literacy and Numeracy Secretariat. (2008). Building capacity with a focus on results: The literacy and numeracy strategy. Paper presented to the Canadian Society for the Study of Education. Retrieved from: http://www.edu.gov.on.ca/eng/research/buildingCapacity.pdf

Canadian Education Statistics Council. (2014). Education indicators in Canada: An international perspective 2013. Retrieved from http://www.cmec.ca/ Publications/Lists/Publications/Attachments/322/Education-Indicators-Canada-International-Perspective-2013.pdf

CIEB. (2015). Statistic of the month: Education performance, equity, and efficiency. Retrieved from http://www.ncee.org/2015/01/statistic-of-the-month-education-performance-equity-and-efficiency/

Clandinin, D. J., Shaefer, L., Long, J., Steeves, P., McKenzie-Robblee, S., Pinnegar, E., Wnuk, S., & Downey, C.A. (2012). Early career teacher attrition: Problems, possibilities, potentials. http://www.elementaryed.ualberta.ca/en/ Centres/CRTED/~/media/elementaryed/Documents/Centres/CRTED/ECA_-_ FINAL_Report.pdf

CMEC. (2014). Pan Canadian Assessment Program (PCAP) 2013 Public Report. Retrieved from: http://www.cmec.ca/docs/pcap/pcap2013/PCAP-2013-Public-Presentation-EN.pdf

CMEC. (2015). Education in Canada: An overview. Retrieved from http:// www.cmec.ca/299/Education-in-Canada-An-Overview/index.html#02

CMEC. (2015b). CMEC educators' forum on Aboriginal education. Retrieved from http://www.cmec.ca/314/Programs-and-Initiatives/Aboriginal-Education/CMEC-Educators-Forum-on-Aboriginal-Education/Overview/index .html

Collective agreement between the Toronto District School Board and the Elementary Teachers Federation of Ontario, 2008–2012. (2008). Retrieved from: http://www.ett.ca/collective-agreement-2008--2012/

Collective agreement between the Toronto District School Board and the Ontario Secondary School Teachers' Federation, September 1, 2008– August 31, 2012. Retrieved from: http://osstftoronto.ca/wp-content/ uploads/2014/01/2008--2012-SecondaryCA-Nov11—091.pdf

Couture, J. C. (November 2012). Lead the change series: Interview with J-C Couture. Retrieved from http://www.AERA.NET/EDUCATIONAL_ CHANGE_SIG.HTM

Directions Evidence and Policy Research Group. (2014). *Teacher workload and professionalism study.* Retrieved from http://www.edu.gov.on.ca/ eng/policyfunding/memos/nov2014/ETFO_TeacherWorkloadReport_ EN.pdf

Dyck, G. (29 August 2014). Edmonton's 2014 census confirms strong population growth. Accessed 2 September 2015, from http://www.edmonton .ca/city_government/news/2014/edmontons-2014-census-confirms-strong-population-growth.aspx

Early Childhood Development Mapping Project. (2014). How are our young children doing? Community profiles of early childhood development in Alberta. ECMap, Community-University Partnership for the Study of Children, Youth and Families, University of Alberta.

Education funding in Alberta handbook. (2014). Retrieved September 4, 2014, from http://education.alberta.ca/media/8309883/education%20fund-ing%20in%20alberta%20handbook%202014--2015%20v2.pdf

Education Quality and Accountability Office. (2013a). *Programme for International Student Assessment (PISA), 2012: Highlights of Ontario student results.* Retrieved from http://www.eqao.com/pdf_e/13/2012_ PISA_Highlights_en.pdf

Education Quality and Accountability Office. (2013b). *EQAO: Ontario's Provincial Assessment Program. Its history and influence, 1996–2012.* Retrieved from http://www.eqao.com/Research/pdf/E/ON_ProvAssess-mentPgm_9612_eng.pdf

Education Quality and Accountability Office. (2014). *Pan-Canadian Assessment Program (2013): Ontario results.* Retrieved from http://www.eqao .com/pdf_e/14/PCAP-ontario-report-2013.pdf

Fullan, M. (2010). *All systems go: The change imperative for whole system reform.* Thousand Oaks, CA: Corwin Press.

Fullan, M., & Rincón-Gallardo, S. (2016). Developing high quality public education in Canada: The case of Ontario. In F. Adamson, B. Astrand, & L. Darling-Hammond (Eds.), *Global education reform: How privatization and public investment influence education outcomes.* New York: Routledge.

Gambhir, M., Broad, K., Evans, M., & Gaskell, J. (2008). *Characterizing initial teacher education in Canada: Themes and issues.* Canadian submission to the Alliance for Excellent Education, Ontario Institute for Studies in Education, University of Toronto.

Gambhir, M., Broad, K., Evans, M., & Gaskell, J. (September, 2008). *Characterizing initial teacher education in Canada: Themes and issues.* Toronto: University of Toronto. Ontario Institute for Studies in Education.

Garvey, D. (2000). A report on a model project for implementing a mentorship program. Alberta Teachers' Association. Retrieved on September 2, 2015, from http://www.teachers.ab.ca/Publications/Other%20Publications/Mentorship%20Program%20A%20Model%20Project/Pages/A%20Report.aspx

Garvey, D. (2003). Mentoring beginning teachers. *Alberta Teachers Association Magazine.* Vol. 84. No. 3. Retrieved September 2, 2015, from http://www.teachers.ab.ca/Publications/ATA%20Magazine/Volume%2084/Number%203/Articles/Pages/Mentoring%20the%20Beginning%20Teacher.aspx

Gereluk, D. (2015). University of Calgary Werklund School of Education 2-year consecutive & 5-year concurrent bachelor of education student handbook 2015–2016. Retrieved April 2, 2015, from: http://werklund.ucalgary.ca/upe/files/upe/consecutive-concurrent-bed-student-handbook-march-2015--2016.pdf.

Glaze, A., & Campbell, C. (2007). Putting literacy and numeracy first: Using research and evaluation to support improved student achievement. Paper presented to the American Educational Research Association Annual Meeting. Retrieved from: http://www.edu.gov.on.ca/eng/research/litNumFirst.pdf

Glaze, A., Mattingley, R., & Andrews, R. (2013). *High school graduation: K–12 strategies that work.* Thousand Oaks, CA: Corwin Press and Toronto, ON: Ontario Principals' Council.

Government of Alberta Ministerial Order #016/97. (1997). Teaching quality standard.

Government of Canada. (1995). Employment Equity Act. Accessed 2 September, 2015, from http://www.labour.gc.ca/eng/standards_equity/eq/emp/index.shtml

Government of Canada. (2008). Statement of apology to former students of Indian residential schools. Retrieved from https://www.aadnc-aandc.gc.ca/eng/1100100015644/1100100015649

Government of Ontario. (2014a). *Ontario fact sheet October 2014.* Retrieved from http://www.fin.gov.on.ca/en/economy/ecupdates/factsheet.html

Government of Ontario. (2104b). *About Ontario.* Retrieved from: www.ontario.ca/government/about-ontario

Government of Ontario. (2014c). *Ontario to repeal Putting Students First Act.* Retrieved from: http://news.ontario.ca/edu/en/2013/01/ontario-to-repeal-putting-students-first.html

Government of Ontario. (2014d). *Ontario strengthening education sector for students: Improved collective bargaining process supports stronger, more stable schools.* Retrieved from http://news.ontario.ca/edu/en/2014/04/ontario-strengthening-education-sector-for-students.html

Grimmett, P. (2008). Canada. In T. O'Donoghue & C. Whitehead (Eds.). *Teacher education in the English speaking world* (pp. 23–44). Charlotte, N.C.: Information Age Publishing.

Grimmett, P., & Young, J. (2011). *Teacher certification and the professional status of teaching in North America: The new battleground for public education.* Charlotte, N.C: Information Age Publishing.

Gunn, T. M., Pomahac, G., Striker, E., & Tailfeathers, J. (2011). First Nations, Metis, and Inuit education: The Alberta Initiative for School Improvement approach to improve Indigenous education in Alberta. *Journal Of Educational Change, 12*(3), 323–345.

Hansen, J. (2012). 2011 Census of Canada: Language characteristics of Albertans. Retrieved September 4, 2014, from http://www.finance.alberta.ca/aboutalberta/census/2011/2011-census-language.pdf

Hansen, J. (2014). Quarterly population report: First quarter 2014. Retrieved September 4, 2014, from http://www.finance.alberta.ca/aboutalberta/population_reports/2014--2015/2014--1stQuarter.pdf

Hargreaves, A., & Braun, H. (2012). *Leading for all: Final report of the review of the development of essential for some, good for all: Ontario's strategy for special education reform devised by the council of directors of education.* Toronto, Ontario: Council of Directors of Education.

Hargreaves, A., & Shirley, D. (2009). *The fourth way: The inspiring future for educational change.* Thousand Oaks, CA: Corwin.

Hargreaves, A., & Shirley, D. (2012). *The global fourth way: The quest for educational excellence.* Thousand Oaks, CA: Corwin.

Hargreaves, A., Crocker, R., Davis, B., McEwen, L., Sahlberg, P., Shirley, D., Sumara, D., & Hughes, M. (2009). *The learning mosaic: A multiple perspective review of the Alberta Initiative for School Improvement AISI.* Edmonton, Alberta: Alberta Education. http://education.alberta.ca/

Hart, D. (2012). *The 18th OISE survey of educational issues: Public attitudes towards education in Ontario 2012.* Retrieved from http://www.oise.utoronto.ca/oise/UserFiles/File/OISE%20Survey/18th_OISE_Survey/OISE%20SURVEY%2018.pdf

Herbert, M., Broad, K., Gaskell, J., Hart, D., Berrill, D., Demers, S., & Heap, J. (2010). Teacher preparation and success in Ontario. Prepared for the Ministry of Education of Ontario.

Herman, J. (2013). *Canada's approach to school funding: The adoption of provincial control of education funding in three provinces.* Center for American Progress.

Horner, D. (2014). The Building Alberta Plan Budget 2014: Operational plan. Edmonton, Alberta: Treasury Board and Finance. Retrieved September 4, 2014, from http://finance.alberta.ca/publications/budget/budget2014/fiscal-plan-operational-plan.pdf

Johnson, D. R. (2013). *Teachers and their salaries—Some evidence from the Labour Force Survey.* Laurier Centre for Economic Research & Policy Analysis. Retrieved from: http://navigator.wlu.ca/content/documents/Link/career%20new%20website/LCERPA_LFNews_Jan_2013.pdf

Leithwood, K. (2012). *Ontario Leadership Framework 2012: With a discussion of the research foundations.* Ontario: The Institute for Education Leadership.

Lieberman, A., Campbell, C., & Yashkina, A. (2015). Teacher learning and leadership: Of, by and for teachers. In J. Elmers & R. Kneyber (Eds.), *Flip the system: Changing education from the ground up.* London: Routledge.

Lieberman, A., Campbell, C., & Yashkina, A. (2017). *Teacher learning and leadership: Of, by, and for teachers.* London: Routledge.

Literacy and Numeracy Secretariat. (2010). Collaborative teacher inquiry: New directions in professional practice. Retrieved from: http://www.edu.gov.on.ca/eng/literacynumeracy/inspire/research/CBS_Collaborative_Teacher_Inquiry.pdf

Mourshed, M., Chijioke, C., & Barber, M. (2010). *How the world's most improved school systems keep getting better.* New York, NY: McKinsey & Co.

National Center for Children in Poverty. "Child Poverty." Retrieved September 4, 2014, from http://www.nccp.org/topics/childpoverty.html

Neilson, M., Dowdell, V., & Kolkman, J. (2013). *Tracking the trends 2013: 12th edition.* Edmonton, Alberta: Edmonton Social Planning Council.

NTIP induction elements manual. (2010). Retrieved from: http://www.edu.gov.on.ca/eng/teacher/pdfs/NTIP-English_Elements-september2010.pdf

OECD. (2010). *Strong performers and successful reformers in education: Lessons from PISA for the United States: Ontario, Canada: Reform to support high achievement in a diverse context.* pp. 65–81. Retrieved from: http://www.oecd.org/pisa/pisaproducts/46580959.pdf

OECD. (2011). *Strong performers and successful reformers in education: Lessons from PISA for the United States: Ontario, Canada: Reform to support high achievement in a diverse context.* pp. 65–81. Retrieved from: http://www.oecd.org/pisa/pisaproducts/46580959.pdf

OECD. (2013a). "Teachers' salaries", Education: Key Tables from OECD, No. 1. DOI: http://dx.doi.org/10.1787/teachsal-table-2013-1-en

OECD. (2013b). Education at a glance country note: Canada. Retrieved from http://www.oecd.org/edu/Canada_EAG2013%20Country%20Note.pdf

OECD. (2014). Education at a glance country note: Canada. Retrieved from http://www.oecd.org/edu/Canada-EAG2014-Country-Note.pdf

OECD. (2015). Education policy outlook: Canada. Retrieved from http://www.oecd.org/edu/EDUCATION%20POLICY%20OUTLOOK%20CANADA.pdf

OECTA. (2006). Workload study—Executive summary. Retrieved from http://www.aloecta.on.ca/elemworkload.pdf

O'Grady, K., & Houme, K. (2014). PCAP 2013: Report on the Pan-Canadian assessments of science, reading and mathematics. Retrieved from: http://cmec.ca/Publications/Lists/Publications/Attachments/337/PCAP-2013-Public-Report-EN.pdf

Ontario College of Teachers. (2009). *Principals' Qualification Program.* Retrieved from https://www.oct.ca/-/media/PDF/Principals%20Qualification%20Program%202009/principals_qualification_program_e.pdf

Ontario College of Teachers. (2011). *Transition to teaching 2011: Early-career teachers in Ontario schools.* Retrieved from: http://www.oct.ca/-/media/PDF/Transition%20to%20Teaching%202011/EN/transitions11_e.ashx

Ontario College of Teachers. (2012). *Transition to teaching 2012: Teachers face tough entry-job hurdles in an increasingly crowded Ontario employment market.* Retrieved from: http://www.oct.ca/-/media/PDF/Transition%20to%20Teaching%202012/T2T%20Main%20Report_EN_web_accessible0313.ashx https://www.oct.ca/public/professional-standards/ethical-standards

Ontario Ministry of Education. (2007a). *Ontario First Nation, Métis, and Inuit education policy framework: Delivering quality education to Aboriginal Students in Ontario's provincially funded schools.* Aboriginal Education Office. Retrieved from: http://www.edu.gov.on.ca/eng/aboriginal/fnmiframework.pdf

Ontario Ministry of Education. (2007b). *Report to the partnership table on teacher professional learning. Recommendations of the working table on teacher development.* Retrieved from: http://www.edu.gov.on.ca/eng/teacher/pdfs/partnerReport.pdf

Ontario Ministry of Education. (2011). *The Teaching profession: Teacher assignment in Ontario schools: A resource guide.* Retrieved from: http://www.edu.gov.on.ca/eng/teacher/assign.html

Ontario Ministry of Education. (2013b). *Modernizing teacher education in Ontario.* Retrieved from: http://news.ontario.ca/edu/en/2013/06/modernizing-teacher-education-in-ontario.html

Ontario Ministry of Education. (2013c). *School Effectiveness Framework: A support for school improvement and student success.* Retrieved from http://www.edu.gov.on.ca/eng/literacynumeracy/SEF2013.pdf

Ontario Ministry of Education. (2014). *Education facts.* Retrieved from: http://www.edu.gov.on.ca/eng/educationFacts.html

Ontario Ministry of Education. (2014a). *2014–2015 grants for student needs technical briefing.* Retrieved from: http://www.edu.gov.on.ca/eng/funding/1415/webcast2014.pdf

Ontario Ministry of Education. (2014b). *2014–2015 school year education programs—Other (EPO) funding.* Retrieved from http://faab.edu.gov.on.ca/Memos/B2014/B05E.pdf

Ontario Ministry of Education. (2014c). *Achieving excellence: A renewed vision for education in ontario.* Retrieved from: http://www.edu.gov.on.ca/eng/about/renewedVision.pdf

Ontario Universities' Application Centre. (2014). Teacher education application statistics—January 2014. Retrieved from: http://www.ouac.on.ca/statistics/teacher-education-applications/tapp_january/

Parkin, A. (2015). International report card on public education: Key facts on Canadian achievement and equity. The Environics Institute. Retrieved from http://www.environicsinstitute.org/uploads/institute-projects/environics%20institute%20-%20parkin%20-%20international%20report%20on%20education%20-%20final%20report.pdf

Parsons, J. (2015). "The erosion of efficacy" *in the Alberta Teachers Association Magazine.* Vol. 95, No. 3. Retrieved on September 2, 2015, from http://www.teachers.ab.ca/Publications/ATA%20Magazine/Volume%2095%202014--15/Number-3/Pages/TheErosionOfEfficacy.aspx

Parsons, J., & Beauchamp, L. (2012). Action research: The Alberta Initiative for School Improvement (AISI) and its implications for teacher education. *Action Researcher in Education,* 3(1), 120–131.

Parsons, J., McRae, P., & Taylor, L. (2006). *Celebrating school improvement: Six lessons from Alberta's AISI projects.* Edmonton, Alberta: School Improvement Press.

Pervin, B., & Campbell, C. (2011). Systems for teacher and leader effectiveness and quality: Ontario, Canada, in L. Darling-Hammond & R. Rothman (Eds). *Teacher and leader effectiveness in high-performing education systems.* Washington, D.C.: Alliance for Excellent Education and Stanford, CA: Stanford Center for Opportunity Policy in Education.

Pollock, K., with Wang, F., & Hauseman, C. (2014). The changing nature of principals' work. Retrieved from http://www.edu.uwo.ca/faculty_profiles/cpels/pollock_katina/opc-principals-work-report.pdf

Pruegger, V., Cook, D., & Richter-Salomons, S. (2009). Inequality in Calgary: The racialization of poverty. Retrieved September 4, 2014, from http://www.calgary.ca/_layouts/cocis/DirectDownload.

aspx?target=http%3a%2f%2fwww.calgary.ca%2fCSPS%2fCNS%2fDoc
uments%2finequality_in_calgary.pdf&noredirect=1&sf=1

Richards, J. (2008). Closing the Aboriginal/non-Aboriginal education gaps (Issue Brief No. 116). Retrieved September 2, 2015, from C. D. Howe Institute website: http://www.cdhowe.org/pdf/Backgrounder 116.pdf.

Sahlberg, P. (2009). AISI: A global perspective. In A. Hargreaves, R. Crocker, B. Davis, L. McEwan, P. Sahlberg, D. Shirley, & D. Sumara (Eds.), *The learning mosaic: A multiple perspectives review of the Alberta Initiative for School Improvement (AISI).* (pp. 77–89). Alberta: the Crown in Right of Alberta.

Shirley, D. & McEwen, L. (2009). AISI: A qualitative case study. In A. Hargreaves, R. Crocker, B. Davis, L. McEwan, P. Sahlberg, D. Shirley, & D. Sumara (Eds.), *The learning mosaic: A multiple perspectives review of the Alberta Initiative for School Improvement (AISI).* (pp. 51–61). Alberta: the Crown in Right of Alberta.

Standing Senate Committee on Aboriginal Peoples. (2011). Reforming First Nations education: From crisis to hope. Retrieved from http://www.parl .gc.ca/content/sen/committee/411/appa/rep/rep03dec11-e.pdf

Statistics Canada. (2014). Number of full-time and part-time educators in public elementary and secondary schools, by age group and sex, Canada, provinces and territories (Table 477–0028). Retrieved from: http://www5 .statcan.gc.ca/cansim/pick-choisir?lang=eng&p2=33&id=4770028

Statistics Canada. (2015). Education Indicators in Canada: An International Perspective. Retrieved from: http://www.statcan.gc.ca/pub/81—604- x/81—604-x2014001-eng.pdf

Stewart V. (2012). *A world-class education: Learning from international models of excellence and innovation.* Alexandria,VA: ASCD (pp.45–55: material on Canada, Alberta, and Ontario).

Sumara, D. & Davis, B. (2009). Using complexity science to study the impact of AISI on cultures of education in Alberta. In A. Hargreaves, R. Crocker, B. Davis, L. McEwan, P. Sahlberg, D. Shirley, & D. Sumara (Eds.), *The learning mosaic: A multiple perspectives review of the Alberta Initiative for School Improvement (AISI).* (pp. 34–50). Alberta: The Crown in Right of Alberta.

Task Force for Teaching Excellence. (2014). Report to the Minister: Task Force for Teaching Excellence. Retrieved 18 December 2015 from: https:// inspiring.education.alberta.ca/wp-content/themes/inspiringeducation/_ documents/GOAE_TaskForceforTeachingExcellence_WEB_updated.pdf

The City of Calgary Civic Census Results. (2014). Retrieved September 2, 2015, from http://www.calgary.ca/CA/city-clerks/Pages/Election-and-information- services/Civic-Census/2014-Results.aspx

The City of Calgary: Community and Neighbourhood Services. Calgary at a Glance: Results of the 2011 Federal Census Program. (2013). Retrieved September 4, 2014, from http://www.calgary.ca/CSPS/CNS/Documents/ Social-research-policy-and-resources/Calgary_at_a_glance.pdf

The School Act. (2000). Alberta Queen's Printer. Retrieved 20 July 2015 from: http://www.qp.alberta.ca/documents/acts/s03.pdf.

Truth and Reconciliation Commission of Canada. (2015). Honouring the truth; Reconciling for the Future: Summary of the final report of the Truth and Reconciliation Commission of Canada. Retrieved from: http://www.trc .ca/websites/trcinstitution/File/2015/Honouring_the_Truth_Reconciling_ for_the_Future_July_23_2015.pdf

University of Alberta. (2004). Alberta Initiative for School Improvement: What have we learned: An assessment of district qualitative reports and promising practices from Cycle 1, 2000–2003. Retrieved January 4, 2005, from www.education.govab.ca/K_12/special/AISI/pdfs/UniversityofA_Cycle1_ Report_June 2004.pdf in J. Parsons, P. McRae, & L. Taylor (2006). *Celebrating school improvement: Six lessons from Alberta's AISI projects.* School Improvement Press: Edmonton, Alberta.

University of Lethbridge. Faculty of Education. Retrieved March 22, 2015, from: http://www.uleth.ca/education/.

Weiner, L., & Compton, M. (Eds). (2008). *The global assault on teaching, teachers and their unions.* New York: Palgrave Macmillan.

Zeichner, K. (2014). The struggle for the soul of teaching and teacher education. *Journal of Education for Teaching.* 40(5), 551–568.

Printed and bound by CPI Group (UK) Ltd, Croydon, CR0 4YY

13/04/2025

14656500-0001